COLORADO
CAMPGROUNDS

The 100 Best
And All the Rest

Text by
Gil Folsom

Photography by
Bill Bonebrake

WESTCLIFFE PUBLISHERS

westcliffepublishers.com

Diana Zivkovic

ISBN 10: 1-56579-334-X
ISBN 13: 1-978-56579-334-7

COVER AND BOOK DESIGN: Paulette Livers Lambert
PRODUCTION MANAGER: Craig Keyzer
EDITORS: Steve Grinstead and Jenna Samelson

PUBLISHER: Westcliffe Publishers, Inc.
  P.O. Box 1261
  Englewood, Colorado 80150
  westcliffepublishers.com

PRINTED IN CHINA BY: C & C Offset Printing Co., Ltd.

LIBRARY OF CONGRESS CATALOGING-IN-PUBLICATION DATA:
Folsom, Gil, 1953–
   Colorado campgrounds : the 100 best and all the rest / text by Gil Folsom ; photography
by Bill Bonebrake
      p. cm.
   Includes index.
   ISBN: 1-56579-334-X
   1. Camp sites, facilities, etc.—Colorado—Guidebooks. 2.
Camping—Colorado—Guidebooks. 3. Colorado—Guidebooks. I. Bonebrake, Bill, 1960–
II. Title.

GV191.42.C6 F65 2002
647.94788'09—dc21

2002066188

For more information about other fine books and calendars from Westcliffe Publishers, please call your local bookstore, contact us at 1-800-523-3692, or visit us on the web at westcliffepublishers.com

PLEASE NOTE:
Risk is always a factor in backcountry and highcountry travel. Many of the activities described in this book can be dangerous, especially when weather is adverse or unpredictable, and when unforeseen events or conditions create a hazardous situation. The author has done his best to provide the reader with accurate information about backcountry travel, as well as to point out some of its potential hazards. It is the responsibility of the users of this guide to learn the necessary skills for potentially hazardous areas, especially on glaciers and avalanche-prone terrain. The author and publisher disclaim any liability for injury or other damage caused by backcountry traveling, mountain biking, or performing any other activity described in this book.

COVER PHOTOGRAPH: *Hikers trace the lakeshore near the Lake Irwin Campground beneath the majestic Ruby Range.*

OPPOSITE: *Wildflowers carpet the Redstone Campground, the ultimate camping destination with modern amenities, total wheelchair accessibility, and striking scenery.*

Acknowledgments

Thanks to all the readers who have already purchased this book and made it a success. Everyone that helped in creating this book appreciates all of the wonderful comments and suggestions we have received from our most ardent critics, you the reader. Thank you very much!

As with many labors of love, this project would not have been possible without the help and commitment of others. First of all, thanks to the staff at Westcliffe Publishers for believing in this book and committing the resources to produce a first-class effort. I give special thanks to my editor, Jenna Samelson, and Craig Keyzer for all their hard work. I am grateful to Bill Bonebrake for his superb photography and enthusiasm in bringing these campgrounds to life. Thanks to Paul Marken for his video work and tips on identifying trees. Officials from the Forest Service, campground concessionaires, state parks, national parks, city parks, and county parks went out of their way to provide me with up-to-date campground information and in verifying the accuracy of campground descriptions. A very special thank you goes out to all the campground hosts for the time they spent educating me. Many of these individuals have lived and worked at the same campgrounds for many summers. Their knowledge, insights, tips, and love for the campgrounds entrusted to them could fill encyclopedias.

A grassy meadow at the Sunshine Campground, the most pleasant campground near Telluride, provides the ideal spot for an early autumn picnic.

The Alta Lakes Campground—a longtime favorite getaway for Telluride locals— offers campers a dramatic natural setting with three pristine lakes, as well as the nearby ghost town of Alta for exploring Colorado's past.

To all campers who wish to maximize their camping experiences—and especially those who toil all week long at work, looking forward to a great Colorado camping weekend—I hope this book provides you with some fresh new ideas on where to find the very best in Colorado. Happy Camping!

CONTENTS

COLORADO STATE MAP

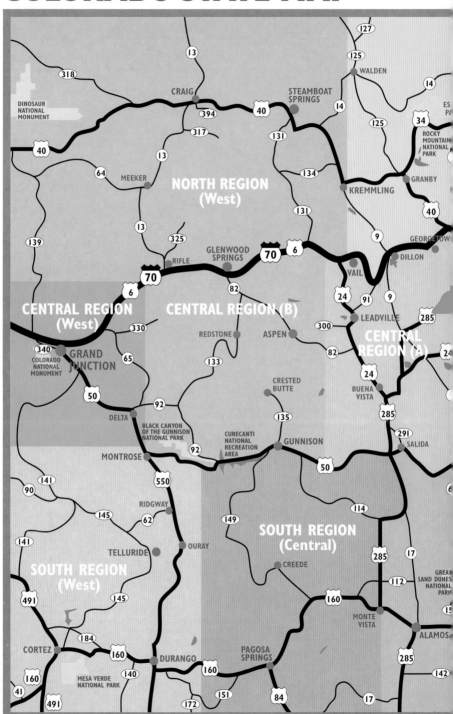

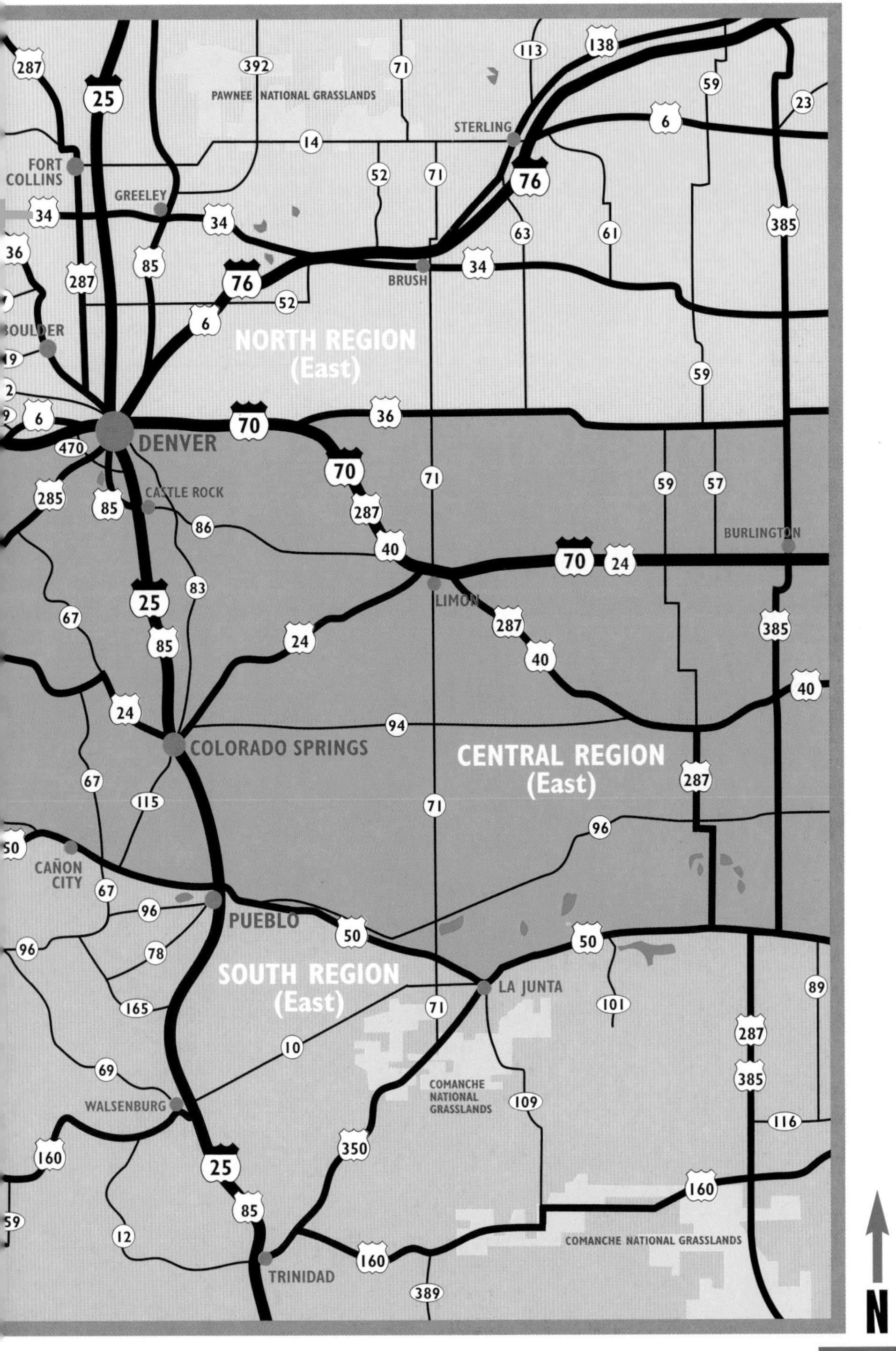

287 · 25 · 392 · 71 · 113 · 138 · 59 · 23

PAWNEE NATIONAL GRASSLANDS

STERLING · 6

14 · 76

FORT COLLINS · 34 · 52 · 71

GREELEY · 34

36 · 85 · 63 · 61 · 385

287 · 76 · 34

BRUSH

52 · 6

BOULDER

NORTH REGION (East)

59

2 · 6

DENVER · 70 · 36

470 · 70

285 · 85 · CASTLE ROCK · 287

67 · 25 · 83 · 86 · 40 · 59 · 57 · BURLINGTON

85 · 70 · 24

24 · LIMON · 287 · 385

40 · 40

94 · 40

67 · COLORADO SPRINGS · **CENTRAL REGION (East)** · 287

115 · 71

50 · 96

CAÑON CITY · 67 · 50 · 50 · 89

96 · 78 · 101 · 287

96 · 165 · PUEBLO · 50 · LA JUNTA · 385

SOUTH REGION (East) · 71

69 · 10 · COMANCHE NATIONAL GRASSLANDS · 109 · 116

WALSENBURG

160 · 350 · 160

25 · 85

59 · 12 · 160

TRINIDAD · 389

COMANCHE NATIONAL GRASSLANDS

N

Introduction

In this revised edition, every attempt was made to ensure that all information is as up to date as possible. Colorado continues to offer some of the nation's best camping experiences and most beautiful campgrounds. However, changes to camping facilities due to time, funding, and natural events are inevitable. Keep in mind that some little-used Forest Service campgrounds have been closed due to a lack of funds. Most are in remote areas, but not all. These closed campgrounds have been noted throughout the book.

The pine beetle problem continues to plague the state, and many trees have been removed at some of the most popular camping areas. In 2005, for instance, 9,000 trees were removed from around Lake Dillon. This also means you may be camping around some partially or fully dead trees that have not yet been removed. Dead trees leave the forest much more susceptible to fire, so please be very, very careful with your fires and obey all fire restriction rules that may be in effect.

Drinking water is no longer available at some campgrounds. Wells have dried up due to a variety of factors, including simply time, but no funds are available to drill new ones. **A word to the wise: If you have a specific campground in mind, always call first to check on current drinking water conditions and general status.** To be on the safe side, always bring some drinking water along, particularly when heading to more remote campgrounds. Most importantly, enjoy your Colorado campground experience. Check the maps in the back of this book of some of the most popular lakes and reservoirs.

This book was born of frustration. Finding the perfect campsite is never easy—and there's nothing as disappointing as driving several hours, taking a side trip down a long, bumpy road, and arriving at your favorite campground to find it full. Equally disappointing is depending on sources that prove to be inadequate or incomplete. I had experienced these frustrations again and again, so I started scouting on my own. Word got out, and friends began calling me for tips on where and when to camp and how to find the best spot. I began to think of the type of book I would write.

Eventually I began to turn my notes and scribbles into something more substantial. Armed with a video camera and the spirit of an explorer, I drove 12,000 miles and spent almost half a year visiting Colorado campgrounds. Each day I was on the road by 7:00 a.m., didn't stop until dark, and was up the next morning for another foray. I spent hundreds of hours questioning campground hosts, and officials of the Forest Service, state parks, and National Park Service. I checked out local recreational opportunities, verified phone numbers, and sought to provide exactly the type of specific, practical,

Nestled in an aspen grove, Silver Jack Campground is an outdoor lover's dream.

down-to-earth information I would appreciate as a Colorado camper myself. The result of this Herculean effort is the book you hold in your hands.

While the subject of camping in Colorado is not new, this book offers a novel and refreshing approach. Rather than merely reiterating existing statistics, *Colorado Campgrounds: The 100 Best and All the Rest* takes a critical look at campgrounds for the discriminating camper. Over 400 public campgrounds administered by a variety of public agencies are covered, including the Forest Service, state parks, and national park campgrounds, in addition to selected Bureau of Land Management (BLM) areas, city, county, and state wildlife areas, and others. Unlike other books that merely list campgrounds, this book, with beautiful photography by Bill Bonebrake, will help you get a much better feel for the campgrounds as well as the surrounding scenery.

Designating 100 campgrounds as the very best Colorado has to offer was a difficult process. As with any list of top choices, there is always room for disagreement. One person's criteria for a great campground are not necessarily the same as another's. However, people tend to think alike in many respects when choosing their favorite campgrounds. Certain factors take precedence— especially scenery and proximity to water. But the greatest scenery in the world may not matter if the area lacks trees, privacy, spacious campsites, or modern facilities. My "Top 100" list takes into account many factors, but scenery and water are two of the most important.

Remember, you don't have to stay at a "top" campground to have a great time. *You* are the ultimate judge as to which campgrounds best satisfy your own criteria! This book is filled with many superb campgrounds that didn't make the "Top 100" list, but offer all you need for a wonderful camping experience. And keep in mind that many of these campgrounds are no secret to their devotees. Plan as far in advance as possible. Use this book to help choose a spot, and *call ahead* for current campground and road conditions and to make reservations. You'll also find helpful tips and secrets to get the best out of your camping experiences. How often and when during the camping season does a campground fill? Which sites are the most popular and closest to the water? How can campers obtain "dream" sites? All this plus many more valuable tips are contained within the following pages.

Finally, reader comments, questions, and suggestions are welcome. Please e-mail your responses to **editor@westcliffepublishers.com** or to **gilfolsom@hotmail.com**.

How to Use This Guide

The 400-plus campgrounds in this book are divided by geographic area and grouped into nine sections. A brief overview of each region is followed by the campgrounds listed according to their geographic proximity to one another.

Although I've provided directions and approximate mileage, **I strongly suggest that you carry a good map when you're looking for a specific campground.** This book is designed to be used in conjunction with DeLorme's *Colorado Atlas and Gazetteer* or Pierson Guides' *Colorado Recreational Road Atlas*, available at book, map, and grocery stores throughout the state. For more information, contact DeLorme at (207) 846-7000 (website: **www.delorme.com**), or Pierson Graphics Corp. at (303) 623-4299 or 1-800-456-8703 (website: **www.coloradomaps.com**).

These two road atlases serve as good general map books, but Forest Service maps and the *Trails Illustrated* series of maps provide even greater detail, offering such valuable information as campground names right on the map. The *Trails Illustrated* maps are my own personal favorite, but they cover a smaller area.

The following sections provide important tips on how to make the most of your Colorado camping experience.

Campground Information

To make it easy for you to find all you need to know for a successful trip, **Top-100 Campground** information is organized as follows (**Other Nearby Campgrounds** offer similar information in a condensed form):

Location: Approximate distance from a nearby town.

Elevation: The elevation of the campground in feet above sea level. Use this figure to make camping plans during a particular time of year. Remember that in the spring, fall, and winter, snow prohibits access to many campgrounds at higher elevations.

Number of Sites: The published number of campsites in a campground. This number, provided by campground administrators, is not always correct, but is close enough to plan around.

Recommended RV Length: The recommended maximum length of an RV parking space, or "spur." Most of these figures come directly from the public agencies that oversee the campgrounds; when this information was unavailable, I have described the site capacities in more general terms. Keep in mind that this figure does not reflect how many sites can accept this length, and use it as a general guideline, not the ultimate authority.

Season: Approximate campground opening and closing dates. Because a campground's popularity, elevation, and the weather (especially snow) can

affect opening and closing dates, they can vary dramatically from year to year; the wise camper will check with the agency in charge before traveling to a campground. Some campgrounds open early and stay open much later than the published dates for hunters or anglers to use. Most state parks and wildlife areas, as well as some Front Range county campgrounds, are open year-round, although running water and trash removal services are frequently discontinued outside of the official camping season.

Map: The page number and map coordinates for the campground as found in DeLorme's *Colorado Atlas & Gazetteer* and in Pierson Guides' *Colorado Recreational Road Atlas*.

Phone: The number to call for information about the campground or others in the area. This is *not* the reservation number! To locate reservation numbers, see "Making Reservations" on page 10 or call the information number listed with the campground.

Directions: This information was gathered from campground agencies and from personal experience. Every effort has been made to provide accurate directions, but I *strongly* advise campers to contact the appropriate campground administrators, as some maps may not indicate details such as campground names, landmarks, alternate road names, and route changes. Many RV owners have an aversion to driving on dirt roads, so be advised that over 90 percent of all Forest Service roads mentioned are dirt or gravel.

Distinguishing Features: This is a general description of the campground, its setting, and what makes it special.

Popularity: When and how often a campground typically fills can be the most important piece of information I can pass along to you. Reservation information is listed here, and if a campground is on the reservation system, I have included what campground officials consider the most heavily requested reservable site numbers. Site numbers are listed in order of popularity within the campground wherever possible. Because the reservable sites can change from year to year, make sure to plan ahead.

Facilities: This section lists basic facilities such as picnic tables, toilets, fire grates or pits, firewood for sale, and wheelchair accessibility. Because some campgrounds do not offer trash removal services, you may want to bring trash bags. And remember that not all campgrounds have drinking water, especially outside of the official camping season.

RV Notes: This section highlights important points for RV campers such as the quality of the road leading to the campground, site lengths, the number of pull-thru sites, availability of dump stations for public use, whether sites are level, whether hookups are available, and whether the campground is more tent- or RV-oriented.

The Cache la Poudre River burbles by the grassy Ansel Watrous Campground.

Tent Notes: This section highlights important points for tent campers such as the amount of shade, degree of seclusion, whether the ground is level or bumpy, whether the campground is more tent- or RV-oriented, and the availability of tent pads (designated spots for tents, usually square with a level, sandy surface that maximizes water drainage). Note that to access a "walk-in" tent site, campers must carry their gear from the parking lot to the campsite (normally no more than a two-minute walk). The Tent Notes sections are typically shorter than the RV Notes because it is fairly easy to find a good spot to pitch a tent in most campgrounds.

Recreational Opportunities: This section provides a general overview of some of the activities available in the campground's immediate vicinity. They are illustrated by the following icons:

 ATVs: This symbol indicates trails that are typically narrower than a four-wheel-drive road and designated for any or all of the following: motorcycles, ATVs (all-terrain vehicles), and/or dirt bikes. A license plate is often not necessary on these trails. Dirt bikes, ATVs, and motorcycles are also referred to as OHVs (off-highway vehicles).

 Biking: Road and/or mountain-biking opportunities exist in the area.

 Fishing: Opportunities for anglers exist in the area.

 Four-wheeling: This symbol indicates roads that are open to four-wheel-drive vehicles, and often motorcycles and ATVs as well. Motorcycles and ATVs often need to be licensed to travel on jeep roads; please check with the area's governing agency first, and remember your driver's license, too.

 Hiking: Hiking trails exist in the area.

 Horseback Riding: Equestrian trails and/or outfitters exist in the area.

 Motorized Boats: This symbol indicates lakes and reservoirs suitable for motorized boats of any horsepower.

 Rafting/Kayaking: This symbol indicates waterways suitable for rafting and/or kayaking. These waterways are typically too hazardous for canoes.

 Rock Climbing: Rock climbing opportunities exist in the area.

Sailing: This symbol indicates lakes and reservoirs popular for sailing.

 Small Boats: This symbol indicates lakes and reservoirs with any or all of the following restrictions: the area is only open to nonmotorized boats or small boats with electric motors, small gas motors, and/or wakeless boating.

Swimming: This symbol indicates waterways open to swimming, although it is often restricted to designated areas; please check before diving in. Remember that swimming in high mountain lakes can be extremely hazardous.

Waterskiing: This symbol indicates lakes or reservoirs where waterskiing is allowed.

Joined in summer by colorful wildflowers, the aspen trees that fill the soul-stirring Vaughn Lake Campground make it the perfect fall destination.

Campground Rating System

For the Top-100 Campgrounds, a five-star rating system is used to rate scenery, suitability for RVs and tents, amount of shade, and privacy. Ratings are as follows:

★ Poor
★★ Fair
★★★ Good
★★★★ Excellent
★★★★★ Outstanding

Scenery: As a longtime Colorado resident and traveler to some of the world's most majestic mountain regions, I have taken a critical look at each campground's aesthetic qualities. This is my personal, subjective rating of the scenic beauty of the campground and/or its surroundings. Note that in many campgrounds, the scenery often differs from site to site.

RVs: This rating takes into account the quality of the road leading to the campground, site lengths, the number of pull-thru sites, whether sites are level, and if hookups are available. In many campgrounds, the RV friendliness factor varies quite a bit from site to site.

A "Colorado secret," the Hahns Peak Campground provides tranquility amidst rolling, pine-enshrouded hills, as well as trout at 40-acre Hahns Peak Lake.

Tents: This takes into account the amount of shade, degree of seclusion, the availability of tent pads, and whether the ground is level or bumpy. In many campgrounds, the tent friendliness factor varies quite a bit from site to site.

Shade: This takes into account the density of the trees in a campground and whether they are located in places of benefit to campers. In many campgrounds, shade varies widely from site to site. *NOTE:* The rating system for shade only goes as high as four stars, as sometimes there can be too much of a good thing.

Privacy: This takes into account the sites' size, how closely they are spaced, and whether there are trees or other natural features that allow for privacy from other campers. In many campgrounds, the amount of privacy varies quite a bit from site to site.

Understanding Public Campgrounds

Understanding the differences between types of campgrounds can help you plan the type of outdoor experience you desire. Here is a brief summary:

Bureau of Land Management Campgrounds: These campgrounds are generally in remote locations, not heavily used, and often similar to primitive Forest Service campgrounds. They may or may not provide basic campground amenities. Camping fees vary but are usually only a few dollars or free. Not well publicized, they can be hard to locate.

City Campgrounds: These campgrounds vary considerably. They can be very primitive or quite deluxe. Sometimes a campground is owned by the city but operated by private concessionaires. They are almost always located very close to town, and usually within city limits (it's common to find them next to the city park). Most are not well publicized, and it is easy to pass them without noticing their existence. Camping fees typically range between $8 and $12.

County Campgrounds: Operated by the county, most of these campgrounds are located near reservoirs that act as county water supplies. Normally very popular, they are often close to population centers and offer a quick escape for city dwellers. Camping fees typically range between $10 and $20.

Forest Service Campgrounds: Colorado is fortunate to have over 300 of these jewels, the most common of all public campgrounds. Most are in great camping locations, and some are starting to add very modern amenities. Almost all are operated by private concessionaires and will likely have a host (many of the campground hosts have returned to manage the same campground year after year). The hosts can be your best friends—they are sensitive to individual camper needs, and provide a wealth of information on activities available in the area. Treat the hosts like gold, and you will not be disappointed. Some Forest Service campgrounds are located in "Fee Demo Areas", where there's a charge to enter the area in addition to a camping fee of generally $8 to $20. Outside of the official camping season, many Forest Service campgrounds are free (if open).

National Park Campgrounds: Most of the campgrounds in national parks are large, and sites are tightly spaced and don't offer much privacy. However, their location overcomes many faults, and interpretative programs led by rangers provide excellent learning opportunities. Some of these campgrounds are on the reservation system, but campers are not permitted to make a specific site request. Camping fees range between $8 and $20 per night.

State Park Campgrounds: For those looking for deluxe and modern facilities, the state parks are the most obvious choices when it comes to public campgrounds. Extremely RV- and tent-friendly, they accommodate all campers' needs quite well. These campgrounds are continually being upgraded and expanded. Most are near large reservoirs that offer a wide variety of water recreation possibilities. Camping is often possible all year long at state parks. The only downside to these campgrounds is that many of the mountain campgrounds offer very little shade or privacy. Almost every campsite in the state park system can be reserved. State parks generally require an entrance fee (or annual pass) plus a camping fee of $6 to $20.

State Wildlife Campgrounds: These are primitive public campgrounds and campers are lucky if even a basic toilet exists. Not really campgrounds in the conventional sense, campsites are mostly undefined and campers have a wide latitude in choosing where to camp. They can be tough to locate, but are almost always free. Not all wildlife areas permit camping, or it may be limited to certain times of the year. Pick up a copy of Westcliffe Publishers' *Guide to Colorado State Wildlife Areas* or the *Colorado Fishing Season Information and Property Directory* to unravel the mysteries of these areas.

Making Reservations

Camping is most popular from Memorial Day to Labor Day, and you should make reservations whenever possible (from Sunday through Thursday, however, this is usually not as critical). If you don't have a reservation, arriving early in the day will give you the best chance to land a prime campsite. **The key to stress-free camping is to utilize the reservation system as much as possible—and as early as possible.**

Forest Service Campgrounds: You can make reservations at Forest Service Campgrounds up to 240 days in advance, or sometimes as close as 24 hours prior to arrival, by calling toll-free **1-877-444-6777** or visiting the National Recreation Reservation Service website at **www.reserveusa.com.** (For the hearing impaired, the TDD number is **1-877-833-6777**.) Phone reservations are available seven days a week from 8:00 a.m. to midnight (Eastern Time) during the high season, and from 10:00 a.m. to 7:00 p.m. (Eastern Time) during the winter months. ("Early Birds" can capture popular weekends ahead of the 240-day window if their stay extends from the arrival date through the holiday.) Reservation agents have access to campground maps and should be able to help campers out with site selection. When you call, be prepared to pay a reservation fee plus the cost of each night's camping. Campers may be

Dinner Station Campground has mountain vistas and campsites by the Taylor River.

charged an additional "Premium Site" fee for prime sites. Sites will be held for 24 hours from the arrival check-in date and time (usually 1:00 to 2:00 p.m). Canceling a reservation on short notice will invoke an additional fee.

Internet reservations can be made 24 hours a day, and a wealth of information—campground maps, site details, information on availability, and more—is all on the web.

National Park Campgrounds: With the National Park Service, camping reservations may be made up to five months in advance by calling **1-800-365-CAMP (2267)**, 10:00 a.m. to 10:00 p.m. (Eastern Time), seven days a week or by visiting the website (see below). The fifteenth of each month is a key date, as that's when the reservation system opens up an additional month. It is now possible to reserve individual sites, walk-in tent sites, generator-free sites, disabled accessible sites, and group sites. The reservation fee is built into the daily camping fee, and the price is the same whether making reservations or showing up on a first-come, first-served basis—so making a reservation is always a wise move. Your place in the campground is held for 24 hours, and failing to show up or canceling invokes additional fees.

In Colorado, the only national park campgrounds currently on the reservation system are Glacier Basin and Moraine Park, both located in Rocky Mountain National Park. For Internet reservations and additional information, visit the national parks website at **http://reservations.nps.gov**.

State Park Campgrounds: Reservations are possible for almost all sites in state parks and can be made up to 180 days in advance. Reserve online at **www.reserveusa.com.** Call **303-470-1144** (Denver metropolitan area) or toll-free **1-800-678-CAMP (2267)**. Campers must pay a reservation fee in addition to campground fees. Reservations are possible up to a minimum of three days prior to your arrival date. Most state parks are open year-round. Further information about the state parks, as well as detailed campground information, can be obtained online at **www.parks.state.co.us** and also at **www.coloradoparks.org.**

Campground Common Sense
Campground Know-How

Plants and Trees: Leaving trees and plants alone preserves the beauty for others to enjoy. This is especially true for aspen trees, which are very fragile and usually part of an interconnected system. Pounding nails or carving initials into, or cutting branches off of just one tree can often cause diseases that affect other aspen trees. If you see anyone engaging in such activity, please report him or her to campground officials.

Wildlife: Keep a safe distance from wildlife, especially during breeding, nesting, and birthing seasons. Please don't feed any animals, even the cute little chipmunks. Chipmunks and squirrels often store food, which can rot. Human food is generally bad for them, and can make them sick or even kill them. It can also make them dependent on humans, and thus leaves them ill-prepared to survive the winter. Feeding animals can also cause them to lose their fear of humans, become aggressive, endanger campers, and might eventually require officials to destroy them.

Food Storage: Keep food away from wildlife. Bears have a keen sense of smell and will eat almost anything, so keep garbage out of reach by using bear-proof trash containers. Store food, toiletries, and coolers properly and away from your living area—never inside a tent. Keep all edibles in bear-proof food containers, a hard-sided vehicle or RV, or suspended from a tree.

Trash Disposal: Place trash in bear-proof or provided trash containers, or pack it out. Do not throw trash down toilets, as it is difficult and expensive to remove.

Campground Fires: Be very careful with fires, especially in windy, dry conditions. In certain places or during dry times of the year, fires may be prohibited. Build campfires only in established fire grates or rings. Never leave campfires unattended. Make sure they are completely extinguished by dousing them thoroughly with water and dirt, then repeating the process.

Children: Please watch your children closely, especially around lakes, streams, and rivers. It only takes a few seconds for a child to get into trouble around water, steep mountainsides, wild animals, and other natural hazards. Teach them to respect others in the campground, and don't let them tramp through the middle of other occupied campsites.

Tent Pitching: If formal tent pads exist in the campground, please use them. Not only does this minimize your environmental impact, but it also provides a level, well-drained spot free of tree roots and rocks. If no tent pads exist, try to find a level spot with good drainage.

Basic Essentials

Almost every camper remembers to bring the tent, sleeping bags, rain gear, warm clothing, food, cooking stove, and utensils. However, campers can frequently be in for some unpleasant surprises if certain basics are not available, so check before leaving home to make sure these items are among your gear.

Firewood: It is usually best to bring firewood or, if available, buy it at the campground. Even though it is permissible to use any dead wood found on the ground (not found on trees!), it is often in short supply in or near a campground.

Toilet Paper: This is often missing in the outhouses.

Trash Bags: Trash receptacles are not always available at campgrounds, especially outside of the normal camping season.

The famed Colorado Trail runs just north of the tent-only Green Mountain Campground, a secluded place to experience the wilderness at its best.

Water: Outside of the summer camping season, water systems are often turned off to prevent possible damage from freezing. Even during the summer, some campgrounds do not offer drinking water or can experience problems with water systems, so bringing drinking water with you is a good idea. Never drink water from streams, rivers, and lakes without first purifying it with chemicals, filtration systems, or boiling it for 15 minutes.

Sun Protection: In sunny Colorado, high-altitude sunshine is much rougher on skin than at lower elevations. Suntan lotion, sunglasses, protective clothing, and a hat help combat sunburn, sunstroke, and skin cancer.

Insect Repellent: Insects are most active at dawn and dusk. Insect repellent and thick clothes are your best defense.

Rules to Camp By

Here are a few general camping rules to keep in mind, but remember to also look over each campground's rules, usually posted at the entrance.

Check-In and Check-Out Times: A typical check-in time is normally around 1:00 to 2:00 p.m., and check-out time is usually around noon.

Firearms: It is illegal to discharge firearms or other weapons within a campground or within 150 yards of a residence, building, developed recreation area, or occupied area. Firing a weapon on or across a Forest Road or body of water is also prohibited.

Fireworks: Possessing or igniting fireworks is strictly prohibited in national forests and public campgrounds.

Maximum Limits: Many campgrounds limit the number of people, vehicles, and/or nights allowed per campsite. Check with the campground administrator.

Noise Restrictions and Quiet Hours: Please respect quiet hours, which are usually between 10:00 p.m. and 6:00 a.m. Leave the boom box at home; other campers may not share your love of music in the peaceful wilderness. Please don't ride dirt bikes or ATVs around and around a campground. And RVers, try to restrict generator usage as much as possible.

Pets: Most campgrounds require that pets be leashed at all times. Please do not allow them to disturb or chase wildlife, and remember to pick up after them. Horses and other pack animals are normally prohibited in campgrounds, but nearby corrals are sometimes provided.

Picnicking: In many campgrounds, you cannot picnic at a campsite without paying a fee. These campgrounds will often have a free picnic area nearby.

Speed Limits: When driving through campgrounds, please go slowly and pay close attention, as small children or wild animals could dart into the road.

Fall colors explode in a kaleidoscope of gold, green, orange, and crimson at Jumbo Campground, an angler's paradise on the northern edge of the Grand Mesa.

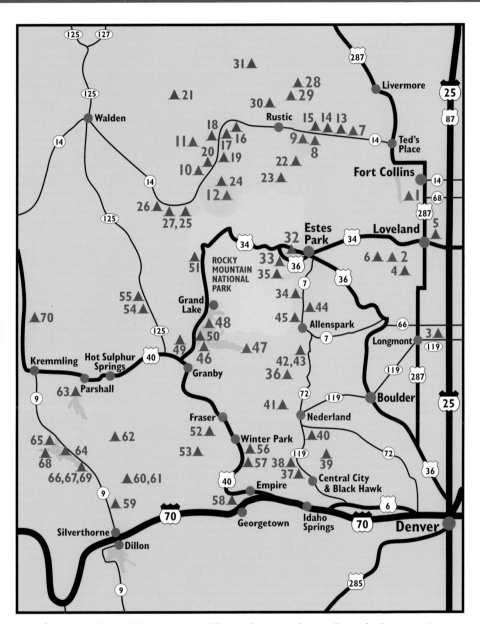

▲ **71, 72, 73** and **74** are not visible on the map above. Consult the maps in DeLorme's *Colorado Atlas & Gazetteer* or Pierson Guides' *Colorado Recreational Road Atlas* for the locations of these campgrounds on the Eastern Plains. For locations of campgrounds by Carter Lake, Green Mountain Reservoir, Horsetooth Reservoir, Jackson Reservoir, and Lake Granby, refer to pages 288-289.

Not far from some of Colorado's largest metropolitan areas—Den~~~~~, Boulder, Longmont, and Fort Collins—are some of the state's most popular recreational areas. The northern Colorado campgrounds near Horsetooth Reservoir, Carter Lake, Pinewood Reservoir, Flatiron Reservoir, and Boyd Lake provide quick getaways from the city, and fishing, waterskiing, and swimming are popular summertime sports. Horsetooth Mountain Park offers 26 miles of trails for hikers and horseback riders.

Another standout attraction in northern Colorado is the immensely popular and scenic Poudre Canyon. Within this canyon lies the Cache la Poudre, Colorado's only National Wild and Scenic River, which is a favorite of anglers, whitewater kayakers, and rafters. The subdued charm of the campgrounds and pretty lakes near Red Feather Lakes are target weekend destinations of many city dwellers in northern Colorado.

The Grand Lake area offers breathtaking views, opportunities for both lake and stream fishing, and wonderful hiking opportunities in Rocky Mountain National Park. Closer to Denver, the Fraser–Winter Park area is great for hiking and mountain biking.

Due to their proximity to the Front Range, the campgrounds in this entire North Region (East) area are extremely popular on summer weekends—almost all of the areas are accessible within a three-hour drive. If planning a weekend stay, campers should make reservations as far in advance as possible where reservations are accepted. Otherwise, plan to arrive on Thursday or early Friday to secure a spot.

▲ 100 BEST   ▲ All The Rest

▲ 100 BEST	▲ All The Rest		
▲1 Inlet Bay/South Bay/ Horsetooth Reservoir	▲3 Barbour Ponds State Park	▲35 Glacier Basin	▲60 South Fork
▲2 Flatiron Reservoir	▲4 Carter Lake	▲37 Columbine	▲61 Sugarloaf
▲7 Ansel Watrous	▲5 Boyd Lake State Park	▲38 Cold Springs	▲62 Horseshoe
▲8 Mountain Park	▲6 Pinewood Lake	▲39 Golden Gate Canyon State Park	▲63 Williams Fork Reservoir
▲9 Kelly Flats	▲13 Stove Prairie		▲64 Prairie Point
▲10 Chambers Lake	▲14 Narrows	▲40 Kelly Dahl	▲65 Willows
▲11 Tunnel	▲15 Dutch George Flats	▲41 Rainbow Lakes	▲66 Davis Springs
▲12 Grandview	▲16 Big Bend	▲42 Camp Dick	▲67 McDonald Flats
▲28 Dowdy Lake	▲17 Bliss State Wildlife Area	▲43 Peaceful Valley	▲68 Elliot Creek
▲29 West Lake	▲18 Sleeping Elephant	▲44 Meeker Park	▲69 Cataract Creek
▲32 Aspenglen	▲19 Big South	▲45 Olive Ridge	▲70 Wolford Mountain Reservoir
▲33 Moraine Park	▲20 Aspen Glen	▲49 Willow Creek	▲71 Crow Valley
▲36 Pawnee	▲21 Browns Park	▲50 Stillwater	▲72 North Sterling State Park
▲46 Sunset Point	▲22 Jacks Gulch	▲51 Timber Creek	▲73 Jackson Lake State Park
▲47 Arapaho Bay	▲23 Tom Bennett	▲52 St. Louis Creek	▲74 Brush Memorial Campground
▲48 Green Ridge	▲24 Long Draw	▲53 Byers Creek	
	▲25 State Forest	▲54 Sawmill Gulch	
	▲26 Aspen	▲55 Denver Creek	
	▲27 Pines	▲56 Idlewild	
	▲30 Bellaire Lake	▲57 Robbers Roost	
	▲31 North Fork Poudre	▲58 Mizpah	
	▲34 Longs Peak	▲59 Blue River	

FORT COLLINS—LOVELAND AREA

photo by Gil Folsom

1. Inlet Bay/South Bay/Horsetooth Reservoir

Location: About 5 miles west of Fort Collins (see map on p. 289)
Elevation: 5,340 feet
Number of Sites: 53
Recommended RV Length: Up to 45 feet
Season: Year-round
Maps: *Colorado Atlas & Gazetteer*, page 20, D1
Colorado Recreational Road Atlas, page 7, B3.5
Phone: 970-679-4570

Scenery: ★★★
RVs: ★★★★
Tents: ★★★
Shade: ★★★
Privacy: ★★

Directions
From the Denver/Longmont/Boulder area, take I-25 north to the Harmony Road/Timnath exit (265). Travel west on Harmony Road, which eventually becomes County Road 38E, and wind around the southern edge of the reservoir. After about 10 miles, you will reach the reservoir. Proceed past the first entrance to Horsetooth Reservoir ("South Bay Area") for another 1.7 miles to Shoreline Drive (County Road 25G). Turn right, and go 0.2 mile.

Distinguishing Features
Recently renovated, two campgrounds lie at the south end of Horsetooth Reservoir: Inlet Bay and South Bay. South Bay features RV-friendly pull-thru electric sites, cabins, and tent sites. Inlet Bay offers 53 sites and is split into two separate campgrounds. Inlet Bay North is near the marina and boat ramps and has 14 lakeside pull-thru sites. Inlet Bay South (formerly Shoreline) is prettier. Most south sites line the lake edge, some with good shade as well.

Popularity

These campgrounds fill quickly and reservations are highly recommended. The south area of Inlet Bay offers the best mix of ambience and scenery. Sites I-16–I-21 are the choice sites, with sites I-22–I-25 a close second. Reservations are accepted online (www.larimer.org/parks) or by phone at (800) 397-7795.

Facilities

Facilities include picnic tables, fire grates, water faucets, and accessible toilets. The marina has a store, boat rental, and boat docking.

RV Notes

Sites are all mostly medium to long pull-thrus and all have electricity. Dump stations are nearby.

Tent Notes

If you are overwhelmed by the RVs, you are not imaging things. There are only four designated tent sites (at South Bay) at Horsetooth. However, sites I-16–I-25 in Inlet Bay offer a grassy setting with many shade trees.

Recreational Opportunities

Northern Colorado's largest reservoir, Horsetooth is 6.5 miles long with 25 miles of shoreline. Anglers will find cutthroat, lake, and rainbow trout as well as smallmouth bass, walleye, wiper, and bluegill. Waterskiing, swimming (in designated areas), and other water activities are allowed, but the wind is rarely conducive to sailing or windsurfing. Hikers, horseback riders, and mountain bikers should check out the 26 miles of interconnected trails in Horsetooth Mountain Park, about a mile west of the reservoir.

---

2. Flatiron Reservoir

Location: About 9 miles southwest of Loveland
Elevation: 5,470 feet
Number of Sites: 37 plus 2 cabins
Recommended RV Length: Up to 30 feet
Season: Year-round
Maps: *Colorado Atlas & Gazetteer*, page 30, A1
Colorado Recreational Road Atlas, page 7, B4
Phone: 970-679-4570

Scenery: ★★★
RVs: ★★★
Tents: ★★★
Shade: ★★
Privacy: ★★★

Directions

From Denver, take I-25 north to Highway 34 (exit 257B) and go west at the cloverleaf to Loveland. Stay on Highway 34 through Loveland, and from Wilson Street (K-Mart is an easy landmark), continue west for another 5 miles. Watch for the "Carter Lake" sign, and turn left (south) on County Road 29. After about 2 miles, turn right (west) on County Road 18E, and go about 2 miles more. Turn left at the sign for Carter Lake, or go straight ahead to Flatiron Reservoir (about 0.5 mile).

Distinguishing Features

Campers enjoy views of Flatiron Mountain across the small lake, which is 0.5-mile long with 2 miles of shoreline. Mostly spread along the shore, the campground is very large with spacious sites; good to excellent spacing gives campers plenty of privacy. Trees provide excellent shade to some sites, while other sites have no shade, and a well-manicured lawn creates a cool and inviting spot to relax next to the lake. Recently renovated, Flatiron now offers 34 mostly pull-thru electrical sites, three designated tent sites, and two cabins.

Popularity

A short drive from the city, this place can be popular. My top choices would be sites 10 (long back-in), 8, 6, 16, and 20, in that order. In the summer, reservations are highly recommended, particularly on the week-ends. Reservations are accepted from April to September, up to 90 days in advance, online (www.larimer.org/parks) or by phone at (800) 397-7795.

Flatiron Reservoir

Facilities

Facilities include picnic tables, fire grates, water faucets, and accessible toilets. There is also a group-use area and shelter, a day-use area, a volleyball area, and horseshoe pits.

RV Notes

All sites are electric, and you can generally expect medium to long pull-thrus. The nearest dump station is near the south entrance at nearby Carter Lake.

Tent Notes

The three designated tent sites are away from the lake and not very desirable. If you want a good site to pitch your tent, it would probably be better to pay extra for one of the other sites even though you may not need the electrical connections.

Recreational Opportunities

Flatiron Reservoir, a favorite of local anglers, is stocked regularly with rainbow trout. A stroll around the lake offers breathtaking mountain vistas and the soothing sound of water lapping along the shore. Boating and swimming are not allowed. There is a volleyball area and horseshoe pits.

Other Nearby Campgrounds

3. St. Vrain State Park (60 sites); 7 miles east of Longmont. From I-25 take Highway 119 (exit 240). Go west on Highway 119 for about a mile, and turn north onto County Road 7. Adjacent to four ponds are three campgrounds. Most sites offer enough room for RVs of any length. Deciduous trees offer varying amounts of shade. A dump station is within the park. The nearby highway can make things noisy. Most sites offer little privacy. Reservations are accepted. **(303) 678-9402.**

4. Carter Lake (106 sites; see map on p. 288); 13 miles west of I-25 (southwest of Loveland). Take Highway 56 (exit 250) off of I-25, and go west for 9 miles to County Road 23. Turn right (north) on County Road 23 for 0.75 mile, and turn left (west) onto County Road 8E. Head west for 3.5 miles to County Road 31, which follows the lake's shoreline. Choose from six campgrounds around this popular 1,140-acre reservoir. With 12 miles of shoreline, this is the 2nd largest lake in northern Colorado. Campsites vary considerably, but many have excellent lake views, and a few are close to the water. Most can handle large RVs (up to 35 feet), and a dump station is near the south entrance. Eagle (on the northern end) and South Shore (on the southern end) campgrounds offer electrical hookups at all of their sites. Reservations can be made by calling **(800) 397-7795.**

5. Boyd Lake State Park (148 sites); 1 mile east of Loveland. Take Highway 34 (exit 257) west off of I-25. Go 2.5 miles and turn right (north) on Madison Avenue. Follow the signs to 1,800-acre Boyd Lake, northern Colorado's water sports haven. This large campground, which fills every summer weekend, has six paved loops near the lake but no lakeside spots. All sites are large, paved, and RV-friendly with pull-thru spaces, and a dump station is within the campground. Eighty-four sites have electrical hookups. Shade is sparse and there is little privacy. Tents can be pitched on grassy sites. Modern facilities include flush toilets and showers. Reservations are accepted. **(970) 669-1739.**

6. Pinewood Lake (30 sites); 14 miles southwest of Loveland. From I-25, take Highway 34 (exit 257B) and go west about 11 miles to County Road 29. Turn left (south) on County Road 29, and go for about 2 miles to County Road 18E. Turn right (west) on County Road 18E, and proceed for about 5.5 miles to the lake (at 2.5 miles you will pass Flatiron Reservoir on the left). Campsites offer limited shade and privacy, but both tent and RV campers can spend a peaceful afternoon fishing or canoeing on 100-acre Pinewood Lake. Reservations accepted. **(800) 397-7795.**

POUDRE CANYON AREA

7. Ansel Watrous

Location: About 23 miles northwest of Fort Collins
Elevation: 5,800 feet
Number of Sites: 19
Recommended RV Length: Up to 30 feet
Season: Year-round
Maps: *Colorado Atlas & Gazetteer*, page 19, C7
Colorado Recreational Road Atlas, page 7, A2.5
Phone: 970-295-6700

Directions
From Fort Collins, go about 10 miles north on Highway 287 to Ted's Place at the junction of Highway 14, then go west on Highway 14 for about 13 miles.

Scenery: ★★★
RVs: ★★
Tents: ★★★★
Shade: ★★★
Privacy: ★★

Distinguishing Features
The Ansel Watrous Campground, stretching along the Cache la Poudre River (commonly known as the Poudre River), is divided into upper, middle, and lower areas—offering a grassy, parklike setting with sites no more than 50 feet from the river. Ponderosa pines and cottonwoods supply ample shade and give the campground a wonderful ambiance.

The Cache la Poudre's name means "hiding place of powder." Legend has it that in the 1820s a group of French fur traders got caught in a vicious snowstorm, and to lighten their load they hid their gunpowder near the river.

Popularity
The campground in Poudre Canyon closest to Fort Collins, Ansel Watrous fills every weekend from Memorial Day through Labor Day (especially in June). Reservations are not accepted, so if you're planning a weekend trip, try arriving on Thursday.

Facilities
Facilities include picnic tables, fire grates, firewood for sale, a water faucet, and vault toilets. Anglers can find convenient parking as well.

RV Notes
Most of the 12 RV-accessible sites are medium pull-thrus. Sites are fairly

level. The nearest dump station is at the Poudre River Resort, about 18 miles west on Highway 14 past Rustic.

Tent Notes
Tent campers will find level, grassy sites and several walk-ins.

Recreational Opportunities
Ansel Watrous is the gateway to the Cache la Poudre National Wild and Scenic River and near the start of the 101-mile Cache la Poudre–North Park Scenic Byway. The Poudre offers fishing for rainbow and brown trout and is famous for its rafting and kayaking. It's river runners' favorite water along the Colorado Front Range, and commercial outfitters will be happy to take adventurous campers for a run.

The Young Gulch trailhead is just across the road. This easy trail follows an intermittent mountain stream for several miles before dead-ending. The Greyrock Trail, about 4 miles east of the campground on Highway 14, is one of the most heavily used trails in all of northern Colorado. In about 3 miles it climbs 2,040 feet to the top of Greyrock Mountain, where you'll find spectacular views of surrounding peaks. On the return trip, a side loop through Greyrock Meadow takes you back to the main trail.

---

8. Mountain Park
Location: About 33 miles northwest of Fort Collins
Elevation: 6,500 feet
Number of Sites: 55
Recommended RV Length: Up to 50 feet
Season: Memorial Day through September
Maps: *Colorado Atlas & Gazetteer*, page 19, C6
Colorado Recreational Road Atlas, page 7, A2.5
Phone: 970-295-6700

Scenery: ★★★
RVs: ★★★★★
Tents: ★★★
Shade: ★★
Privacy: ★★

Directions
From Fort Collins, go about 10 miles north on Highway 287 to Ted's Place at the junction of Highway 14. Take Highway 14 west about 23 miles.

Distinguishing Features
Mountain Park has been renovated into a thoroughly modern campground, offering deluxe amenities along the beautiful Cache la Poudre River. Ponderosa pines shade the four loops in this large campground. Mountain Park offers a number of double-fee sites as well.

All sites in the Bear Loop (sites 1-25) have electrical hookups. Spacing ranges from satisfactory to good along the outside of the loop, with sites closer together on the inside.

Mountain Park

The McConnel Loop (sites 26-32) has electrical hookups at every site. Farther from the river, these sites offer adequate shade and privacy.

The Crown Loop (sites 33-39) is very near the river and offers great campsites. Number 38 is the best of these sites.

The Comanche Loop (sites 40-57) is closest to the river. Sites 40-43, 47, and 48 are close together with limited shade and privacy, but they're on the river. Sites 50–54 are riverside, with good shade and privacy.

Popularity

Mountain Park is very popular. If you're looking for a weekend spot during the busy summer months, reserve ahead or get there by noon on Thursday. The most popular reservable sites are 6 (close to showers and toilets), 16, 19, 21, and 22. Sites nearest the river are 34, 35, 37, 38, 40-43, 47, 48, and 50-54.

Facilities

Modern facilities include picnic tables, fire grates, firewood for sale, water faucets, wheelchair-accessible vault toilets, and a shower house with sinks, mirrors, and electrical outlets. Other facilities include a playground, volleyball court, horseshoe pits, a pavilion, and a picnic area. A group camping area is available by reservation only.

RV Notes

Sites 1-32 have electrical hookups. Large, fairly level back-ins and three pull-thrus are spaced relatively close together, offering limited privacy. The nearest dump station is in the Poudre River Resort, 10 miles west on Highway 14 past Rustic.

Tent Notes

Tent pads are in all sites. A shower runs you 25 cents for every two minutes.

Recreational Opportunities 🏃 🚣 🎣

The Poudre is stocked with rainbow and brown trout. A volleyball court, horseshoe pits, a pavilion, and a children's playground are all available. The Mount McConnel Trail, which starts from the campground, is a 2.5-mile loop that climbs 800 feet; hikers are rewarded with terrific canyon views. The Kreutzer Interpretative Trail makes for a nice 1-mile side loop.

---

9. Kelly Flats

Location: About 35 miles northwest of Fort Collins
Elevation: 6,600 feet
Number of Sites: 29
Recommended RV Length: Up to 40 feet
Season: May through November
Maps: *Colorado Atlas & Gazetteer*, page 19, C6.5
Colorado Recreational Road Atlas, page 7, A2.5
Phone: 970-295-6700

Scenery: ★★★★
RVs: ★★★
Tents: ★★★★
Shade: ★★
Privacy: ★★

Directions

From Fort Collins, go north on Highway 287 about 10 miles to Ted's Place at the junction of Highway 14. Turn left (west), and travel about 25 miles on Highway 14.

Distinguishing Features

With fantastic river sites, Kelly Flats is the nicest of the 10 campgrounds along the Cache la Poudre. The campground is split into three areas: one long loop on the north side of the river divided into two areas, and one shorter loop on the south side. Campsites offer a range of shade, spacing, and privacy, and all but one are just a few feet from the river.

Popularity

From Memorial Day through mid-November, this campground fills by 7:00 p.m. every Friday night. Reservations are not accepted, so arrive early.

Facilities

Facilities include picnic tables, fire grates, firewood for sale, water faucets, and wheelchair-accessible vault toilets.

RV Notes

The south side of the river offers the best RV sites (sites 7-13). Long, level, wide back-ins are the rule and should handle just about any modern RV. The nearest dump station is 8 miles west on Highway 14 at the Poudre River Resort near Rustic.

Kelly Flats

Tent Notes

Sites on the river offer terrific views and a place to rest tired bones after a week of work. All sites have tent pads. Check out some of the tent-only sites, especially sites 2, 3, 4, 5, and 16.

Recreational Opportunities

The Poudre River is stocked with rainbow and brown trout. Upriver, from Pingree Park Road to Hombre Ranch just past Rustic, only artificial flies and lures are permitted. Anglers are limited to two fish over 16 inches. Across from the campground, FR 168, a difficult four-wheel-drive road, runs north 2,000 feet above the canyon. It parallels the canyon road as it heads northwest for 10 miles before joining the Pingree Hill Road, which hooks up with Highway 14 in Rustic. The road is also a popular mountain-biking route.

10. Chambers Lake

Location: About 63 miles west of Fort Collins
Elevation: 9,200 feet
Number of Sites: 52
Recommended RV Length: Up to 30 feet
Season: Mid-June to Labor Day
Maps: *Colorado Atlas & Gazetteer*, page 18, D4
Colorado Recreational Road Atlas, page 6, A3
Phone: 970-295-6700

Scenery: ★★★★
RVs: ★★★★
Tents: ★★★★
Shade: ★★★
Privacy: ★★★

Directions

From Fort Collins, go north on Highway 287 about 10 miles to Ted's Place at the junction of Highway 14. Go west on Highway 14 for about 53 miles to County Road 103 (Chambers Lake turnoff). Turn right (northwest), and follow the paved road for about a mile.

Distinguishing Features

Just above beautiful Chambers Lake (350 acres), the extraordinary Chambers Lake Campground is designed for both RVs and tents. Families will appreciate the many double sites and the playground. Lodgepole pines give most sites ample shade. Sites 1-20 have limited views and some highway noise, but

are large and private. Sites 26-31 are pleasant and offer average spacing and privacy. Sites 32-51 are the crème de la crème, offering excellent spacing, lake views, and privacy; some are within 50 feet of the lake. Sites 45-51 are walk-in tent sites; most have stunning lake views through the trees. Bears do wander through here from time to time, so don't leave food or coolers out in the open.

Popularity
This campground stays nearly full from Memorial Day through Labor Day. Make reservations by March 1, or arrive early on Thursday to grab a spot for the weekend. Sites 32-51 are most popular, and sites 34, 36, 35, and 37 are the most requested.

Facilities
Facilities include picnic tables, fire grates, firewood for sale, and water faucets. The vault toilets are wheelchair-accessible. Other facilities include a playground, a day-use area, an amphitheater, and a boat ramp.

RV Notes
The long to extra-long, wide, fairly level back-ins have everything but RV hookups. The nearest dump station is about 20 miles east on Highway 14 at the Poudre River Resort, just before Rustic.

Tent Notes
Sites throughout the campground have well-maintained tent pads. The walk-ins are the best, especially site 51. You can take a shower at Mountain Park Campground in Poudre Canyon; the cost is a quarter for two minutes.

Recreational Opportunities
Anglers report that the fishing is great for rainbow trout, brown trout, and mackinaws. If brookies are more your style, hike 1 mile northwest along the lake trail to Fall Creek.

A short drive north on County Road 103 leads you to Lost Lake and the Laramie River. Joe Wright Reservoir is just a few miles south on Highway 14. Motorized boats (up to 10 horsepower) are allowed, but boating must be wakeless. Swimming is prohibited.

For hikers, Blue Lake trailhead is only a short drive south on Highway 14. The trail leads to Blue Lake, Blue Lake Pass, and deep into the Rawah Wilderness. From the same trailhead, the Sawmill Creek Trail also goes into the Rawah Wilderness.

11. Tunnel

Location: About 69 miles west of Fort Collins
Elevation: 8,600 feet
Number of Sites: 49
Recommended RV Length: Up to 40 feet
Season: Memorial Day to Labor Day
Maps: *Colorado Atlas & Gazetteer,* page 18, C3.5
Colorado Recreational Road Atlas, page 6, A2.5
Phone: 970-295-6700

Scenery: ★★★
RVs: ★★★
Tents: ★★★★
Shade: ★★★
Privacy: ★★

Directions
From Fort Collins, drive north on Highway 287 for about 10 miles to Ted's Place at the junction of Highway 14. Take Highway 14 west for about 52 miles. Turn right (north) on County Road 103, a.k.a. Laramie River Road or Forest Road 190. Go about 6 miles.

Distinguishing Features
Tunnel is a large, spacious campground; the abundant wildlife includes moose. Five loops contain a variety of sites. Many sites are closely spaced, but some have excellent spacing and good privacy. Young lodgepole pines provide shade. The Laramie River meanders through the campground near 15 sites, and lovely mountain views can be seen from many others. Mosquitoes can be abundant, so remember the repellent!

Popularity
From Memorial Day to Labor Day, Tunnel can fill by Thursday night for

the weekend. Reservations are not accepted, so get off work early on Thursday —tell your boss the doctor says you have "tunnel vision."

Facilities
Facilities include picnic tables, fire grates, firewood for sale, hand-pumped water, and vault toilets.

RV Notes
Choose among numerous large, fairly level back-in and pull-thru/pull-out spaces.

Tent Notes
Tunnel has such a variety of options that campers should find a wonderful site to pitch their tent. Most sites have tent pads.

Recreational Opportunities
Winding through the campground, the Laramie River offers anglers prime opportunities to bag monster-sized brookies. The nearby West Branch Trail is very popular with horseback riders and leads to several destinations as it heads southwest into the Rawah Wilderness. Four miles along the trail, Camp Lake Trail branches off to the north, leading to the Rawah Lakes. The Rawah trailhead, 5 miles north of the campground, offers additional possibilities.

12. Grandview

Location: About 76 miles west of Fort Collins
Elevation: 10,220 feet
Number of Sites: 9
Season: June through October
Maps: *Colorado Atlas & Gazetteer*, page 28, A4
Colorado Recreational Road Atlas, page 6, B3
Phone: 970-295-6700

Scenery: ★★★★
RVs: No
Tents: ★★★★
Shade: ★★★
Privacy: ★★★

Directions
From Fort Collins on Highway 287, go about 10 miles north to Ted's Place at the junction of Highway 14. Take Highway 14 west for 54 miles. Go left (southeast) on gravel Forest Road 156 (Long Draw Road) for about 11.5 miles.

Distinguishing Features
Set at the south end of 242-acre, 2-mile-long Long Draw Reservoir, Grandview indeed has a grand view. This spectacular tent-only campground near the northern boundary of Rocky Mountain National Park offers many sites close to the reservoir, with beautiful views of the Never Summer Range to the south. Lodgepole pines border most sites, which are set near a grassy meadow. Excellent separation provides ample privacy for most sites. Two free, dispersed campsites are available on the other side of the lake. Don't forget the boat! This indeed is a "grand" tenting campground.

Popularity
Even though it's 75 percent filled on Friday nights in the summer, and nearly full by Saturday night, this campground is rarely filled completely. Visitors should find an available site, especially during the week. No reservations.

Facilities
Facilities are a bit primitive but include picnic tables, fire grates, and hand-pumped water. The vault toilets provide wheelchair access.

Tent Notes
All sites have tent pads, and there isn't an RV in sight!

Recreational Opportunities
Long Draw Reservoir offers tremendous cutthroat trout fishing (flies and lures only). The lake is rich in opportunities for canoeing and non-gas motorized boating, and elk herds frequent the area in the fall. A network of trails takes hikers into the Neota Wilderness and Rocky Mountain National Park. Near the campground, the Corral Creek Trail heads east, leading to the Cache la Poudre River after only 1 mile. Another trail then follows the river north and south for many miles, connecting to several other trails and leading into Rocky Mountain National Park. A few miles south of the campground lies the La Poudre Pass Trail, which also fingers out into the park.

Other Nearby Campgrounds

13. Stove Prairie (9 sites); 26.5 miles northwest of Fort Collins on Highway 14. Stove Prairie offers four well-shaded walk-in tent sites along the river. Other sites have limited shade and privacy but accommodate RVs of up to 30 feet. No reservations. **(970) 295-6700.**

14. Narrows (15 sites); 30 miles northwest of Fort Collins on Highway 14. Most sites are along the river's edge in this popular campground. Seven sites will accept RVs under 30 feet and eight are walk-in tent sites. Shade ranges from fair to good. No reservations. **(970) 295-6700.**

15. Dutch George Flats (20 sites); 32 miles northwest of Fort Collins on Highway 14. This modern, RV-friendly campground accommodates RVs of up to 33 feet. Every site has tent pads, too. Shaded river sites offer incredible views—but those that are treeless can be hot. No reservations. **(970) 295-6700.**

16. Big Bend (6 sites); 50 miles northwest of Fort Collins on Highway 14. A single row of sites near the road and above the river, Big Bend is a wonderful place to view bighorn sheep. Three sites are shaded walk-in tent sites. The campground is short on shade, and privacy is very limited. Maximum RV length is 20 feet. No reservations. **(970) 295-6700.**

17. Bliss State Wildlife Area (dispersed sites); 53 miles northwest of Fort Collins on Highway 14 (between mile markers 82 and 81). Few campers know about this free, primitive camping area next to the Poudre River. Not a conventional campground, undesignated campsites are spread around the edges of a flat, grassy meadow. The only facility is a pit toilet, and there is no drinking water. No reservations. **(970) 472-4300.**

18. Sleeping Elephant (15 sites); 54 miles northwest of Fort Collins on Highway 14. Sleeping Elephant is one of the last Poudre Canyon campgrounds to fill on weekends. Sites are just off the highway and can be small, but they offer excellent views of Sleeping Elephant Mountain. Maximum RV length is 20 feet. No reservations. **(970) 295-6700.**

19. Big South (4 sites); 59 miles northwest of Fort Collins on Highway 14. Bright, open campsites offer limited shade and privacy but do provide river access. Maximum RV length is 25 feet. No reservations. **(970) 295-6700.**

20. Aspen Glen (9 sites); 60 miles northwest of Fort Collins on Highway 14. Aspen Glen is a sunny little campground with good mountain views and sites close to the river. Best suited for smaller RVs and tents, it's very close to the road. No reservations. **(970) 295-6700.**

21. Browns Park (28 sites); 81 miles northwest of Fort Collins. From Fort Collins, go north on Highway 287 about 10 miles to Ted's Place at the junction of Highway 14. Go west on Highway 14 for about 52 miles and turn right (north) on County Road 103, a.k.a. Laramie River Road or Forest Road 190. Go about 16 miles to County Road 190 and turn left (west). Go about 3 miles. Situated near beaver ponds, Browns Park offers peace and seclusion. Most sites offer tent pads, and lodgepole pines and aspens provide sufficient shade. No drinking water is provided, so bring your own. Maximum RV length is 30 feet. Reservations not accepted, but this isolated campground rarely fills. **(970) 295-6700.**

22. Jacks Gulch (70 sites); 35 miles west of Fort Collins. From Fort Collins, go north on Highway 287 about 10 miles to Ted's Place at the junction of Highway 14. Go west on Highway 14 about 19 miles and turn left (south) on County Road 63E (gravel road) and then go about 6 miles. Beautifully designed and quite modern, Jacks Gulch also boasts the finest equestrian campsites in the state. Able to accommodate any RV, 28 sites in the Columbine loop even offer electrical hookups. All sites include tent pads and 10 are walk-in sites. No reservations. **(970) 295-6700.**

23. Tom Bennett (12 sites); 44 miles west of Fort Collins. From Fort Collins, go north on Highway 287 about 10 miles to Ted's Place at the junction of Highway 14. Go west on Highway 14 for about 19 miles and turn left (south) on County Road 63E. Proceed for about 15 miles. This remote tent-oriented campground south of Jacks Gulch offers many sites beside a quiet stream. No reservations. **(970) 295-6700.**

24. Long Draw (25 sites); 73 miles west of Fort Collins. From Fort Collins, go north on Highway 287 about 10 miles to Ted's Place at the junction of Highway 14. Go west on Highway 14 about 54 miles to Forest Road 156 (Long Draw Road). Go left (southeast) on Forest Road 156 for about 9.5 miles. On the way up, campers may want to consider one of the 38 free dispersed sites along Long Draw Road. Sites are close together, and provide fair to good shade. Maximum RV length is 30 feet. Reservations aren't accepted but this campground rarely fills. **(970) 295-6700.**

25. State Forest (164 sites); 75 miles northwest of Fort Collins on Highway 14, over Cameron Pass. This large park can be confusing, so first-time visitors should stop by the visitor center for help.

Four campgrounds miles apart from each other make up this park. The access road up to **The Crags** (26 sites) is steep, narrow, winding, and is not recommended for trailers or most RVs. Set in dense forest, this tent-oriented campground offers excellent mountain views. Sites generally have good separation and privacy. **Ranger Lakes** (32 sites) is good for large RVs, with electrical hookups and a dump station. The campground isn't near the lakes, but sites are well-shaded and private. Boating is not yet allowed at the lakes. **North Michigan Campground** (48 sites and 6 cabins) contains some excellent lakeside campsites around picturesque North Michigan Creek Reservoir. Swimming is not permitted, but wakeless boating is. Sites offer a range of shade and privacy, and 10 are tent-only. **Bockman** (52 sites) is the most isolated and rustic of the four. A recently upgraded mix of open and shaded sites, this campground is RV-friendly. Bring your own drinking water. Reservations accepted. **(970) 723-8366.**

26. Aspen (7 sites); 20 miles southeast of Walden. From Highway 14, turn right (south) on Forest Road 740, and proceed for 1 mile. Aspen may not offer terrific views, but it is a peaceful spot near a mountain stream. Moose roam the area, and tall pines provide plenty of shade. Medium-sized RV spots are available. Reservations accepted. **(970) 723-8204.**

27. Pines (11 sites); 20 miles southeast of Walden. From Highway 14, turn right (south) on Forest Road 740 and proceed for 2–3 miles. Pines is rustic, with sufficient shade and separation between sites. Sites will accommodate medium-sized RVs. Campers will find two wonderful riverside campsites. No reservations. **(970) 723-8204.**

Chambers Lake

RED FEATHER LAKES AREA

28. Dowdy Lake (closed for the 2006 camping season)
Location: About 46 miles northwest of Fort Collins
Elevation: 8,100 feet
Number of Sites: 62
Recommended RV Length: Up to 40 feet
Season: May through September
(some sites year-round)
Maps: *Colorado Atlas & Gazetteer*, page 19, B6
Colorado Recreational Road Atlas, page 6, C2
Phone: 970-295-6700

Scenery: ★★★★
RVs: ★★★
Tents: ★★★★
Shade: ★★
Privacy: ★★

Directions
From Fort Collins, take Highway 287 north to Livermore, about 21 miles.
Go west about 23 miles on County Road 74E (Red Feather Lakes Road).
Turn right (northeast) on Forest Road 218 (Dowdy Lake Road), and proceed
about 2 miles.

Distinguishing Features
Dowdy Lake (115 acres) can cast a spell over first-time visitors, luring them
back year after year. The campground's charm is hard to categorize: there
are no spectacular views, but the ponderosa pines, rock formations, rock
islands jutting above the lake's surface, and boulders scattered around the
campground are captivating. At least 20 sites are within a few feet of the lake,
and none of the others are much farther away. Many sites are compact and
tightly spaced.

Loop A (sites 1-3) is a smaller loop, and site 3 is on the water. Loop B (sites 4-8) is a flatter area on the water and popular for RVs. Loop C (sites 9-24) is a little farther from the lake but contains walk-in tent sites 12-20, which are close to the water. Loop D (sites 25-32) is highly desirable; all but three sites are on the water. Loop E (sites 33-62) is long and contains two mini-loops; sites 33-39 are lakeside.

Popularity
This is an extremely busy campground. From early May through late September, Dowdy Lake fills almost every weekend. Reserve far in advance (by March 1), or arrive by early Thursday afternoon and hope for the best. The most requested waterfront sites are 27, 28, 30-32, 34, 35, 37, and 39. For tent-campers only, sites 15, 16, 18, and 19 (my favorite!) are also lakeside. Reservations accepted.

Facilities
Facilities include picnic tables, fire grates, firewood for sale, water faucets, one hand pump, amphitheater, and wheelchair-accessible vault toilets. A boat ramp is conveniently nearby.

RV Notes
All sites but one have medium to large back-in spaces. Some will require a little leveling. There is no nearby dump station.

Tent Notes
All sites have tent pads, and 12-20 are walk-ins.

Recreational Opportunities
In Dowdy Lake, anglers can catch rainbow, brown, cutthroat, and brook trout. Only wakeless boating is permitted, and small boats are best. A good network of hiking and biking trails starts from the north end of the lake, and Mount Margaret (7,957 feet) is a popular destination. West of the Red Feather Lakes area on County Road 74E (becoming Forest Road 162) is a network of trails and four-wheel-drive roads suitable for hikers, mountain bikers, ATVs, and motorcycles.

photo by Gil Folsom

29. West Lake

Location: About 44 miles northwest of Fort Collins
Elevation: 8,200 feet
Number of Sites: 35
Recommended RV Length: Up to 50 feet
Season: Memorial Day to Labor Day
Maps: *Colorado Atlas & Gazetteer*, page 19, B6
Colorado Recreational Road Atlas, page 6, C2
Phone: 970-295-6700

Scenery: ★★★
RVs: ★★★★
Tents: ★★★
Shade: ★★
Privacy: ★★★

Directions

From Fort Collins, go north on Highway 287 to Livermore, 21 miles. Turn left (west) on County Road 74E (Red Feather Lakes Road), and continue for 23 miles.

Distinguishing Features

Recently renovated, West Lake is an RV-friendly lakeside spot that attracts campers looking for peace and solitude. Sites 6-36 now have electrical hookups. West Lake is a pretty 25-acre lake surrounded by light vegetation. The campground consists of five walk-in tent sites, one long lakeshore loop, and a smaller loop further up the hill from the lake. Several sites on the upper loop offer lovely mountain views to the west. Scattered ponderosa pines on an otherwise open hillside allow views of the lake from most sites.

Popularity

From Memorial Day to Labor Day, this campground fills almost every night. Make reservations in advance to insure a spot. Many of the sites are less than 75 feet from the lake. Sites 6, 7, 9, 10, 12, 14, 15, 17, 18, 20, 23, 25, 26, 27, and 28 all are lakeside. The most popular sites are 6, 25, 26, 27, and 28.

Facilities

Facilities include picnic tables, fire grates, firewood for sale, water faucets, and wheelchair-accessible vault toilets.

RV Notes

This campground offers about 6 pull-thrus, and a mix of medium and longer back-ins. Sites 6-36 all have electrical hookups. Sites 8, 14, 16, 21, and 33 all have 50 amp service. This is a good RV campground, but there is no nearby dump station.

Tent Notes

Although all sites work well for tents, you pay a premium for the electrical hookups that have been added to most of the sites. To save money, you might opt for the five walk-in tent-only sites (sites 1-5). Sites 1 and 3 are the best walk-in sites. Nearby Dowdy Lake would be a better option if spots are available. Tents must be pitched on tent pads.

Recreational Opportunities

Plenty of rainbow and brown trout are there for the catching. Gas motors are prohibited on the lake. For more fishing, or simply to drink in their beauty, check out nearby Dowdy and Bellaire Lakes. The terrain here is fairly gentle, so mountain biking is popular, too. Easy trails fan out from Dowdy Lake and the Mount Margaret/Molly Lake trailhead just a few miles northeast of the campground. Hiking and biking possibilities abound in the Red Feather Lakes area as well. Commercial outfitters offer horseback riding.

Other Nearby Campgrounds

30. Bellaire Lake (26 sites); about 3 miles southwest of Red Feather Lakes. From County Road 74E, turn south on County Road 162, and go 2 miles to Forest Road 163. Turn right (west), and go 0.5 mile. Known as "The Hilton" by area campground hosts, Bellaire Lake accommodates RVs of up to 60 feet, and hookups are available. All sites have tent pads. Shade and privacy range from poor to good. No sites on the lake. No reservations. **(970) 295-6700.**

31. North Fork Poudre (9 sites); about 7 miles west of Red Feather Lakes on gravel County Road 162. Set in dense woods without much sun, sites have good tent pads and can accommodate RVs of up to 30 feet. A creek runs near five sites. Lightly used, it offers solitude. No reservations. **(970) 295-6700.**

ROCKY MOUNTAIN NATIONAL PARK AREA

32. Aspenglen

Location: About 5 miles west of Estes Park
Elevation: 8,230 feet
Number of Sites: 54
Recommended RV Length: Up to 30 feet
Season: Mid-May to mid-September
Maps: *Colorado Atlas & Gazetteer,* page 29, A6
Colorado Recreational Road Atlas, page 6, C4
Phone: 970-586-1206

Scenery: ★★★★
RVs: ★★
Tents: ★★★
Shade: ★★
Privacy: ★★

Directions
From Estes Park, go west on Highway 34 to the Fall River entrance of Rocky Mountain National Park, then turn left just beyond the entrance station.

Distinguishing Features
Set in a quiet section of Rocky Mountain National Park, Aspenglen offers peace, seclusion, and breathtaking views of MacGregor and Deer Mountains. A paved road leads to three loops with paved parking spots. Loop A (sites 1-5) contains five short back-ins for RVs and five great walk-ins for tents (A-E). The walk-in sites put campers close to the river and provide wonderful seclusion. Loop B (sites 6-20) has mostly short back-ins for RVs, with some double parking spots. Most of these spots are in the open with good views of the mountains. Sites 22-31 are medium-sized, and blue spruce, ponderosa pines, and aspens provide plenty of shade. Loop C (sites 32-50) is a very open, sunny loop with great mountain and meadow views. Sites in the interior of this loop have no shade, and a few around the edges have limited shade. Sites 43, 44, and 46 are close to the river.

Popularity
Reservations are not accepted, and from July 1 through Labor Day the campground is usually full by 9:00 a.m. The best way to secure a site is to arrive between 7:00 and 9:00 a.m. and wait for someone to leave.

Facilities

Facilities include picnic tables, an amphitheater, fire grates, and water faucets. Firewood and ice are sold from 5:30 to 7:30 p.m. Bathrooms have flush toilets, sinks, and electrical outlets.

RV Notes

All RV sites are paved, and most are fairly level. The nearest dump station is in the National Park Resort, a private campground a quarter mile from the park entrance.

Tent Notes

Try to grab one of the walk-in tent sites. All sites have tent pads. Showers are available in Estes Park at Dad's Maytag Laundry and Shower, Estes Park Aquatic Center, Colorado Mountain School, Happy Camper, and Estes Park Campground.

Recreational Opportunities

First-timers to the park would be wise to stop at the visitor center and ask a ranger about the unlimited hiking and other activities available. Near the campground, Deer Ridge Trail circles Deer Mountain and intersects Deer Mountain Trail, which climbs 1,083 feet in 3 miles to the top of the mountain. A mile west of the campground, Lawn Lake trailhead leads into the Mummy Range and to several high alpine lakes. Of course, these two suggestions only scratch the surface of the adventures to be had in this park.

---

33. Moraine Park

Location: About 6 miles southwest of Estes Park
Elevation: 8,150 feet
Number of Sites: 247 (fewer after Labor Day)
Recommended RV Length: Up to 40 feet
Season: Year-round (no water after September)
Maps: *Colorado Atlas & Gazetteer*, page 29, B6
Colorado Recreational Road Atlas, page 6, C4
Phone: 970-586-1206

Scenery: ★★★★
RVs: ★★
Tents: ★★
Shade: ★★
Privacy: ★

Directions

In Estes Park, go west on Highway 34 to the middle of town, then turn left at the stoplight onto Highway 36. Carefully follow the "36 West" signs to the Beaver Meadows entrance (about 4 miles). Take the first left past the entrance station, and follow the road for 1.5 miles. Take the first road on the right, and follow the signs.

Distinguishing Features

Of all the campgrounds in Rocky Mountain National Park, this exceptionally large one offers the most spectacular views. Coyotes, deer, and elk are often

spotted in the campground. RV-friendliness, shade, privacy, and site size vary tremendously in such a big area. Choices are limited during the busy season, but rangers do their best to please everyone. The campground is in four loops, with sites varying in shade, privacy, and views.

Loop A (sites 1-140) is the only two-way loop. All other loops connect to Loop A, which offers the greatest variety of sites.

Loop B contains sites 170-225. Located in open, unshaded areas, many sites are spaced close together. Many have formal tent pads.

Loop C (sites 226-249) offers sweeping vistas but the least protection from the elements.

Loop D (sites 141-169) offers some of the best tent sites in the campground among interesting rock formations.

A color scheme allows campers to find the site that will best accommodate them. Brown signs (137 sites) designate sites for tents only. Blue sites (18) are for vans and pickups. Yellow sites (141) are for trailers under 18 feet and mini-homes. Green sites (50) are for trailers over 18 feet and large RVs.

Popularity

It's best to reserve a spot as soon as possible, especially if you're planning to visit in July or August. During these months, Moraine Park fills almost every day. Holiday weekends are generally filled. Campers without reservations should begin showing up at the ranger office as early as 7:00 a.m. to put their name on the waiting list. Those with a reservation should arrive early in the day to have the best chance of finding a decent site.

Facilities

The many modern facilities include picnic tables, fire grates, water faucets, flush toilets, sinks, and electrical outlets in the bathrooms. Firewood and ice are available between 5:30 and 8:30 p.m. from a roving truck (listen for what sounds like an ice-cream truck). Loop B contains chemical toilets. Several sites are wheelchair-accessible, as is one bathroom.

RV Notes

There's a spot for nearly any rig someplace in the campground. Just be patient while searching. Sites 32 through 60 in Loop A and several sites in Loops B and C are the best for RVs. A dump station is just inside the entrance.

Tent Notes

Persistent campers will discover dynamite tent spots. The best are sites 77–130 in Loop A; Loop D offers wonderful tent sites as well. Showers are available in Estes Park at Dad's Maytag Laundry and Shower, Estes Park Aquatic Center, Colorado Mountain School, Happy Camper, and Estes Park Campground.

Recreational Opportunities

Rangers are the best source of information in narrowing down the endless choices for maximizing time spent at the park. First-time visitors should drive to the top of Trail Ridge Road—one of the most breathtaking drives in all of Colorado. Every trail is tempting, but Cub Lake and Fern Lake trailheads are nearest the campground. Free shuttle buses leave from the campground during the summer, taking hikers to the popular trails near Bear Lake. Campers can visit the free museum near the campground, or try one of several nature hikes nearby; a livery offers horseback riding. Campfire programs at the amphitheater are a great way to learn more about this renowned area.

Other Nearby Campgrounds

34. Longs Peak (26 sites); 11 miles south of Estes Park on Highway 7. This immensely popular tent-only campground exists essentially for one purpose—to serve hikers hoping to summit one of Colorado's most popular fourteeners. The tent-only designation is strictly enforced; sleeping in the bed of a pickup or in any other vehicle is prohibited. All sites have tent pads and provide good shade. There's a three-day maximum stay in the summer. Late sleepers, beware: your neighbors will be up at 3:00 a.m. to get an early start on their ascent of Longs Peak. No reservations, so arrive early. **(970) 586-1206.**

35. Glacier Basin (150 sites); about 5 miles south of the Beaver Meadows entrance station on Bear Lake Road. Five paved loops lead to tight, compact campsites and limited privacy. Heavily wooded with lodgepole pines, sites offer campers plenty of shade, but few mountain views. RV sites are short to long back-ins and can accommodate RVs of up to 30 feet. A few have tent pads, and campers can pitch their tents in the deep, wooded areas of the campground. Modern amenities include flush toilets and a dump station. This is a popular campground, and reservations are required; call as far in advance as possible. **(970) 586-1206.**

CENTRAL CITY—NEDERLAND AREA

36. Pawnee

Location: About 17 miles northwest of Nederland
Elevation: 10,400 feet
Number of Sites: 55
Recommended RV Length: Up to 45 feet
Season: July through October
Maps: *Colorado Atlas & Gazetteer,* page 29, D6
Colorado Recreational Road Atlas, page 10, C2
Phone: 303-444-6600

Scenery: ★★★★★
RVs: ★★★
Tents: ★★★
Shade: ★★★
Privacy: ★★★

Directions

From the circular intersection in Nederland, go north on Highway 72 for 11.7 miles, to just past the huge "Brainard Lake Recreation Area/Pawnee Campground" sign on the right. Turn left (west) on County Road 102 (a.k.a. Brainard Lake Road or Forest Road 112), and go about 5 miles to the Brainard Lake Recreation Area.

Distinguishing Features

Incredible views along the many trails make this campground without question one of the top choices for hikers along the Colorado Front Range. The wildflowers are spectacular. Just a short walk from the campsites is Brainard Lake, with a breathtaking backdrop of the Indian Peaks Wilderness. Campers can choose between open sites with spectacular views or those deep within forests of lodgepole pine and blue spruce. Trees growing at an angle in more open areas serve as reminders of the harsh winds that whip through this area. Many sites in the woods offer excellent privacy. South St. Vrain Creek is 150 yards behind sites 43-55.

Popularity

From July 1 through Labor Day, this campground fills every weekend. Reserve in advance or arrive by Thursday or early Friday to secure a spot. Favorites with campers are deeply wooded sites 44, 46, 48, 50, 52, and 54. Sites 22-30 all have great views, but no shade. Sites 29 and 30 are the closest to the lake, and 29 has the best lake and mountain views of any spot in the campground.

Facilities

Facilities include picnic tables, fire grates, firewood for sale, water faucets, and vault toilets.

RV Notes

Two-thirds of the sites accommodate larger RVs, and the long back-ins in the woods are fairly level and offer privacy (although other sites are not as level).

The campground has only two pull-thrus, and the nearest dump stations are in Lyons, Estes Park, or Golden Gate State Park.

Tent Notes
Most sites have tent pads. Be prepared for strong winds and chilly nights.

Recreational Opportunities
In Brainard Lake, anglers will find rainbows, browns, and brookies. Non-motorized boating is permitted. Just west of Brainard Lake is 40-acre Long Lake, where anglers will find cutthroat, rainbows, and the rare emerald green trout. In nearby Left Hand Park Reservoir (100 acres) are lake, rainbow, and brook trout. Fly-fishing is recommended in the surrounding high alpine lakes.

Hikers should plan an extended stay in the campground and try a different trail every day. The Mitchell Lake Trail leads to Mitchell Lake (1 mile), then to Blue Lake (2.5 miles) with an 850-foot total elevation gain. The Mount Audubon Trail climbs 2,773 feet in 3.5 miles to the top of the mountain (13,223 feet). The Pawnee Pass Trail leads to Long Lake (0.5 mile), then to Lake Isabelle (2 miles), and at 4 miles reaches the top of Pawnee Pass (12,541 feet). The Niwot Ridge Trail climbs 1,830 feet in 4 miles to the top of Niwot Ridge (12,284 feet).

Other Nearby Campgrounds

37. Columbine (47 sites); 2 miles northwest of Central City on dirt Highway 279. Sites are well-shaded and RV-friendly, and privacy ranges from fair to adequate. An extensive network of four-wheel-drive roads in this area attracts off-road enthusiasts and mountain bikers. Reservations are accepted, but this campground rarely fills. **(303) 567-3000.**

38. Cold Springs (38 sites); 5 miles north of Black Hawk on Highway 119. Situated very close to the highway, Cold Springs is fairly open with limited shade. All sites have tent pads. Privacy is fair, and this campground is RV-friendly. Reservations accepted. **(303) 567-3000.**

39. Golden Gate Canyon State Park (132 sites) is a favorite quick escape from the city for many, and miles of hiking trails are the main attraction. In addition to the following two campgrounds, the park also offers a group campground, 20 backcountry sites, 5 cabins, and 2 yurts.

Reverend's Ridge (97 sites); 10 miles northeast of Black Hawk. From Highway 119, turn right on Gap Road (mile marker 16). With many electrical hookups (59) and a dump station, Reverend's Ridge works well for both RVs and tents. Flush toilets and showers are also provided. Many sites have tent pads, and some tent-only loops are available. Most sites offer good shade. Reservations accepted. **(303) 582-3707.**

Pawnee

39. Golden Gate Canyon State Park (continued)
   Aspen Meadow (35 sites); 11.5 miles northeast of Black Hawk via Highway 119 and Gap Road (mile marker 16). This primitive tent-only campground offers a mix of drive-in and walk-in sites, some designed for horseback riders. Sites, grouped in clusters around the campground, provide satisfactory privacy. A mix of evergreens and aspens provides shade to most. Reservations accepted. **(303) 582-3707.**

40. Kelly Dahl (46 sites); about 3 miles south of Nederland on Highway 119. A large campground with three loops and a playground, Kelly Dahl offers a variety of sunny and shady sites. Maximum RV length is 40 feet. Reservations accepted. **(303) 444-6600.**

41. Rainbow Lakes (16 sites); 11 miles northwest of Nederland. Take Highway 72 north from Nederland about 6.5 miles to Forest Road 298. Turn left (south), and go 4.5 miles on a rocky, dirt road. This long, narrow campground is close to beaver ponds, fishing, and good hiking opportunities in a remote area. Sites offer good shade and privacy; two are on the creek. No trash service or drinking water is available. Maximum RV length is 20 feet. No reservations. **(303) 444-6600.**

42. Camp Dick (41 sites); 17 miles north of Nederland on Highway 72. Camp Dick is a modern campground with a paved road and tent pads. It has a reputation for being windy and offers a mix of open and shaded sites, some near the river. Sites 29-38 are sheltered and are the most popular in the campground. Maximum RV length is 55 feet. Reservations accepted. **(303) 444-6600.**

43. Peaceful Valley (17 sites); 17 miles north of Nederland on Highway 72. A few sites are by the river, and privacy is limited. Maximum RV length is 55 feet. Reservations accepted. **(303) 444-6600.**

44. Meeker Park (29 sites); 12.5 miles south of Estes Park, 1 mile south of Meeker Park Lodge, on Highway 7. A primitive campground without drinking water or picnic tables. Maximum RV length is 25 feet. No reservations. **(303) 444-6600.**

45. Olive Ridge (56 sites); 15 miles south of Estes Park on Highway 7. Popular with families and national park visitors looking for seclusion, this campground offers shade and privacy. Special facilities include a playground with a "Big Toy" and amphitheater programs on Friday and Saturday evenings. Maximum RV length is 30 feet. Reservations accepted. **(303) 444-6600.**

LAKE GRANBY—GRAND LAKE AREA

46. Sunset Point

Location: About 6 miles northeast of Granby (see map on p. 289)
Elevation: 8,300 feet
Number of Sites: 25
Recommended RV Length: Up to 35 feet
Season: May to September
Maps: *Colorado Atlas & Gazetteer*, page 28, C3
Colorado Recreational Road Atlas, page 10, A1.5
Phone: 970-887-4100

Scenery: ★★★
RVs: ★★★
Tents: ★★★★
Shade: ★★★
Privacy: ★★★

Directions

From the intersection of Highways 40 and 34 just west of Granby, go north on Highway 34 for about 5.2 miles. Turn right (east) on Forest Road 125 (a.k.a. County Road 6 or Arapaho Bay Road), go 1.25 miles, then turn left into the campground.

photo by Gil Folsom

Distinguishing Features

With 17 shaded lakeside sites, this new, modern campground on Lake Granby has quickly become a favorite destination in the area. The boat ramp is only a short distance away, boats can be moored on the shoreline, and no sites are more than a minute's walk down to the lake.

A paved one-way road leads through the campground, with campsites on either side of it. Sites to the right of the road are all lakeside, while those on the left enjoy mountain views and are more open with less shade. Lakeside sites 1-11 are located higher up on the shore, while sites 14 and higher have a more gently sloping shoreline with easier lake access. Site 1 is for motorcyclists or bicyclists, and sites 9, 19, and 23 are all double sites.

Popularity

Sunset Point fills every weekend, so your best bet is to get there Thursday or early Friday. For those who find it full, a shadeless parking lot that moonlights as an overflow camping area is just across from the campground. At press time, this campground was not on the reservation system. The prime lakeside sites are 21, 23 (double fee), 25, 20, 18, 17, and 14-16 (tents only). Other lakeside sites are 11, 10, 7, 6, 4, 3, 2, and 1.

Facilities

Facilities are all wheelchair-accessible and include picnic tables, fire grates, lantern posts with double hangers, firewood for sale, water faucets, and vault toilets.

RV Notes

Most sites are wide, medium to long back-ins that are fairly level. However, there isn't enough room to easily park a boat trailer in the parking spaces. Stillwater Campground several miles to the north offers the nearest dump station.

Tent Notes

All sites work great for tents and every site has a formal tent pad with tie-down points. Tents must be pitched *only* on tent pads. Sites 14-16 and 1 (for motorcyclists or bicyclists) are lakeside tent-only sites.

Recreational Opportunities

Here, boating and fishing are the big draws. The Sunset Point boat ramp is about a two-minute drive, and campers are allowed to moor boats on the shoreline adjacent to their campsites. For a change of pace, the more intimate Willow Creek Reservoir, better suited for small boats, lies just a few miles to the west. (See also Arapaho Bay and Green Ridge Campgrounds.)

---

47. Arapaho Bay

Location: About 14 miles northeast of Granby (see map on p. 289)
Elevation: 8,320 feet
Number of Sites: 84
Recommended RV Length: Up to 35 feet
Season: Memorial Day to early September
(Big Rock Loop open through hunting season)
Maps: *Colorado Atlas & Gazetteer*, page 29, C4
Colorado Recreational Road Atlas, page 10, B2
Phone: 970-887-4100

Scenery: ★★★★
RVs: ★★★★
Tents: ★★★★
Shade: ★★★
Privacy: ★★

Directions

From the intersection of Highways 40 and 34 just west of Granby, go north on Highway 34 for 5.2 miles. Turn right (east) on Forest Road 125 (a.k.a. County Road 6 or Arapaho Bay Road), and go 8.6 miles; the last 7.5 miles are gravel.

Distinguishing Features

Adjacent to Lake Granby (7,256 acres with 45 miles of shoreline) and at the far southeast edge of the lake, this campground is remote. In such a large campground, spacing and privacy vary tremendously.

The Big Rock Loop (sites 1-22), in the middle of a lodgepole pine forest, is a pleasant area. This loop is the farthest from the water, and sites lack lake and mountain views. Dust from passing motorists on their way to the other loops can be a problem for sites 1-8. The Moraine Loop (sites 23-51) is much nicer, with several lakeside sites and shade throughout. The Roaring Fork Loop (sites 52-84) has fantastic lakeside walk-in sites for tents and many additional lakeside sites that offer boaters a chance to dock next to their campsites. Most lakeside sites have poor to fair shade, but excellent lake and mountain views. Sites 69, 71, 73, and 83 are doubles.

Popularity

Campers must call for reservations far in advance if they wish to spend a weekend at the campground during peak season, from Memorial Day through Labor Day. Try sites 70-78 or 83 if you're bringing a boat or looking for a lakeside haven. Sites 35, 26, 31, and 51 are also lakeside. The best tent site on the lake is 62.

Facilities

Facilities include picnic tables, fire grates, firewood for sale, water faucets, wheelchair-accessible vault toilets, and a boat ramp.

RV Notes

All sites have medium to large back-ins that are fairly level. Stillwater Campground, 8.6 miles north of Granby on Highway 34, contains the nearest dump station.

Tent Notes

Most sites have tent pads. Sites 57-66 (except 63) in the Roaring Fork Loop are all walk-ins near the lake. Site 62 is a superb walk-in, and 57-61 are all lovely lakeside sites but spaced close together. Sites 59 and 60 are next to the river and lake.

Recreational Opportunities

If you brought a boat and are lucky enough to have grabbed a lakeside site, life couldn't be better. Kokanee salmon and lake, rainbow, brown, and brook trout await anglers. Monarch Lake (147 acres) is only 1 mile to the southeast and offers a chance to catch rainbows, brookies, and cutthroats. Only hand-powered boats are allowed in Monarch Lake. Hikers can access the Indian Peaks Wilderness from the Roaring Fork or Monarch Lake trailheads. Hikers can head northwest for many miles along and above the lakeshore on the Knight Ridge Trail.

---

48. Green Ridge

Location: About 13 miles northeast of Granby (see map on p. 289)
Elevation: 8,360 feet
Number of Sites: 78
Recommended RV Length: Up to 35 feet
Season: Memorial Day to early September (loop B open through October or November)
Maps: *Colorado Atlas & Gazetteer,* page 28, C3.5
Colorado Recreational Road Atlas, page 10, A1
Phone: 970-887-4100

Scenery: ★★★★
RVs: ★★★★
Tents: ★★★★
Shade: ★★★
Privacy: ★★

Directions

From Granby, go about 11.5 miles north on Highway 34, then right on County Road 66 at the "Green Ridge Complex" sign. Go about 1.5 miles to the southern end of Shadow Mountain Lake.

Distinguishing Features

Shadow Mountain and the Never Summer Range are just two of the breathtaking vistas that greet campers. The Colorado River, just a stream at this point, is nearby. Green Ridge sits just south of 1,356-acre Shadow Mountain Lake, which is 3 miles long with 8.5 miles of shoreline. Lodgepole pines shade the campground and protect campers from the wind. Green Ridge sites do not look out onto the lake, but do put campers within a short walking distance. Sites are close together.

Loop A features adequate shade in all sites and is a bit closer to the lake. Sites 2, 3, 6, 7, 9, 10, 12, and 14 back up to a tiny hill. A 10- to 15-foot walk from the back of these sites will lead campers to a great view of the lake!

Loop B features shade in all sites except 64, 66, 67, 69, and 72, which are in an open, treeless meadow. The mountains are visible from some sites in Loop B. This loop is closer to the spillway and the Colorado River. Sites 53 and 57-60 are near the spillway, the river, and fantastic fishing.

Popularity
Sites fill almost every weekend during the summer, so make reservations far in advance for any weekend from Memorial Day through Labor Day.

Facilities
Facilities include picnic tables, fire grates, firewood for sale, water faucets, flush and vault toilets, a parking area for anglers, and a boat ramp next to the campground.

RV Notes
Loop A sites are medium and large back-ins with some doubles and pullouts. Loop B offers medium and large back-ins with many doubles and no pull-outs. A dump station is near the picnic area.

Tent Notes
Loop A sites 18-22 are away from the RVs and are walk-ins. Tent pads are available in most every site.

Recreational Opportunities

Visitors to Shadow Mountain Lake can try their luck at both lake and stream fishing. The spillway below the lake offers rainbows, browns, cutthroats, and brookies. The islands make great picnicking and canoeing destinations (except where posted). A boat ramp is next to the campground.

The Knight Ridge Trail lies just across the spillway, leading north along the eastern lakeshore and to the top of Shadow Mountain. Heading south on this trail, hikers travel along the eastern edge of the river and eventually to the southeastern shore of Lake Granby. Rocky Mountain National Park is only a few miles north of the campground, and to the northwest is an extensive network of ATV and mountain-bike trails.

Other Nearby Campgrounds

49. Willow Creek (34 sites); 9 miles northwest of Granby. From Highway 34, turn left (west) on County Road 40. Recently renovated, this relatively open campground has widely scattered evergreens and aspens that provide some shade. Sites are spaced close together, so privacy is poor. Sites will now accommodate RVs up to 25 feet, and each one also has a tent pad. Willow Creek Reservoir (750 acres) is popular with canoeists and anglers. In addition to the usual amenities, each site now has a lantern post and a bear proof food storage container. New toilets are now wheelchair accessible and of the SST (sweet smelling toilets) design. Reservations accepted. **(970) 887-4100.**

50. Stillwater (129 sites; see map on p. 289); 8.6 miles north of Granby on Highway 34. In many campers' minds, this is a top-100 campground. Stillwater offers beautiful views of Lake Granby and every convenience a camper could want—hot showers, flush toilets, and RV hookups. But sites are close together and provide little shade or protection from the fierce afternoon winds that can whip up out of nowhere. Maximum RV length is 45 feet. On the far side of the lake, off in the distance, look for "sleeping Abe." Reservations are necessary for a weekend spot. **(970) 887-4100.**

51. Timber Creek (100 sites); 10 miles north of Grand Lake on Highway 34 in Rocky Mountain National Park. Four paved loops with paved parking lead to a mix of multi-use sites and walk-in tent sites. Shade is good, but privacy isn't great. A number of sites accommodate RVs up to 30 feet long; some have double parking areas. All sites have tent pads, and 32 are walk-ins. Timber Creek is the only national park campground on the west side of Rocky Mountain National Park. Facilities include flush toilets and a dump station. No reservations. **(970) 586-1206.**

FRASER—WINTER PARK AREA

52. St. Louis Creek (16 sites); 3 miles southwest of Fraser on gravel County Road 73 (Forest Road 160.2). Popular with hikers and mountain bikers, this campground offers spacious sites with adequate shade. It features long, wide back-ins and pull-thrus for RVs of up to 32 feet. A short walk leads to the creek. No reservations. **(970) 887-4100.**

53. Byers Creek (6 sites); 7.5 miles southwest of Fraser on gravel County Road 73 (Forest Road 160.2). Heavily wooded sites offer ample spacing and privacy. Two sites are on the creek. Popular with the hiking and mountain-biking crowd, this campground can accommodate RVs of up to 32 feet. No reservations. **(970) 887-4100.**

54. Sawmill Gulch (6 sites); 13 miles northwest of Granby. Go 2.75 miles west of Granby on Highway 40 and turn right (north) on Highway 125. Go about 10 miles. Sites offer decent shade, ample space for RVs, and sufficient privacy. Four sites are on or near a stream. Maximum RV length is 32 feet. No reservations. **(970) 887-4100.**

55. Denver Creek (22 sites); 15 miles northwest of Granby. Go 2.75 miles west of Granby on Highway 40 and turn right (north) on Highway 125. Go about 12 miles. Located on both sides of the highway, this campground is best suited for tents and smaller RVs (up to 25 feet) and rarely fills. The more desirable sites are west of the road; seven sites are creekside, but lack shade and privacy. Sites on the east side offer more shade. No reservations. **(970) 887-4100.**

56. Idlewild (24 sites); 1 mile south of Winter Park on Highway 40. Two loops make up this campground. The loop closest to the road has most of the sites, and the second loop is set down by the Fraser River, farther away from traffic noise. All sites are well shaded. Several are near the water, but they're not very RV-friendly. No reservations. **(970) 887-4100.**

57. Robbers Roost (11 sites); about 6 miles south of Winter Park on Highway 40. This campground is suited for both tents and small RVs. Sufficient spacing allows for privacy and many sites are well-shaded. Highway noise can be very invasive to what would otherwise be a quiet campground. Five sites are close to the Fraser River. No water. No reservations. **(970) 887-4100.**

58. Mizpah (10 sites); 5.5 miles west of Empire on Highway 40. This campground, on the south side of Berthoud Pass and close to Denver, features generally large sites with adequate spacing, privacy, and shade. Because of its proximity to the Front Range, Mizpah fills almost every day in the summer, often by early afternoon. Clear Creek runs alongside two sites. RVs will have some leveling to do, depending on site selection. No reservations. **(303) 567-3000.**

Grandview

SILVERTHORNE—KREMMLING AREA

59. Blue River (24 sites); 7.5 miles north of Silverthorne (I-70 exit 205) on Highway 9. Two loops make up this campground. The upper loop (sites 1-9) has four sites in a small loop by the road, and five more on the side of the road leading into the lower loop. The lower loop includes 10 closely spaced riverside sites. Shade and privacy range from poor to good. Upper-loop sites accommodate medium-sized RVs. No reservations. **(970) 468-5400.**

60. South Fork (21 sites); 27 miles northeast of Silverthorne. Go north on Highway 9 about 13 miles, and turn right (east) on County Road 15 (Ute Pass Road). Follow County Road 15 about 9-10 miles to County Road 30 (Forest Road 138). Turn right (south) on County Road 30, and go about 6 miles. Sites offer sufficient shade and privacy. Most are rather ordinary, but seven riverside spots are delightful, and a horse corral is nearby. Maximum RV length is 23 feet. Reservations accepted. **(970) 887-4100.**

61. Sugarloaf (11 sites); 27.5 miles northeast of Silverthorne. Go north on Highway 9 about 13 miles, and turn right (east) on County Road 15 (Ute Pass Road). Follow County Road 15 about 9-10 miles to County Road 30 (Forest Road 138). Turn right (south) on County Road 30, and go about 6.5 miles. This campground is a bit better than average, with good shade, privacy, and spacing in one loop. Only one site is by the river. What makes it special is the wheelchair-accessible boardwalk and trail that crosses the river to marvelous views and picnic tables. Most sites accommodate medium-sized RVs up to 23 feet. No reservations. **(970) 887-4100.**

62. Horseshoe (7 sites); 24 miles northeast of Silverthorne. Go north on Highway 9 about 13 miles, and turn right (east) on County Road 15 (Ute Pass Road). Follow County Road 15 about 9-10 miles to County Road 30 (Forest Road 138). Turn left (north) on County Road 30, and go about 3 miles. This is a small, open campground with compact sites and sparse shade in all but three sites. One site offers views of the river, and in three others a short stroll through the trees leads to the water. Good for smaller RVs. No reservations. **(970) 887-4100.**

63. Williams Fork Reservoir (dispersed); about 3.5 miles southwest of Parshall on County Road 3. Camping is free at this 1,800-acre reservoir, but swimming is prohibited. You'll find developed sites at several spots around the reservoir, many large RV sites, and little shade. You can camp very close to the water at many sites. No reservations. **(303) 628-6526.**

Green Mountain Reservoir (2,125 acres; see map on p. 288) is situated in an open sagebrush setting with few trees. With no boating or swimming restrictions, it attracts water sports lovers and anglers. The following five very primitive campgrounds (64-68) are clustered along the shoreline and rarely fill. Most campsites are better for RVs than tents. No reservations.

64. Prairie Point (31 sites; see map on p. 288); 18 miles north of Silverthorne (I-70 exit 205) on Highway 9. Set in the open prairie above Green Mountain Reservoir, this is a parking-lot style campground that is best for RVs. Most sites have no privacy or shade. A few work well for tents. Sites 1-8 are less than 50 feet from the water. No reservations. **(970) 468-5400.**

65. Willows (35 sites; see map on p. 288); 25.5 miles northwest of Silverthorne (I-70 exit 205). Go north on Highway 9 for 25 miles, and then left (west) on County Road 30 (north end of reservoir). Near the western edge of Green Mountain Reservoir, this free campground is very large but offers no water, trash service, or tables. Sites are not defined, and camping is possible along a lengthy stretch of the reservoir and slightly above it. Most sites are treeless, but a few by the reservoir have good shade; this area also has the best views and the best boating. Sites accommodate any RV. No reservations. **(970) 468-5400.**

66. Davis Springs (7 sites; see map on p. 288); 18.5 miles northwest of Silverthorne (I-70 exit 205). Go north on Highway 9 for 16.5 miles to County Road 30 (Heeney Road). Turn left (northwest) on County Road 30, and go about 2 miles. This free, dirt parking lot for RVs lies slightly above Green Mountain Reservoir. It's very primitive, with no water, trash service, tables, or defined sites. Large cottonwoods and aspens ring the lot. Campers have no privacy in their sites. A short trail leads down to the lake. There are no reservations. **(970) 468-5400.**

67. McDonald Flats (13 sites; see map on p. 288); 19 miles northwest of Silverthorne (I-70 exit 205). Go north on Highway 9 for 16.5 miles to County Road 30 (Heeney Road). Turn left (northwest) on County Road 30, and go about 2.5 miles. Campers will find themselves in a level, treeless meadow with no privacy. They will, however, have easy access to Green Mountain Reservoir and a boat ramp. A few sites are less than 25 feet from the water, but most are 200 to 400 feet away. Sites accommodate most RVs. No reservations. **(970) 468-5400.**

68. Elliot Creek (24 sites; see map on p. 288); 27.8 miles northwest of Silverthorne (I-70 exit 205). Go north on Highway 9 for about 25 miles, and then left (west) on County Road 30 (Heeney Road). Follow County Road 30 for about 3 miles. This very primitive, free campground consists of a huge dirt parking lot above Green Mountain Reservoir with no privacy, and a couple of additional smaller camping areas. This campground offers no water, trash service, or tables, but accommodates most RVs. Sites are not defined, and shade is sparse. No reservations. **(970) 468-5400.**

69. Cataract Creek (4 sites; see map on p. 288); 24.6 miles northwest of Silverthorne (I-70 exit 205). Go north on Highway 9 about 16.5 miles to County Road 30 (Heeney Road). Turn left (northwest) on County Road 30, and go about 6.5 miles to Forest Road 1725. Turn left (west) on Forest Road 1725, and go about 2 miles. This primitive campground with a rough road leading through it is only suitable for tents and pickup campers. Shade is decent, privacy is fair, and sites are small. A short walk down the hill leads to the creek. No reservations. **(970) 468-5400.**

70. Wolford Mountain Reservoir (48 sites); 6.3 miles north of Kremmling on Highway 40. Boating and fishing are the main attractions at this 1,440-acre reservoir. The large, modern campground is devoid of trees and—usually—tenters. Sites are all long RV pull-thrus with electrical hookups and little privacy, but every camper enjoys a great view of Wolford Mountain and the reservoir. With rock monoliths towering overhead, this one wins the award for the most elaborate covered picnic tables. Reservations accepted. **1-866-472-4943** or **(970) 724-3460.**

Arapaho Bay

NORTHEASTERN PLAINS AREA

71. Crow Valley (10 sites. Map coordinates: *Colorado Atlas & Gazetteer*, page 94, B1; *Colorado Recreational Road Atlas*, page 17, A1.5); 40 miles east of Fort Collins. Go east from Fort Collins on Highway 14 about 40 miles to County Road 77. Turn left (north), and go 1 mile. This small campground is located in a woodland oasis on the southeastern corner of 193,000-acre Pawnee National Grassland, which offers wonderful wildlife viewing (primarily birds). A map is mandatory for exploring! Most sites are well-shaded by towering elms and cottonwoods. All the basic amenities are provided. Maximum RV length is 35 feet. No reservations. **(970) 353-5004.**

72. North Sterling State Park (141 sites. Map coordinates: *Colorado Atlas & Gazetteer*, page 95, A4.5; *Colorado Recreational Road Atlas*, page 18, A1); about 20 miles northwest of Sterling. From Sterling, take Highway 138 northeast about 7.5 miles to Highway 113. Turn left (north) on Highway 113, go about 2 miles to County Road 46, and go left (west). Go for about 8 miles to County Road 33, turn right (north), and go 2 miles. Sterling Reservoir (3,000 acres) offers many nooks and crannies to explore along its 40-mile shoreline, making this a boater's paradise. Campers are permitted to moor their boats along the shore near their campsites. Sterling Reservoir has gained a reputation as one of the best warm-water fishing destinations in the state. Anglers will find walleye, wiper, crappie, perch, catfish, and trout to test their fishing expertise. The park also boasts a wonderful swim beach, with water temperatures climbing into the 80s in the heat of the summer.

Elks Campground (sites 1-50) is on a small hill overlooking the lake, and is the most established campground in the park. A mixture of pull-thrus and back-ins, sites are grassy and spacious with good separation. Very little shade is available except for what is provided by the shade shelters over the picnic tables at many sites. All sites offer electrical hookups, and a dump station is available for RVs. Amenities include pay showers, flush toilets, a nearby marina and store, and a boat ramp. **Chimney View Campground** (sites 51-94) is on a bluff about 500 yards from the lake, with some sites overlooking the reservoir. Sites are all RV-friendly pull-thrus with no hookups. There is no shade except for some shade shelters. Formal tent pads exist in all sites. Showers, laundry facilities, and flush and vault toilets are provided. **Inlet Grove Campground** (sites 95-141) is just down the hill from Chimney View and adjacent to the reservoir. Sites are long pull-thrus with electrical hookups. A number of sites are along the shoreline, with large cottonwoods providing shade to some lakeside sites. Most of the sites have no shade except for under the shade shelters, but all sites have tent pads. Flush toilets are provided. In addition, a building shared with Chimney View has pay showers and laundry facilities. Reservations are accepted, and are a good idea on summer weekends. **(970) 522-3657.**

73. Jackson Lake State Park (260 sites; see map on p. 289. Map coordinates: *Colorado Atlas & Gazetteer*, page 94, C1; *Colorado Recreational Road Atlas*, page 17, B2.5); 22 miles northwest of Fort Morgan. From Fort Morgan, go west 13 miles on I-76 to Highway 39 (exit 66). Turn right (north) on Highway 39, and go 7 miles until the road ends at County Road Y.5 (past Goodrich). Turn left (west) on County Road Y.5 and go 3.5 miles. Jackson Reservoir is a large, 2,700-acre lake with 11 miles of shoreline. It's known for its shoreline camping, warm water, sandy bottom, and beaches. All water sports are allowed, and there are two designated swim areas. The lake is home to trout, saugeye, bass, walleye, perch, catfish, crappie, and wiper, making it a popular fishing spot. Hunting is also a favorite activity during the fall and winter. Seven campgrounds lie along the lake, so campers are never too far from the water. The following seven campgrounds are listed from south to north, which is the order in which campers will find them. Most of them are adjacent to each other, and it can be difficult to determine where one ends and another begins. Some of the facilities are located between campgrounds. Amenities include water faucets, showers, laundry facilities, and a mix of vault and flush toilets. There is a dump station near the park office.

Dunes Campground is a group campground on the south shore of the lake, and offers seclusion from the other campgrounds. Limited shade is available, but each site has a shade shelter. **Lakeside Campground** (62 sites) offers many lovely lakeside sites in a grassy, parklike setting with fair, widely varying shade. An abundance of long pull-thrus makes life easy for RVers. **Cove Campground** (16 sites) has no prime lakeside sites because heavy brush lies between the campsites and the lake, obscuring the view. All sites have electrical hookups and shade shelters over the picnic tables. Natural shade ranges widely. At **Pelican Campground** (37 sites), half of the sites are by the lake. Most sites are medium back-ins with minimal shade. **Sandpiper Campground** (28 sites) has all its sites in one loop with electrical hookups at every site. Sites on the outside are all long pull-thrus, and those on the inside are medium back-ins. Sites are generally large and spacious, but in the open with no shade. Only a few sites are lakeside and this is not a great place for tents. **Fox Hills Campground** (89 sites) is the largest campground in the park and probably the least appealing. Campsites are in the open without shade and offer little privacy, but have lake views. RVers will find a mix of long pull-thrus and back-ins. Those with tents are better off elsewhere. **Northview Campground** (10 sites) is best for RVs. Very popular, it offers the best lake views, even though sites are not close to the lake. All sites are pull-thrus with electrical hookups. Sites are in the open without shade, but the picnic tables all have shade shelters over them. Reservations are accepted and highly recommended for summer weekends. **(970) 645-2551.**

74. Brush Memorial Campground (34 sites. Map coordinates: *Colorado Atlas & Gazetteer*, page 94, D3; *Colorado Recreational Road Atlas*, page 17, C3); about 10 miles east of Fort Morgan. Take I-76 east 8 miles from Fort Morgan. Turn right (south) at exit 90, and go 1 mile to Brush City Park. This well-shaded and grassy campground offers all the amenities of a commercial campground but is operated by the town of Brush. Twenty-four of the sites have electrical hookups, while the other 10 are tent sites. Amenities include flush toilets, showers, picnic tables, water faucets, and a dump station. Recreational facilities include a swimming pool, wading pool, playground, tennis courts, basketball courts, and a softball field. Across the street is a new stocked fishing pond with an accessible fishing dock. The first night is free, and there is a $10 fee per night thereafter! No reservations, but it rarely fills. Open all year round. **(970) 842-5001.**

Mountain Park

NORTH REGION (West)

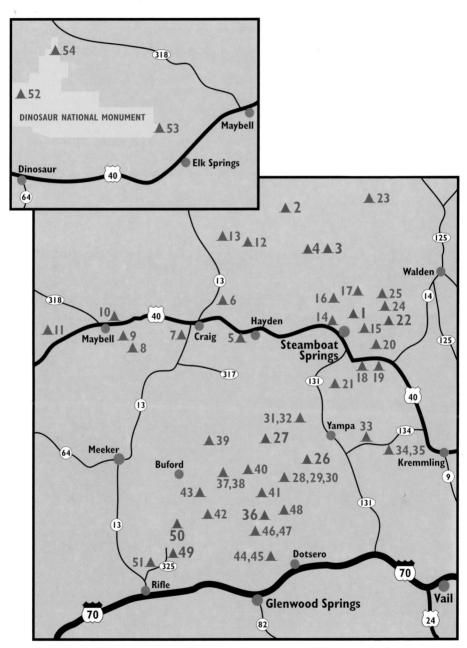

Inset (Dinosaur National Monument):

▲54

318

▲52

DINOSAUR NATIONAL MONUMENT

▲53

Maybell

Dinosaur

40

Elk Springs

64

Main map:

▲2

▲23

▲13 ▲12

125

▲4 ▲3

13

Walden

▲6

16▲ 17▲ ▲25

14

▲24

318

10▲

40

Hayden

14▲ ▲1

▲22

125

▲11

Maybell ▲9

7▲ Craig

5▲

▲15

Steamboat
Springs

▲20

▲8

317

131

▲21

▲▲ ▲
18 19

40

31,32 ▲

▲27

Yampa 33
▲

134

▲39

▲26

▲34,35

64 Meeker

Buford

▲
37,38

▲40

▲28,29,30

Kremmling

9

43▲

▲41

131

13

▲42 36▲ ▲48

▲
50

▲46,47

51▲ ▲49
325

44,45 ▲

Dotsero

70

Rifle

70

Glenwood Springs

Vail

82

24

Inset above shows campgrounds that are northwest of this map. For locations
of campgrounds by Steamboat Lake, refer to map on p. 290.

The Steamboat Springs area is beautiful—and popular. Call ahead for a schedule of spring and summer events in the town of Steamboat Springs and stop on your way to take in an arts or music festival. Keep in mind, however, that nearby campgrounds tend to fill up quickly on festival weekends.

There are many exceptional areas to camp in the Steamboat Springs area. At 10,300 feet, the Summit Lake campground opens later in the summer than many campgrounds but offers nice views from the top of Buffalo Pass—and the nearby Strawberry Park Hot Springs can soothe tired muscles after a long day of hiking. The campground at Hahns Peak Lake is considered a "Colorado secret," with abundant fishing and good roads for mountain bikers and four-wheelers. Pearl Lake State Park offers a little more privacy along with its scenic views. Steamboat Lake, stretching over 1,000 acres, is indeed one of the crown jewels of the Colorado state park system.

The Walden area is famous for its wildflowers, and the aspen trees burst into spectacular colors in the fall. Vaughn Lake is also well-known for its aspen and is worthy of an autumn visit. Deep Lake, 43 miles northwest of the town of Eagle, was where one lucky angler broke the Colorado record with a 36-pound mackinaw.

Looking for a great family destination? Dinosaur National Park offers not only spectacular campsites in remote settings near canyon rivers, but exciting opportunities for river rafting as well.

▲ 100 BEST

- ▲ 1 Summit Lake
- ▲ 2 Hahns Peak Lake
- ▲ 3 Pearl Lake State Park
- ▲ 4 Steamboat Lake State Park
- ▲ 22 Hidden Lakes
- ▲ 26 Bear Lake
- ▲ 27 Vaughn Lake
- ▲ 36 Deep Lake
- ▲ 49 Rifle Falls
- ▲ 50 Rifle Mountain Park

▲ All The Rest

- ▲ 5 Yampa River State Park
- ▲ 6 Elkhead Reservoir
- ▲ 7 South Beach
- ▲ 8 Duffy Mountain
- ▲ 9 Juniper Canyon
- ▲ 10 Maybell Bridge
- ▲ 11 East Cross Mountain
- ▲ 12 Sawmill Creek
- ▲ 13 Freeman Reservoir
- ▲ 14 Dry Lake
- ▲ 15 Granite
- ▲ 16 Hinman Park
- ▲ 17 Seedhouse
- ▲ 18 Meadows
- ▲ 19 Walton Creek
- ▲ 20 Dumont Lake
- ▲ 21 Stagecoach State Park
- ▲ 23 Big Creek Lakes
- ▲ 24 Grizzly Creek
- ▲ 25 Teal Lake
- ▲ 28 Bear River Dispersed
- ▲ 29 Horseshoe
- ▲ 30 Cold Springs
- ▲ 31 Chapman Reservoir
- ▲ 32 Sheriff's Reservoir
- ▲ 33 Lynx Pass
- ▲ 34 Blacktail Creek
- ▲ 35 Gore Pass
- ▲ 37 East Marvine
- ▲ 38 Marvine
- ▲ 39 North Fork
- ▲ 40 Himes Peak
- ▲ 41 Trapper's Lake
- ▲ 42 Meadow Lake
- ▲ 43 South Fork
- ▲ 44 Coffee Pot Spring
- ▲ 45 White Owl
- ▲ 46 Klines Folly
- ▲ 47 Supply Basin
- ▲ 48 Sweetwater Lake
- ▲ 51 Rifle Gap State Park
- ▲ 52 Echo Park
- ▲ 53 Deerlodge Park
- ▲ 54 Gates of Lodore

STEAMBOAT SPRINGS AREA

photo by Gil Folsom

1. Summit Lake

Location: 13 miles northeast of Steamboat Springs
Elevation: 10,300 feet
Number of Sites: 16
Recommended RV Length: Up to 18 feet
Season: July through October
Maps: *Colorado Atlas & Gazetteer*, page 17, D4
Colorado Recreational Road Atlas, page 2, C2
Phone: 970-879-1870

Scenery: ★★★
RVs: ★
Tents: ★★★
Shade: ★★★
Privacy: ★★

Directions
From downtown Steamboat Springs, take County Road 36 (Strawberry Park Hot Springs Road) north, then go right (east) on County Road 38 (Buffalo Pass Road) about 12 miles to the campground. Past Dry Lake Campground, County Road 38 becomes Forest Road 60; the Forest Service recommends high-clearance vehicles only.

Distinguishing Features
Situated at the edge of the Mount Zirkel Wilderness, Summit Lake opens later in the summer than most campgrounds. Near small Summit Lake at the summit of Buffalo Pass, this campground is popular with hikers and backpackers. Nine of the campsites are arranged in a loop, with good separation and shaded by spruce and fir trees; the rest are walk-in only tent

sites on the lake, offering little shade or privacy. Mosquitoes and deer flies can be horrendous in July after the snowmelt, so remember bug repellent!

Popularity
The campground is usually full only on holiday weekends, but arrive early on Friday to secure a site. No reservations.

Facilities
Facilities include picnic tables, fire grates, water faucets, and vault toilets.

RV Notes
Buffalo Pass Road is not suited for most RVs. Small RVs (up to 18 feet) are best, but check with the Forest Service before heading up the road. Nine sites —eight medium back-ins and one medium pull-thru—are suitable for RVs.

Tent Notes
Five sites are walk-ins and offer campers wonderful views of the lake. The nights are very chilly, so don't forget the long johns.

Recreational Opportunities
Tiny Summit Lake is a nice fishing spot, and boating is restricted to hand-powered craft. You'll find other fishing (for brookies) and boating opportunities 4 miles south via Forest Road 310 (okay for ATVs) at 78-acre Fish Creek Reservoir.

The Wyoming (or Continental Divide) Trail, which leads into the Mount Zirkel Wilderness, is a magnet for hikers and backpackers. The trailhead is near the campground. The commercially run Strawberry Park Hot Springs, nestled in a spectacular natural outdoor setting outside of Steamboat Springs, is a not-to-be-missed soaking experience.

---

2. Hahns Peak Lake
Location: 33 miles north of Steamboat Springs
Elevation: 8,500 feet
Number of Sites: 25
Recommended RV Length: Up to 30 feet
Season: Memorial Day to mid-October
Maps: *Colorado Atlas & Gazetteer*, page 16, B2
Colorado Recreational Road Atlas, page 2, C1
Phone: 970-879-1870

Scenery: ★★★
RVs: ★★★
Tents: ★★★
Shade: ★★★
Privacy: ★★★

Directions
From Steamboat Springs, go west on Highway 40 to County Road 129 and turn right (north). Continue for about 30 miles to the intersection of Forest

Hahns Peak Lake

Road 486 (a narrow dirt road with turnouts). Head west on Forest Road 486 for about 2.5 miles.

Distinguishing Features
This tranquil campground offers peace and quiet to campers needing a respite from the noise and rush of the city. The campground host considers it a "Colorado secret." A pine forest provides ample shade to the campsites, but blocks the view of the stunning mountain lake. Satisfactory spacing gives campers adequate privacy.

Loop 1 (sites 1-11) is the closest to the lake, which is accessible via a little path that winds through the trees. A day-use area is available to anglers.

Popularity
The campground can fill on busy holiday weekends or during one of Steamboat Springs' many festivals. Reservations are accepted; the most popular reservable sites are 7, 5, 3, and 8.

Facilities
Facilities include picnic tables, fire grates, water faucets, vault toilets, and a boat ramp.

RV Notes
Medium to long back-ins and eight long pull-thrus (all in Loop 1) provide adequate access to campsites for most RVs. Some leveling may be required. The nearest dump station is near Steamboat Lake State Park about 7 miles to the south, but you must purchase a day pass or have a valid park pass to use it.

Tent Notes

Spacious, fairly level sites give campers many options. Pay showers are available at the Hahns Peak Guest Ranch and Columbine Cabins.

Recreational Opportunities

Abundant rainbow trout lure many campers to 40-acre Hahns Peak Lake. No boats with gas motors are allowed. Pearl Lake (190 acres) and Steamboat Lake (1,053 acres) are other fishing options. Hiking is popular, and numerous roads offer thrills for mountain bikers, four-wheelers, and motorcyclists. The fantastic Strawberry Park Hot Springs are nearby in Steamboat Springs.

3. Pearl Lake State Park

Location: 25 miles north of Steamboat Springs
Elevation: 7,800 feet
Number of Sites: 38
Recommended RV Length: Up to 35 feet
Season: Year-round (full facilities early June to late October)
Maps: *Colorado Atlas & Gazetteer,* page 16, B2 *Colorado Recreational Road Atlas,* page 2, C1
Phone: 970-879-3922

Scenery: ★★★★
RVs: ★★
Tents: ★★★
Shade: ★★★
Privacy: ★★

photo by Gil Folsom

Directions

From Steamboat Springs, go west on Highway 40 to County Road 129. Turn right (north), and go 23 miles to Pearl Lake Road (County Road 209). Turn right and go east 2 miles on a flat dirt road.

Distinguishing Features

For those seeking a more intimate wilderness experience than Steamboat Lake offers, this is the place. Set on 167-acre Pearl Lake, the campground is made up of two wooded loops. The always-busy lower loop contains sites spaced close to one another and near the water. The upper loop is for those seeking more solitude, but campers lose the lake atmosphere; from here, the lake is down the hill and through a thick forest.

Popularity

The campground often fills on summer weekends. The lower loop is considerably more popular, as it features many sites near the water. The most requested sites are 24-33. Reservations accepted.

Facilities

Facilities include picnic tables, fire grates, water faucets, flush and vault toilets. Some toilets are wheelchair-accessible. Two yurts are also available.

RV Notes

The lower loop, with mostly pull-thrus and pull-outs, is best suited to smaller RVs; several small to medium back-ins are also available. In the upper loop are pull-thrus and pull-outs that better accommodate medium-sized RVs. Several medium back-ins are also available. Most parking spots are fairly level. The nearest dump station is 5 miles away at Steamboat Lake State Park.

Tent Notes

All sites have tent pads. Pearl Lake campers may use the shower and laundry facilities at nearby Steamboat Lake.

Recreational Opportunities

Cutthroat trout fishing is the big draw, but anglers can only keep fish over 18 inches long. Pearl also offers excellent grayling fishing just after the "ice off" (usually early May). Wakeless boating is permitted. Anglers should also try nearby Hahns Peak Lake and Steamboat Lake. Hiking, mountain biking, horseback riding, and four-wheeling adventures are all minutes away.

4. Steamboat Lake State Park

Location: 26 miles north of Steamboat Springs (see map on p. 290)
Elevation: 8,000 feet
Number of Sites: 198 (10 camper cabins)
Recommended RV Length: Unlimited
Season: Year-round (full facilities Memorial Day to late October)
Maps: *Colorado Atlas & Gazetteer*, page 16, B2
Colorado Recreational Road Atlas, page 2, C1
Phone: 970-879-3922

Scenery: ★★★
RVs: ★★★★
Tents: ★★★★
Shade: ★★★
Privacy: ★★

Directions

From Steamboat Springs, go west on Highway 40 to County Road 129. Turn right (north), and go 26 miles.

Distinguishing Features

A 1,000-acre man-made lake in a valley a few miles from the Continental Divide, Steamboat Lake is a crown jewel of the state park system. In fact, Colorado park rangers voted the lake their favorite vacation destination. Mature trees shade most sites, and nearby mountain-biking and hiking trails abound.

Of the two campgrounds in the park, **Dutch Hill** is the most popular. The three loops within the campground include sites 116-165 (110 to 290 yards above the lake), which are very popular for those needing electrical hookups. Sites 129-132 and 145-147 have varying lake views and are especially popular.

For those wanting to camp as close to the lake as possible, **Bridge Island** (part of Dutch Hill) is the place to be. Sites 166-180 are 50 to 85 yards from the lake and are suitable for RVs and tents. Campers with RVs can ask for one of the pull-thru sites facing the lake. Sites 181-200 are 20 to 70 yards from the lake and are walk-in sites for tents only. Lakeside sites 187, 188, 185, 186, 192, and 193 (in that order) offer the best views of the mountains.

Most sites within the seven loops of **Sunrise Vista** are farther from the lake (60 to 455 yards) and not as popular. Sites 76-113 are now electrical. Campers who prefer less shade find these open sites more pleasant. The Yarrow Loop is the closest to the lake—from 60 to 150 yards. Yarrow Loop's sites 105-110 are nearest to the lake. Reserve heated camper cabins in sites 156-165 by calling 970-879-7019.

Popularity

Although you might find a campsite on a weekday without making a reservation, the only safe way to get a spot between Memorial Day and Labor Day is to reserve ahead. Steamboat Lake's popularity is tied to festivals and other events in Steamboat Springs, so watch the calendar.

Facilities

These renovated campgrounds include picnic tables, fire grates, firewood for sale, water faucets, pay showers, flush and vault toilets (some with wheelchair access), electrical outlets and mirrors in the bathrooms, laundry facilities, an amphitheater, boat ramps, rental cabins, and a visitor center.

RV Notes

Sites offer a wide variety of back-ins and pull-thrus that accommodate any RV. Ninety sites have electrical hookups. You'll find a dump station in the park. Most sites are very level.

Tent Notes

All Dutch Hill and Sunrise Vista sites have pads. Bridge Island's walk-in sites—lying close to the lake and offering breathtaking views—rank as some of the best in the state.

Recreational Opportunities

The park is a haven for every imaginable water-related sport. You can rent watercraft from the marina, and anglers can catch rainbow and other trout in Steamboat Lake; anglers with free time might also try the much quieter Pearl Lake and Hahns Peak Lake. Hikers can choose from myriad trails, many leading into the Mount Zirkel Wilderness. All-terrain-vehicle and four-wheel-drive roads are never far. Nearby guest ranches offer horseback riding, and the park offers ranger and amphitheater programs. Fifteen kilometers of cross-country ski trails are available in the winter.

Steamboat Lake

Other Nearby Campgrounds

Yampa River State Park. This state park actually consists of eight public access points (including campgrounds 5-11) designed to help facilitate recreation along a 172-mile stretch of the Yampa River between Stagecoach Reservoir and Dinosaur National Monument. The smaller campgrounds primarily serve as overnight stopovers for boaters floating the Yampa River. All the campgrounds work fine for both RVs and tents (except South Beach) although the roads leading to the smaller campgrounds via county roads are sometimes not good places for RVs. Check road conditions first.

5. Yampa River State Park (50 sites); 2.5 miles west of Hayden on Highway 40. This is the park headquarters for Yampa River State Park. Nestled in an agricultural high-prairie setting just above the river, this campground is built on historic hayfields. In an open field with a few mature cottonwoods, campers will discover a mix of RV and tent sites, all less than 200 yards from the river. Only a few sites have natural shade. Facilities include a mix of flush and vault toilets, showers, laundry, five tepees for rent, and a dump station. Reservations accepted. **(970) 276-2061.**

6. Elkhead Reservoir (30 sites); 10 miles northeast of Craig. Take Highway 40 east for 5.5 miles to County Road 29. Go left (northeast) on County

Road 29 for 4.5 miles. Two campgrounds in an open, treeless area overlook 600-acre Elkhead Reservoir and gently rolling hills of dry wheat, sagebrush, and range land. The reservoir supports all water sports and also offers warm-water fishing possibilities. **Elks Campground** contains about ten sites 200 yards up a steep grade from the spillway overlooking the reservoir. The **East Beach Campground** contains about 18 undesignated sites in an open, grassy field next to the swim beach. Some sites at East Beach are within 30 feet of the water. Facilities are vault toilets, picnic tables, and fire grates. There is no drinking water. No reservations. **(970) 276-2061.**

7. South Beach (4 sites); 3 miles south of Craig on Highway 13. Walk-in tent sites are on the banks of the Yampa River with mature cottonwoods providing shade to three sites. RVers may camp in the parking lot. Facilities are limited to picnic tables, fire grates, a vault toilet, and a boat ramp. There is no drinking water. No reservations. **(970) 276-2061.**

8. Duffy Mountain (4 sites); 29 miles southwest of Craig. From Craig, go west about 18 miles on Highway 40, and turn left (south). Go 10 miles on County Road 17, turn left (north) onto BLM Road 1593, and go 1 mile. All sites are along the banks of the Yampa River, but there are no trees. Facilities are limited to picnic tables, fire grates, a vault toilet, and a boat ramp. There is no drinking water. No reservations. **(970) 276-2061.**

9. Juniper Canyon (5 sites); 26 miles southwest of Craig. From Craig, go west on Highway 40 for about 21 miles, and turn left (south) on County Road 53. Go for 4 miles, turn right (west) onto County Road 74, and go 1 mile. Sites are all along the river with no trees. Facilities are picnic tables, fire grates, a vault toilet, and a boat ramp. There is no drinking water. No reservations. **(970) 276-2061.**

10. Maybell Bridge (6 sites); 26 miles west of Craig (4 miles east of Maybell). From Craig, go 26 miles west on Highway 40. Three sites overlook the river, and only one of the sites has good shade. Facilities are picnic tables, fire grates, a vault toilet, and a boat ramp. There is no drinking water. No reservations. **(970) 276-2061.**

11. East Cross Mountain (4 sites); 18 miles southwest of Maybell. From Maybell, go west about 14.5 miles on Highway 40, and turn right (north) on County Road 85. Go 2.5 miles, turn left (west) onto BLM Road 1551, and go 1.5 miles. All sites are along the river without shade. Facilities are picnic tables, fire grates, a vault toilet, and a boat ramp. There is no drinking water. No reservations. **(970) 276-2061.**

12. Sawmill Creek (6 sites); 29 miles northeast of Craig. From Highway 13, turn right (east) on County Road 27 (Forest Road 110). This primitive campground offers plenty of solitude away from the crowds. Maximum RV length is 16 feet. No drinking water. No reservations. **(970) 879-1870.**

13. Freeman Reservoir (17 sites); 23 miles northeast of Craig. Drive north on Highway 13 for about 13 miles and right (east) on County Road 11 (Forest Road 112). Although weekends during hunting season can be noisy, Freeman Reservoir is a quiet place the rest of the time. The small lake is limited to nonmotorized boats and is just a short walk from the campground. Maximum RV length is 25 feet. No reservations. **(970) 879-1870.**

14. Dry Lake (8 sites); 6 miles northeast of Steamboat Springs. Go north on County Road 36 for 2 miles, and then right (east) on County Road 38 (Forest Road 60). Proceed about 4 miles. Amply shaded by aspens and pines, this small but very popular campground is most suitable for tents and small RVs (up to 26 feet). Bring your own drinking water. No reservations. **(970) 879-1870.**

15. Granite (8 sites); 17 miles northeast of Steamboat Springs. Go north on County Road 36 for 2 miles, and then right (east) on County Road 38 (Forest Road 60). Follow County Road 38 about 10 miles to Forest Road 310. Turn right (south) on Forest Road 310, and go about 5 miles to Fish Creek Reservoir. On the shore of Fish Creek Reservoir (no gas-powered boats allowed), this campground includes four walk-in tent sites and four drive-in sites with wonderful views. The road is recommended for high-clearance vehicles only, and there is no drinking water. Maximum RV length is 22 feet. No reservations. **(970) 879-1870.**

16. Hinman Park (13 sites); 26 miles north of Steamboat Springs. Go west on Highway 40 about a mile to County Road 129. Turn right (north) and go about 18.5 miles to County Road 64 (a.k.a. Forest Road 400). Turn right (east) and go about 5.5 miles to Forest Road 440. Turn right (south) and go 0.5 mile. This peaceful, primitive campground rarely fills, is heavily shaded, and offers adequate privacy between sites. It's not the best place for RVs (maximum length is 22 feet), but a few pull-thrus are available. Stream fishing and wildlife viewing are the charms of this campground. No reservations. **(970) 879-1870.**

17. Seedhouse (24 sites); 28 miles north of Steamboat Springs. Go west on Highway 40 to County Road 129. Go right (north) on County Road 129 about 18.5 miles to County Road 64 (Forest Road 400). Turn right (east) on County Road 64 (Forest Road 400) and go 8 miles. Heavily wooded and a favorite of weekend hikers and mountain bikers, this is a primitive campground with a narrow road going through it. Anglers love nearby Elk River. Maximum RV length is 25 feet. Reservations accepted. **(970) 879-1870.**

18. Meadows (30 sites); 15 miles southeast of Steamboat Springs on Highway 40. This campground—the closest from Rabbit Ears Pass to Steamboat Springs—is quite busy on weekends. Large sites with a mix of back-ins and pull-thrus accommodate RVs of up to 30 feet. Tall evergreens shade most sites. No drinking water. No reservations. **(970) 879-1870.**

19. Walton Creek (14 sites); 18 miles southeast of Steamboat Springs on Highway 40. Walton Creek Campground is set just off busy Highway 40, so traffic noise can be a problem. Many sites adjoin the creek in the open with little or no shade. The last of the three Rabbit Ears Pass campgrounds to fill, this one is best for tents and small RVs. No reservations. **(970) 879-1870.**

20. Dumont Lake (22 sites); 22 miles southeast of Steamboat Springs on Highway 40. This is a lovely campground set in a lush, wildflower-filled meadow near the summit of Rabbit Ears Pass. There is little shade. The lake is striking, but not close to the campsites. Maximum RV length is 30 feet. No reservations. **(970) 879-1870.**

21. Stagecoach State Park (92 sites); 16 miles south of Steamboat Springs. Go south on Highway 40 for 4 miles, and turn right (west) onto Highway 131. Follow Highway 131 about 7 miles to County Road 14. Turn left (south) onto County Road 14, and go about 6 miles to Stagecoach State Park. Thanks to the awe-inspiring backdrop framing the 3-mile long, 775-acre lake, this state park can be busy. Of the four campgrounds within the park, two offer electrical hookups. Campers won't find much shade or privacy.
Junction City (sites 1-27) offers the best lake view and is near the water. Boaters can moor their boats on shore. Electrical hookups are available. **Pinnacle** (sites 28-64) is close to the swim beach and is popular with families. Long pull-thru sites are spaced together in a parking lot setting, and electrical hookups are available. **Harding Spur** (66-83), in a cove on the lake, gives campers the option of mooring their boats within 50 feet of their site. Campers use **McKindley** (sites 84-92) when the other campgrounds are full or they're trying to save money. You won't find even one token tree in this loop high on a hill, and no drinking water is available. Reservations accepted. **(970) 736-2436.**

WALDEN AREA

photo by Gil Folsom

22. Hidden Lakes

Location: About 30 miles southwest of Walden
Elevation: 8,900 feet
Number of Sites: 9
Recommended RV Length: Up to 20 feet
Season: Mid-June through September
Maps: *Colorado Atlas & Gazetteer*, page 17, D5
Colorado Recreational Road Atlas, page 5, A3
Phone: 970-723-8204

Scenery: ★★★
RVs: ★★
Tents: ★★★
Shade: ★★★
Privacy: ★★★

Directions
From Walden, take Highway 14 southwest 13 miles to Hebron. Turn right (west) onto County Road 24 (which becomes a well-graded dirt road beyond Grizzly Lakes Campground), and go 11 miles to the forest boundary, where the road becomes Forest Road 60. Proceed a mile farther. Turn left (south) onto Forest Road 20, and go about 5 miles.

Distinguishing Features
The gem of the three campgrounds in the area, Hidden Lakes offers more solitude and beauty than the more popular Teal Lake Campground nearby. Several sites are next to Hidden Lake (10 acres). Sites are well-spaced, offering privacy and a good mix of sun and shade.

Popularity
This campground frequently fills on weekends. During the week, it is normally very quiet. No reservations.

Facilities
Facilities include picnic tables, fire grates, hand-pumped water, and a wheel-chair-accessible vault toilet.

RV Notes

Six medium to long back-ins, two long pull-thrus, and one terrible pull-out are available for RVs. Some leveling will be required. The nearest dump station is in Walden at Hanson Park, next to the high school.

Tent Notes

Campers can pitch their tents close to the lake to better enjoy its tranquility. In Walden, the Jackson County Swimming Pool and several hotels offer showers.

Recreational Opportunities

Anglers need only walk a few feet to try their luck fishing for rainbow trout in the lake, or they can seek out nearby streams. Campers who don't mind a little bushwhacking will quickly discover four more lakes. The fishing is much better at nearby Teal Lake (10 acres), which is stocked more often. Only small boats (no gas motors) are suitable for Hidden Lakes and Teal Lake.

The nearby Percy Trail leads to Percy and Round Lakes. The most popular trail in the area, the Newcomb Trail, leads into the Mount Zirkel Wilderness. Buffalo Pass Road is a scenic drive suitable for high-clearance vehicles. Four-wheel-drive and ATV enthusiasts won't leave disappointed.

Other Nearby Campgrounds

23. Big Creek Lakes (54 sites); 35 miles northwest of Walden. Take Highway 125 north from Walden for 9 miles to County Road 6W. Turn left (west) onto County Road 6W, and go about 20 miles to County Road 6A. Go left (southwest) onto county Road 6A, and proceed for about 5.5 miles to Forest Road 600. Turn left (south) onto Forest Road 600, and continue for 1 mile to the campground. Power boats and waterskiing are allowed on the 343-acre lake, and abundant options await hikers in the Mount Zirkel Wilderness. Maximum RV length is 45 feet. Reservations recommended. **(970) 723-8204.**

24. Grizzly Creek (12 sites); 28 miles southwest of Walden. Take Highway 14 southwest for 13 miles to County Road 24, and turn right (west). Go for 11 miles (the road becomes Forest Road 60). Grizzly Creek is an excellent place to spend time in the fall. Nestled in an aspen grove filled with gorgeous wildflowers, this primitive campground offers quiet solitude and never fills. Maximum RV length is 20 feet. Reservations accepted. **(970) 723-8204.**

25. Teal Lake (17 sites); 31 miles southwest of Walden. Take Highway 14 southwest for 13 miles to County Road 24, and go right (west) for 11 miles (the road becomes Forest Road 60). Turn right (north) onto Forest Road 615, and proceed for about 3 miles. Sites fill during summer weekends, so campers should arrive Friday morning to secure a site. Teal Lake offers superb fishing and is stocked frequently. No power boats are allowed. The sites provide little shade but ample spacing. Several pull-thrus accommodate RVs of up to 35 feet. Reservations accepted. **(970) 723-8204.**

YAMPA AREA

26. Bear Lake

Location: About 14 miles southwest of Yampa
Elevation: 9,600 feet
Number of Sites: 43
Recommended RV Length: Up to 60 feet
Season: June through October
Maps: *Colorado Atlas & Gazetteer*, page 26, D1
Colorado Recreational Road Atlas, page 2, B3
Phone: 970-638-4516

Scenery: ★★★
RVs: ★★★
Tents: ★★★
Shade: ★★★
Privacy: ★★

Directions

From Yampa, go southwest on County Road 7 for about 7 miles, where the pavement gives way to dirt and becomes Forest Road 900. Continue for another 7 miles.

Distinguishing Features

Bear Lake provides campers a serene campground close to the Bear River, which runs just below. Several lakes, Bear Lake (46 acres), Yamcolo Reservoir (188 acres), and Stillwater Reservoir (110 acres), are nearby. Some of the sites along the campground's outer edges are well-spaced, and all are nestled among spruce, fir, and aspens that provide plenty of shade. The Flat Tops Wilderness, with its stunning canyons and volcanic cliffs, is nearby.

Popularity
Campsites fill during the busy summer months. Arrive early Friday morning for the best chance at securing a site. No reservations.

Facilities
Facilities include picnic tables, fire grates, water faucets, and vault toilets.

RV Notes
Eight long pull-thrus and many medium back-ins are available. Some may require leveling.

Tent Notes
Tent-pitching options are good in some spots, somewhat restricted in others.

Recreational Opportunities
Motorized boats are prohibited on trout-stocked Bear Lake, but anglers will find the fishing wonderful. Yamcolo Reservoir does allow motorized boats on the water. A few miles down the road, Stillwater Reservoir offers additional fishing possibilities.

Across the road from the campground is the Mandall trailhead, which leads to several lakes. From Stillwater Reservoir, trails lead into the Flat Tops Wilderness and to many other lakes: Trapper's Lake, Causeway Lake, Hooper Lake, and Keener Lakes. Heart Lake is a popular designated ATV trail that is also used by hikers.

---

27. Vaughn Lake
Location: 37 miles southwest of Yampa
Elevation: 9,500 feet
Number of Sites: 6
Recommended RV Length: Up to 36 feet
Season: June through October
Maps: *Colorado Atlas & Gazetteer*, page 25, C7
Colorado Recreational Road Atlas, page 2, B3
Phone: 970-638-4516

Scenery: ★★★★★
RVs: ★★
Tents: ★★★
Shade: ★★★
Privacy: ★★★★

Directions
From Yampa, go west on County Road 17 for about 5 miles to Forest Road 16 (a.k.a. Flat Tops Scenic Byway, a well-maintained gravel road). Turn left (west), and proceed for about 32 miles (outside of Routt National Forest, the road becomes County Road 8).

Distinguishing Features

Vaughn Lake is one of those rare, idyllic campgrounds that captures your soul. Campsites are nestled in the aspens several hundred yards above 36-acre Vaughn Lake, with views below of a brilliant field of wildflowers framed by green, forested hills. Thousands of aspens in the area make this a beautiful fall destination.

Popularity

This campground's location is remote, but campers can occasionally fill it during busy summer weekends. No reservations.

Facilities

Facilities include picnic tables, fire grates, and a vault toilet. No drinking water.

RV Notes

Sites have medium to long back-in spaces that require some leveling. The access road is a bit narrow and constricted, so some skilled maneuvering may be necessary to get into the sites. The campground is a long way down the Flat Tops Scenic Byway, but most RVs can easily navigate the well-maintained gravel road.

Tent Notes

Good tent-pitching options abound. Remember to bring drinking water.

Recreational Opportunities

Fishing is currently poor at Vaughn Lake and Poose Creek. Nonmotorized boating is permitted in Vaughn. Flyfishing is better at 300-acre Trapper's Lake, one of the most stunning lakes in Colorado; nonmotorized boating is also permitted. Popular hiking trails begin at the top of Ripple Creek Pass and at the Pyramid Guard Station.

Other Nearby Campgrounds

28. Bear River Dispersed (32 sites); 10 to 20 miles southwest of Yampa along Forest Road 900. A few of these campsites—scattered along a dusty road near the Bear River—are great, but some leave a lot to be desired. It's primitive camping, the only amenity a fire grate. Maximum RV length is 60 feet. No reservations. **(970) 638-4516.**

29. Horseshoe (7 sites); 16 miles southwest of Yampa on Forest Road 900. Sites are on the outside of a small loop, with little shade. Campers have

Vaughn Lake

N

pretty views of the Flat Tops. Maximum RV length is 25 feet. No reservations. **(970) 638-4516.**

30. Cold Springs (5 sites); 17 miles southwest of Yampa on Forest Road 900. A favorite of Yampa forest rangers, this place fills quickly on Fridays. It's located in an open, sunny meadow with a little creek flowing through it. The Flat Tops form an impressive backdrop. Maximum RV length is 30 feet. No reservations. **(970) 638-4516.**

31. Chapman Reservoir (12 sites); 13 miles northwest of Yampa. Go west on County Road 17 for about 5 miles to Forest Road 16. Go left (west) on Forest Road 16 for about 7 miles, and then turn left (south) on Forest Road 940. Proceed for about 1.5 miles. Very few people visit this campground. Aspens and evergreens provide decent shade, and the reservoir is within walking distance. No drinking water is provided. Maximum RV length is 40 feet. No reservations. **(970) 638-4516.**

32. Sheriff's Reservoir (5 sites); 17 miles west of Yampa. Go west on County Road 17 for about 5 miles to Forest Road 16, and go left (west) for about 9 miles to Forest Road 959/960. Go left (south) on Forest Road 959/960 for about 3.5 miles. As with Chapman Reservoir, this primitive campground is near a pristine mountain lake with few other campers around. Picnic tables and drinking water are not provided. Sites are well-shaded and accommodate RVs of up to 18 feet. No reservations. **(970) 638-4516.**

33. Lynx Pass (11 sites); 21 miles southeast of Yampa. Take Highway 131 southeast 9.5 miles to Highway 134, and turn left (east). Take Highway 134 for 8.5 miles to Forest Road 270, and turn left (north). Proceed for about 3 miles. This campground is rarely crowded and always quiet. Sites provide adequate shade and spacing and are best suited for tents or small RVs. A small, nearby lake offers fishing opportunities. No reservations. **(970) 638-4516.**

34. Blacktail Creek (8 sites); 25 miles southeast of Yampa. Take Highway 131 southeast 9.5 miles to Highway 134, and turn left (east). Follow Highway 134 for about 15 miles to the campground. A former Wells Fargo stage stop, this campground is set just far enough below the highway to eliminate some of the traffic noise. Sites provide satisfactory shade and privacy. Five medium to long pull-thrus are available for RVs of up to 40 feet. A tiny, hard-to-access creek runs near the campground. No reservations. **(970) 638-4516.**

35. Gore Pass (12 sites); 27 miles southeast of Yampa. Take Highway 131 southeast 9.5 miles to Highway 134, and turn left (east). Follow Highway 134 for about 17 miles. Mainly used by overnighters, this wooded campground offers adequate shade, medium to long parking spaces for RVs up to 60 feet long, and satisfactory privacy. Highway noise is prevalent. No reservations. **(970) 638-4516.**

MEEKER AREA

36. Deep Lake

Location: 31 miles northwest of Dotsero
Elevation: 10,460 feet
Number of Sites: 37
Recommended RV Length: Up to 36 feet
Season: July through September
Maps: *Colorado Atlas & Gazetteer,* page 35, B7
Colorado Recreational Road Atlas, page 2, B4
Phone: 970-328-6388

Scenery: ★★★
RVs: ★★
Tents: ★★
Shade: ★★
Privacy: ★★

Directions
Turn off I-70 at Dotsero (exit 133), and follow the signs to Sweetwater and
Burns, turning north on the Colorado River Road (County Road 301). Follow
the road for 1.8 miles, and turn left onto Coffee Pot Road (a.k.a. Deep Creek
Road or County Road 17, which becomes Forest Road 600). Stay on the dirt
road for 29 miles, then turn right into the campground.

Distinguishing Features
Far off the beaten path, this campground overlooks 37-acre Deep Lake
(65 feet deep, to be exact). Nestled in a gossamer spruce-fir forest, some
campsites have wonderful views of the lake. Two-thirds of the sites are in the

open; the rest have partial shade. Campers should stock up on provisions before arriving, as the nearest supplies are 42 miles away—and don't forget the bug repellent. Deep Lake was a Ute hunting camp in the early 1800s; nearly a century later, Teddy Roosevelt hunted and camped here as well.

Popularity

This is the most popular campground in the Eagle Ranger District, but it only fills on occasional holiday weekends. No reservations.

Facilities

Somewhat primitive facilities include picnic tables, fire grates, vault toilets, and firewood for sale. Deep Lake Campground has no water for campers, but a continually flowing faucet is available at Broken Rib Spring, between mile markers 18 and 19, next to the road on your way up to the campground.

RV Notes

You'll find 29 miles of well-graded dirt road that is steep in spots. Many won't make the trek; others visit every year.

Tent Notes

Tent campers should find a site with trees for protection from the wind.

Recreational Opportunities

Deep Lake is a favorite of anglers who fish for rainbow, brook, and lake trout. One lucky fisherman caught a 36-pound mackinaw here, breaking the Colorado record at the time. Gas-powered boats are prohibited.

Hunters use Deep Lake Campground as a base camp in the fall. Ute Trail 2031 is a rough, four-wheel/hiking trail just north of the lake. An extensive network of four-wheel-drive roads attracts many ATVers and motorcyclists to the area.

Other Nearby Campgrounds

37. East Marvine (7 sites); 36 miles east of Meeker. Take Highway 13 east for 1 mile to County Road 8, and turn right (east). Take County Road 8 about 28 miles to County Road 12. Turn right (east) on County Road 12, and go about 7 miles to the campground. This small campground offers solitude within 100 yards of East Marvine Creek. Sites provide good separation and some shade. Maximum RV length is 50 feet. No reservations. **(970) 878-4039.**

38. Marvine (24 sites); 37 miles east of Meeker. Take Highway 13 east for 1 mile to County Road 8, and turn right (east). Take County Road 8 about 28 miles to County Road 12. Turn right (east) onto County Road 12, and go 8 miles. A bit more popular than East Marvine, but still never busy, this campground is close to horse corrals. Aspens and pines provide adequate shade. This campground is a little better for RVs than East Marvine. No reservations. **(970) 878-4039.**

39. North Fork (40 sites); 35 miles east of Meeker. Take Highway 13 east 1 mile to County Road 8, and turn right (east). Go 34 miles to the campground. Set in an aspen forest, North Fork is a quiet place to relax and just enjoy camping. Many large pull-thrus make it easy for RVs, with a maximum length of 60 feet. The campground is rarely busy, except during hunting season. Reservations accepted. **(970) 878-4039.**

40. Himes Peak (11 sites); 47 miles east of Meeker. Take Highway 13 east 1 mile to County Road 8, and turn right (east). Follow County Road 8 for 41 miles to Forest Road 205. Turn right (southeast) onto Forest Road 205, and go about 5 miles. Only a few miles from Trapper's Lake, this campground set in an aspen forest is a terrific spot for enjoying fall foliage. It's often crowded on weekends. Several pull-thrus are available for RVs up to 36 feet long. No reservations. **(970) 878-4039.**

41. Trapper's Lake (58 sites); 53 miles east of Meeker. Take Highway 13 east 1 mile to County Road 8, and turn right (east). Follow County Road 8 for 41 miles to Forest Road 205. Turn right (southeast) onto Forest Road 205, and go about 11 miles. A forest fire affected nearly 15,000 acres around Trapper's Lake in 2002, but the campgrounds were untouched.

The five campgrounds in this area—**Bucks** (10 sites), **Cutthroat** (14 sites), **Horse Thief** (7 equestrian sites with corrals), **Shepherds Rim** (15 sites), and **Trapline** (12 sites)—are immensely popular. Sites are located well above one of the the most beautiful lakes in Colorado, but don't offer lake views or easy access to Trapper's Lake. Most sites are small, very tightly spaced, and have little privacy. Shade ranges widely, but it's fair at best for most sites. Campers should arrive on Thursday or early Friday to find a weekend site. Maximum RV length is 36 feet. No reservations. **(970) 878-4039.**

42. Meadow Lake (10 sites); 37 miles southeast of Meeker. Take Highway 13 east 1 mile to County Road 8, and turn right (east). Follow County Road 8 for about 20 miles to Buford, and turn right (south) onto County Road 17 (Buford-New Castle Road). Take County Road 17 (which becomes Forest Road 245) about 13 miles to Forest Road 601, and turn left (east). Follow Forest Road 601 for about 3 miles, and then turn right (south) onto Forest Road 823. Go about 1.5 miles to the campground. A five-minute walk from captivating Meadow Lake (60 acres), this isolated but quite popular campground offers sites with good shade and privacy. Maximum RV length is 16 feet. No reservations. **(970) 625-2371.**

43. South Fork (18 sites); 31 miles southeast of Meeker. Take Highway 13 east 1 mile to County Road 8, and turn right (east). Go 17.5 miles to County Road 10, and turn right (east). Follow County Road 10 for about 12 miles. This is one of the few campgrounds that offers a trail leading to a cave. Near a lovely river, sites are tucked under tall evergreens. Maximum RV length is 36 feet. No reservations. **(970) 878-4039.**

44. Coffee Pot Spring (10 sites); 18.3 miles northwest of Dotsero (I-70 exit 133). Go north on County Road 301 for 1.8 miles, and turn left (west) onto Coffee Pot Road (Deep Creek Road or County Road 17, which becomes Forest Road 600). Follow Coffee Pot Road for 16.5 miles. Situated at the edge of a forest in an open meadow with beautiful wildflowers, Coffee Pot Spring offers views of three snowcapped mountain ranges. Only three sites have shade, but all can handle medium-sized RVs. Drinking water is 3 miles up the road at Broken Rib Spring. No reservations. **(970) 328-6388.**

45. White Owl (11 sites); 28 miles northwest of Dotsero (I-70 exit 133). Go north on County Road 301 for 1.8 miles, and turn left (west) onto Coffee Pot Road (Deep Creek Road or County Road 17, which becomes Forest Road 600). Follow Coffee Pot Road for about 26 miles to Forest Road 614, and go left (west). Proceed for about a mile. This extremely primitive campground by White Owl Lake has no drinking water or trash service. Three sites have some shade, while the rest have none. Maximum RV length is 20 feet. No reservations. **(970) 328-6388.**

46. Klines Folly (4 sites); 29.2 miles northwest of Dotsero (I-70 exit 133). Go north on County Road 301 for 1.8 miles, and turn left (west) onto Coffee Pot Road (Deep Creek Road or County Road 17, which becomes Forest Road 600). Follow Coffee Pot Road for about 27 miles to Forest Road 601, and go left (west). Proceed for about a mile. This tiny, primitive, tent-oriented campground is in an open subalpine meadow at the edge of a small lake. It's lightly used, and the bugs can be vicious. No trash service is available. Drinking water is 8 miles back on Forest Road 600 at Broken Rib Spring. Maximum RV length is 20 feet. No reservations. **(970) 328-6388.**

47. Supply Basin (8 sites); 30 miles northwest of Dotsero (I-70 exit 133). Go north on County Road 301 for 1.8 miles, and turn left (west) onto Coffee Pot Road (Deep Creek Road or County Road 17, which becomes Forest Road 600). Follow Coffee Pot Road for about 27 miles to Forest Road 601, and go left (west). Proceed for about 1.5 miles. Just up the road from Klines Folly, this campground also sees few campers (and many insects). Partially shaded sites are set at the edge of a small lake; no trash service or drinking water are provided. Five-hundred-acre Heart Lake is nearby. Maximum RV length is 20 feet. No reservations. **(970) 328-6388.**

48. Sweetwater Lake (9 sites); 17.2 miles northwest of Dotsero (I-70 exit 133). Go north on County Road 301 for about 7 miles to County Road 40 (Sweetwater Road). Turn left (west), and follow the road for 10 miles (County Road 40 becomes County Road 150). This campground is adjacent to lovely, 72-acre Sweetwater Lake, with high limestone cliffs on two sides. The campsites leave much to be desired. There's little shade and no drinking water; RVs should head elsewhere. No reservations. **(970) 328-6388.**

RIFLE AREA

49. Rifle Falls

Location: 13 miles northeast of Rifle
Elevation: 6,800 feet
Number of Sites: 20
Recommended RV Length: Up to 35 feet
Season: Year-round
Maps: *Colorado Atlas & Gazetteer*, page 34, C4
Colorado Recreational Road Atlas, page 4, A2
Phone: 970-625-1607

Scenery: ★★★★
RVs: ★★★★
Tents: ★★★★
Shade: ★★★
Privacy: ★★

Directions
From I-70, turn off at Rifle (exit 90). Go north on Highway 13 through Rifle for 3 miles. Turn right (north) on State Highway 325, and go north 9.8 miles.

Distinguishing Features
Truly an exceptional family campground, Rifle Falls showcases a beautiful triple waterfall and captivating caves in this small, lush state park. Film crews from around the world have flocked to these attractions. Upgraded in 1998, an already great campground became even better. A paved road leads to 13 drive-in grassy sites and seven secluded walk-in tent sites. Box elder, cottonwood, hawthorn, and chokecherry trees provide ample shade to most sites.

Popularity
Beautiful views and scenic hikes combine to make Rifle Falls extremely popular, especially during summer weekends. Make reservations as far in advance as possible. Top sites for tents are 20 and 17, followed by 15, 16, 18, and 19.

Facilities

Facilities include picnic tables, fire grates, water faucets, vault toilets, and a kiosk for watching wildlife. Picnic tables and vault toilets are wheelchair-accessible.

RV Notes

Campsites 1-13 supply electrical hookups. Six sites offer large pull-thrus, and another seven offer medium to long back-ins; these 13 sites are level as well. Sites 2-4, 6, 8, and 11-13 back up to the creek. The nearest dump station is in Rifle Gap State Park, 7 miles southwest on Highway 325.

Tent Notes

Walk-in sites 14-20 offer campers a close wilderness experience within a developed campground. Each site provides remarkable privacy.

Recreational Opportunities

Anglers will find rainbow and brown trout, largemouth and smallmouth bass, channel catfish, and walleye at nearby 350-acre Rifle Gap Reservoir. Rainbow and brown trout await in nearby East Rifle Creek. All types of water recreation are permitted in the reservoir. Squirrel and Coyote Trails allow easy access up to and beyond the falls, the dark limestone caves, and East Rifle Creek. Water cascades from the falls year-round.

---

50. Rifle Mountain Park

Location: 17 miles northeast of Rifle
Elevation: 6,900 feet
Number of Sites: 30
Recommended RV Length: Up to 30 feet
Season: Year-round (road plowed only to Huffman Gulch in winter)
Maps: *Colorado Atlas & Gazetteer*, page 34, B4
Colorado Recreational Road Atlas, page 4, A2
Phone: 970-625-2121

Scenery: ★★★★
RVs: ★★
Tents: ★★★
Shade: ★★★
Privacy: ★★★

Directions

From I-70, turn off at Rifle (exit 90). Go north on Highway 13 through Rifle 3 miles. Turn right (north) on Highway 325, and go 12 miles (the road turns into County Road 217) to the entrance of Rifle Mountain Park. You'll find three camping areas within the next 2.2 miles.

Distinguishing Features

Rifle Mountain Park contains three small campgrounds on either side of a road running along a narrow stretch of the canyon, with climbers hanging for dear life on the near-vertical canyon walls (or at least it looks that way!). Privacy and shade vary.

Sawmill Gulch (sites 1-5), the first campground, has three walk-in sites, and the next is Huffman Gulch (sites 6-15). Of these sites, seven are near the stream and provide shade. Rifle Creek (sites 16-30) contains the crème de la crème of the campsites in Rifle Mountain Park. Most sites are on the stream, are well-shaded, and accommodate any RV.

Popularity
All three campgrounds can fill during summer weekends, but they rarely fill during the week. No reservations.

Facilities
Facilities include picnic tables, fire grates, hand-pumped water, vault toilets, a community house, and a group camping area for rent.

RV Notes
Rifle Creek Campground offers the best RV spots. Many work well for medium-sized RVs. The nearest dump stations are in Rifle Gap State Park and the rest area just off I-70.

Tent Notes
All sites work well for tents.

Recreational Opportunities
This is a world-famous climbing area. In fact, the city of Rifle estimates that 70 percent of day-visitors to the park are climbers. Fishing for pan-sized rainbow trout is also popular.

Other Nearby Campgrounds

51. Rifle Gap State Park (49 sites); 9 miles north of Rifle. Go north on Highway 13 for 3 miles, and turn right (north) on Highway 325. Go 6 miles to the east side of Rifle Gap Reservoir, and turn left (west) on the dirt road. Four campgrounds are clustered around the northeast side of the reservoir. Rifle Gap Reservoir (350 acres) permits all water sports, and it's a busy place. Many sites offer lake views, and some are not far from the lake; all are sparsely shaded and provide little privacy or protection from the elements. Unlimited RV length. Reservations accepted. (970) 625-1607.

DINOSAUR NATIONAL MONUMENT AREA

Dinosaur National Monument contains six campgrounds, of them, three are in Colorado and offer a remote setting near canyon rivers. The three in Utah are more conducive to RVs and closer to the Dinosaur Quarry, particularly Green River Campground. These campgrounds are northwest of the map on page 60.

52. Echo Park (18 sites); 38 miles north of Dinosaur. Go east on Highway 40 for 2 miles to Dinosaur National Monument Headquarters, and turn left (north) onto Dinosaur National Monument Road. Follow the road for about 30 miles to Echo Park Road, and turn right (east). (Echo Park Road is a steep, narrow dirt road not recommended for RVs.) Take Echo Park Road (it becomes 14N Road) to 156 Road. Go left (northwest) on 156 Road, and continue for 5 miles. This primitive campground is in an idyllic spot. Situated at the confluence of the Green and Yampa Rivers, campsites are set among cottonwoods and box elders with captivating views of Steamboat Rock, lofty cliffs, and the rivers. No reservations. **(970) 374-3000.**

53. Deerlodge Park (8 sites); 20 miles northwest of Elk Springs. From Elk Springs, go northeast on Highway 40 for 7 miles to Twelvemile Gulch Road, and turn left (north). Follow the road for 13 miles. Offering campers a chance to really get away from it all, this rustic campground beside the Yampa River is mainly used by river runners. A few cottonwoods provide limited shade, but most sites are fairly open. No drinking water is available. No reservations. **(970) 374-3000.**

54. Gates of Lodore (17 sites); 50 miles northwest of Maybell. Take Highway 40 west for 0.5 mile to Highway 318, and turn right (northwest). Follow Highway 318 for 38 miles to County Road 34, and go left (southwest). Take County Road 34, a graded dirt road, 10 miles to the campground. This campground is dramatically set at the base of the Canyon of Lodore. A few cottonwoods and box elders provide limited shade, but most campsites are in the open. Don't miss the overlooks of the Green River at the end of an easy 1.5-mile nature trail, which includes interpretive signs. No reservations. **(970) 374-3000.**

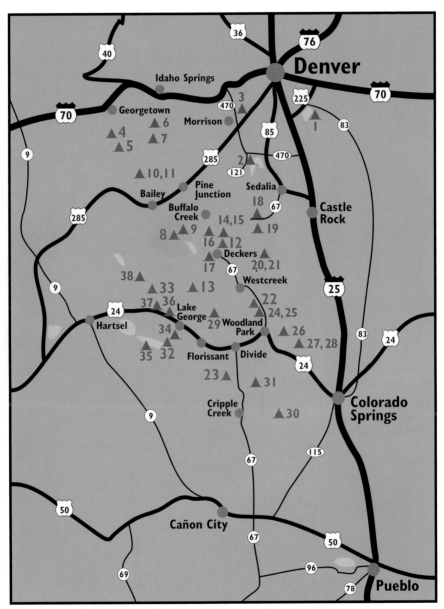

▲ **39** is not visible on the map above. Consult the maps in DeLorme's *Colorado Atlas & Gazetteer* or Pierson Guides' *Colorado Recreational Road Atlas* for the location of this campground on the Eastern Plains. For locations of campgrounds by Bonny Reservoir and Elevenmile Reservoir, see pages 290-291.

In an hour or less, city dwellers from Denver and Colorado Springs can escape the summer heat and find a special camping retreat. Excellent camping experiences are possible, but advance planning is a good idea to prevent disappointments at the most popular campgrounds. In the Denver area, the campgrounds at Cherry Creek and Chatfield Reservoirs fill almost every summer night, often by noon.

West of Denver on I-70, the historic mining settlement of Georgetown serves as a gateway to Guanella Pass, as well as a slew of outdoor activities such as mountain biking, fishing, hiking, off-roading, and wildlife watching.

The Deckers area just southwest of Denver is a favorite of many people. Anglers, tubers, and river runners all share a busy and scenic stretch of the South Platte River by Deckers. The Rampart Range motorcycle trail system in this vicinity offers some of the best single-track riding in the state. Mountain bikers have an extensive network of trails to pick from near Buffalo Creek. The Colorado Trail attracts many nature lovers as it runs through this area on its nearly 500-mile trip from Waterton Canyon (near Chatfield Reservoir) to Durango.

Just northwest of Colorado Springs, Woodland Park serves as the center of activity for weekend fun seekers. The Rampart Reservoir and small Manitou Lake are the biggest draws. Many out-of-towners use the campgrounds in this area as a base camp for exploring the Pikes Peak area. A few miles to the southwest, Mueller State Park offers modern camping facilities and 85 miles of hiking trails. Just southwest of Lake George, spectacular Elevenmile Canyon receives heavy visitation every summer weekend from campers, rock climbers, and anglers. Elevenmile Canyon Reservoir is also close to Lake George. Several miles long, it offers some of the best fishing in the state.

▲ 100 BEST

- ▲4 Clear Lake
- ▲5 Guanella Pass
- ▲8 Green Mountain
- ▲12 Platte River
- ▲13 Goose Creek
- ▲22 Painted Rocks
- ▲23 Mueller State Park
- ▲32 Spillway
- ▲33 Spruce Grove

▲ All The Rest

- ▲1 Cherry Creek State Park
- ▲2 Chatfield State Park
- ▲3 Bear Creek Lake Park
- ▲6 West Chicago Creek
- ▲7 Echo Lake
- ▲9 Buffalo
- ▲10 Deer Creek
- ▲11 Meridian
- ▲14 Ouzel
- ▲15 Osprey
- ▲16 Kelsey
- ▲17 Lone Rock
- ▲18 Indian Creek
- ▲19 Flat Rocks
- ▲20 Devil's Head
- ▲21 Jackson Creek
- ▲24 South Meadows
- ▲25 Colorado
- ▲26 Springdale
- ▲27 Meadow Ridge
- ▲28 Thunder Ridge
- ▲29 Wildhorn (closed)
- ▲30 Wye
- ▲31 The Crags
- ▲34 Elevenmile Canyon
- ▲35 Elevenmile State Park
- ▲36 Happy Meadows
- ▲37 Round Mountain
- ▲38 Twin Eagles Trailhead
- ▲39 Bonny State Park

SOUTH DENVER AREA

1. Cherry Creek State Park (102 sites); southeast of Denver. Take Highway 225 (I-225) to the Highway 83 (Parker Road) exit. Go south on Highway 83 for 1 mile. A summer mecca for Denverites in search of a quick escape, the 880-acre Cherry Creek Reservoir plays host to a multitude of visitors year-round. The campground is not near the lake and is full almost every day from mid-May through mid-September. Five paved loops contain sites offering paved RV pull-outs and back-ins. There is a mix of full and electrical hookups. Both shaded and open sites are available. Amenities include flush toilets and showers. Reservations accepted. **(303) 699-3860.**

2. Chatfield State Park (153 sites); southwest of Denver. From Highway 470 (C-470), take Highway 121 (S. Platte Canyon Road, also known as the Wadsworth exit) and go about 1 mile south. From April through October, the 1,450-acre Chatfield Reservoir is packed. Many sites offer lake views, but none are lakeside. Loop A (51 sites) is the most popular; its sites have the biggest trees (poor to fair shade), and full hookups are available for RVs. Only one site in Loop B has shade, and Loop C has no shade. Sites are all RV-friendly with large, paved pull-thru spaces, and offer electric or full hookups. A dump station is nearby. Modern amenities include flush toilets and showers. Reservations accepted. **(303) 791-7275.**

3. Bear Creek Lake Park (52 sites); west of Denver. From Highway 470 (C-470), take the Morrison Road exit and go east on Morrison Road (a.k.a. Highway 8). On the western edge of the Denver metro area and close to the foothills, the park makes you feel as if you are out of town even though you're not. Bear Creek Lake has a 2.2-mile shoreline and is stocked with rainbow trout, smallmouth bass, and tiger muskie. Soda Lakes Marina rents nonmotorized watercraft. The campground, which isn't near the lake, offers sites with super-long, grassy, pull-thru spaces, but little shade or privacy. Sixteen sites have electrical hookups. Coin-operated showers are also available. This campground is frequently filled on summer weekends. No reservations. **(303) 697-6159.**

GEORGETOWN AREA

4. Clear Lake

Location: About 6 miles south of Georgetown
Elevation: 10,000 feet
Number of Sites: 8
Recommended RV Length: Up to 15 feet
Season: Memorial Day to mid-September
Maps: *Colorado Atlas & Gazetteer*, page 39, C5
Colorado Recreational Road Atlas, page 14, B1
Phone: 303-567-3000

Scenery: ★★★★
RVs: ★★
Tents: ★★★
Shade: ★★
Privacy: ★★

Directions
From I-70, turn off at Georgetown (exit 228), and follow the signs to
Georgetown and the Guanella Pass Road (County Road and Forest Road
381). Go south on Guanella Pass Road about 6 miles to the campground.

Distinguishing Features
This small, tent-oriented campground is located on Guanella Pass Road, and
would be an outstanding fall campground if only they didn't lock the gate!
Clear Lake is an open and sunny campground that allows campers to fully
appreciate the magnificent 360-degree mountain vistas and towering aspen
trees. A mixture of aspen and spruce trees provides half of the sites with good
shade, while other sites have very little shade. The campsites have satisfactory
spacing, allowing for some privacy. Only 1 mile south of Clear Lake, the
campground is a favorite of anglers.

Popularity

This popular campground fills frequently on weekends and sometimes on weekdays from Memorial Day to Labor Day. Arriving early in the day is the best strategy. Mondays and Tuesdays are the least crowded days. No reservations.

Facilities

Picnic tables, fire grates, firewood for sale, hand-pumped water, and vault toilet.

RV Notes

RV sites include medium to long back-in spaces that require a little leveling (the Forest Service's recommended RV length of 15 feet is very conservative). The nearest dump station is located near the Idaho Springs Chamber of Commerce about 12 miles east of Georgetown on I-70.

Tent Notes

One of the sites has a formal tent pad and the others have good, flat areas in which to pitch a tent.

Recreational Opportunities

Anglers can catch rainbow trout in either the creek that runs near the campground, or just down the road at Clear Lake. Swimming and boating are not allowed in Clear Lake. Excellent four-wheeling opportunities await about 3.5 miles to the north. Also popular with mountain bikers, the Waldorf Road (Forest Road 248) is an easy 6-mile four-wheel-drive road that leads to a few old mines. An extremely scenic, easy-to-moderate four-wheeling experience begins at the remains of the Waldorf Mine, and one road leads to the top of Argentine Pass, offering stunning views of the Peru Creek area. Another road leads to McClellan Mountain and views of Grays and Torreys Peaks. Hiking opportunities exist near the top of Guanella Pass.

---

5. Guanella Pass

Location: About 9.25 miles south of Georgetown
Elevation: 10,900 feet
Number of Sites: 18
Recommended RV Length: Up to 35 feet
Season: Early June to mid-September
Maps: *Colorado Atlas & Gazetteer*, page 39, D5
Colorado Recreational Road Atlas, page 14, B1.5
Phone: 303-567-3000

Scenery: ★★★
RVs: ★★★
Tents: ★★★★
Shade: ★★
Privacy: ★★

Directions

From I-70, turn off at Georgetown (exit 228), and follow the signs to the Guanella Pass Road (County Road and Forest Road 381). Go south on Guanella Pass Road about 9 miles to the campground; the last 3 miles are a gravel road.

Distinguishing Features

This modern campground is 2 miles below the summit of Guanella Pass. Campsites are in two loops on either side of the road and next to a creek.

The West Loop contains sites 1-7. All of these sites are suitable for RVs and tents. Four sites have double-wide back-in spaces. Shade is poor to fair. Fair separation between sites offers campers some privacy. For a super spot near the creek, try to reserve site 5. Site 7 is next to the creek too, but views of the water are obscured.

In the East Loop are sites 8-18. This loop has seven walk-in tent sites and three spots that are suitable for RVs. Reservable tent sites 11, 10, and 12 are near the creek. Creekside site 8 is good for both RVs and tents. Sites 13-15 are walk-in tent sites set in the open with no shade trees or privacy. Up the hill, sites 16-18 are suitable for all campers and offer ample shade and privacy.

Popularity

Guanella Pass typically fills every weekend from Memorial Day to Labor Day. As always, the best options are reserving in advance or getting to the campground on a Wednesday or Thursday.

Facilities

Facilities at the Guanella Pass Campground include picnic tables, fire grates, firewood for sale, hand-pumped water, and wheelchair-accessible vault toilets.

RV Notes

Fairly level, medium to long back-in sites are satisfactory for RVs. The nearest dump station is located near the Idaho Springs Chamber of Commerce about 12 miles east of Georgetown on I-70.

Tent Notes

All campsites have tent pads, and seven are walk-in tent-only sites, the best of which are sites 11, 10, and 12.

Recreational Opportunities

Anglers can catch trout in the creek that flows through the campground. A short, easy 1-mile hike leads to Naylor Lake, which offers satisfactory trout fishing above timberline. In less than 2 miles, the South Park Trail climbs above timberline from the top of Guanella Pass to the Square Top Lakes, where anglers can fish for trout. The trail continues beyond the lake for many miles, leading hikers to spectacular mountain vistas.

The Silver Dollar Lake trailhead is about 0.75 mile from the campground up a steep road. The Rosalie Trail heads southeast into the Mount Evans Wilderness. Many campers head to the other side of Guanella Pass for mountain-biking, hiking, and four-wheel-drive opportunities. (See the Whiteside [page 138], Burning Bear, and Geneva Park Campgrounds [page 141] for more camping options on the other side of Guanella Pass, and see Clear Lake Campground [page 93] for more recreational opportunities.)

Other Nearby Campgrounds

These two campgrounds are located southwest of Idaho Springs on Highway 103 (Squaw Pass Road) on the west side of Squaw Pass.

6. West Chicago Creek (16 sites); 9.3 miles southwest of Idaho Springs via Highway 103 (Squaw Pass Road) and Forest Road 188. One of the closest mountain campgrounds to Denver. Pine and aspen provide varying shade. Sites have large parking spots (RV friendly), are closely spaced, and not very private. Maximum RV length is 30 feet. Reservations accepted. **(303) 567-3000.**

7. Echo Lake (18 sites); 14 miles southwest of Idaho Springs on Highway 103 (Squaw Pass Road). Only a half mile from Echo Lake, it is extremely busy every day during the summer and it is tough to get a campsite. Nearby trails lead into the Mount Evans Wilderness. Seven sites are walk-in tent sites. Heavily wooded, all sites have good shade and poor to good privacy. Maximum RV length is 20 feet. Reservations accepted. **(303) 567-3000.**

577-
444-6777 Mountain.Gov

BUFFALO CREEK AREA

8. Green Mountain

Location: 11 miles southwest of Buffalo Creek

Elevation: 7,600 feet

Number of Sites: 6

Season: Year-round (weather permitting)

Maps: *Colorado Atlas & Gazetteer,* page 49, B7 *Colorado Recreational Road Atlas,* page 15, A3

Phone: 303-275-5610

Scenery: ★★★★
RVs: No
Tents: ★★★★★
Shade: ★★★★
Privacy: ★★★★

Directions

From Buffalo Creek, go about 3.5 miles south on County Road 126 (a.k.a. S. Deckers Road) to Forest Road 550. Turn right (west) onto Forest Road 550 (a well-maintained gravel road), and go about 5.5 miles until it intersects Forest Road 543. Go left (south), and proceed about 2 miles.

Distinguishing Features

This tent-only campground is a superb place for those seeking to get away from the crowds and noise. The sites are private, level, on the creek, and well-shaded by mature spruce trees—all of which combines for a delightful wilderness experience. Three of the six sites are on the other side of the creek.

Popularity

As this tent-only campground is off the beaten path, a site is usually still available early on Friday evening in the summer. Summer occupancy can average 95 percent on weekends. No reservations.

Facilities

Facilities are a bit primitive but include picnic tables, fire grates, hand-pumped water, and vault toilets. No trash service is available, so remember to pack out your trash.

Tent Notes

Campers may think they've died and gone to tent heaven!

Recreational Opportunities

Anglers might catch small brookies in the creek. Privately owned Wellington Lake, 1 mile southwest, is open to the public for a fee. The Colorado Trail crosses Forest Road 543 just north of the campground. Heading west, it leads up to a ridge with pretty views of a granite outcropping called "The Castle," and in 4 miles it drops down to Forest Road 543 (a.k.a. Wellington Road) once again. Utilizing the road, visitors with mountain bikes can design a loop trip. If heading east, the Colorado Trail links up to a few other trails, and the nearby Buffalo Creek Mountain Bike Area has 40 miles of trails specifically designed for mountain bikers.

Other Nearby Campgrounds

9. Buffalo (41 sites); 6.5 miles southwest of Buffalo Creek. Go southwest on Forest Road 543 for 6.5 miles to the intersection of Forest Road 550. Ponderosa pines provide good shade, and pretty views of the nearby rocky hills abound. This campground is RV-friendly with many parking spaces suitable for medium-sized RVs. Reservations accepted. **(303) 275-5610.**

10. Deer Creek (13 sites); 10.5 miles northwest of Bailey. Take Highway 285 2.5 miles northeast to County Road 43. Go left (north) on County Road 43 for 8 miles. Here's one of the closest mountain campgrounds to Denver, yet it rarely fills. Hikers have easy access to the Mount Evans Wilderness. Long back-ins are available for RVs. Four sites are on Deer Creek. Shade and privacy range from poor to good. No reservations. **(303) 275-5610.**

11. Meridian (18 sites); 10 miles northwest of Bailey. Take Highway 285 2.5 miles northeast to County Road 43. Go left (north) on County Road 43. Proceed for about 7 miles, and turn right (east) onto County Road 47. Follow this road for about a mile. Popular with retirees, Meridian offers many long back-ins for RVs. Privacy and shade range from satisfactory to adequate. Spaces rarely fill. No reservations. **(303) 275-5610.**

DECKERS—SOUTH PLATTE RIVER AREA

12. Platte River

Location: 4 miles north of Deckers
Elevation: 6,300 feet
Number of Sites: 10
Season: Year-round
Maps: *Colorado Atlas & Gazetteer*, page 50, B1
Colorado Recreational Road Atlas, page 15, B3
Phone: 303-275-5610

Scenery: ★★★
RVs: No
Tents: ★★★
Shade: ★
Privacy: ★

Directions

From Deckers, go 4 miles north on County Road 67 (S. Platte River Road).

Distinguishing Features

Of the four campgrounds along the South Platte River north of Deckers, this is the clear winner (if you have a tent!). This is a lovely setting, with every site overlooking the river. Three sites are near the river. Walk-in sites are scattered on the side of a gently sloping grassy hill. The longest walk from the parking area to the campsites is less than two minutes. Scattered ponderosa pines and some close spacing mean little shade or privacy, but this is a pleasant fishing campground.

Popularity
On summer weekends, the campground is almost always full of anglers; campers should show up on Friday morning or early afternoon to get a site. No reservations.

Facilities
Facilities include picnic tables, fire grates, and a vault toilet that is wheelchair-accessible, as is one campsite and a fishing dock. No drinking water is provided.

RV Notes
This is a terrible spot for RVs: parking is limited to the lot, and the picnic table is many feet away.

Tent Notes
All sites have formal or semiformal tent pads.

Recreational Opportunities
This is a popular stretch of river for both rafters and anglers. Gold Medal water regulations apply. From Wigwam Club to Scraggy View, anglers must use artificial flies and lures. There's a two-trout limit, and trout must be at least 16 inches long. The South Platte River offers a great Class II canoeing and kayaking run from Scraggy View to the confluence; many beginners use this stretch for training. Tubers also use some stretches of the river. The Rampart Range Motorized Recreation Area contains the most popular network of motorcycle trails in the state.

---

13. Goose Creek
Location: 14 miles southwest of Deckers
Elevation: 8,100 feet
Number of Sites: 10
Recommended RV Length: Up to 20 feet
Season: Year-round (weather permitting)
Maps: *Colorado Atlas & Gazetteer*, page 50, C1
Colorado Recreational Road Atlas, page 15, A4
Phone: 303-275-5610

Scenery: ★★★
RVs: ★★★
Tents: ★★★★
Shade: ★★★
Privacy: ★★★

Directions
From Deckers, go west on County Road 126 about 3 miles to Forest Road 211. Go left (southwest) 11 miles on this gravel road; the last few miles can be very "washboardy."

Distinguishing Features

Welcome back from the dead, Goose Creek. Closed for several years because of concerns about upstream flooding from debris from the 2002 Hayman Fire (supposedly, the fire never touched the campground itself), one of Colorado's best kept secrets is once again welcoming lucky campers. Remote and primitive, Goose Creek Campground contains 10 campsites. Five are along the creek, and they are some of the finest river campsites in the entire Deckers area. Campers fortunate enough to grab one will be in no rush to leave. Sites have satisfactory spacing, providing adequate privacy from your neighbors. Large spruces and a few ponderosa pines provide ample shade to the river sites. Of the other five sites, two could be considered walk-ins. The five have less shade and privacy.

Popularity

As this spot is tied for second in Deckers-area campgrounds and can even be busy on weekdays, it's wise to arrive on Thursday or early Friday for a summer weekend. No reservations.

Facilities

Facilities include picnic tables, fire grates, hand-pumped water, and vault toilets. No trash service is available, so pack it out.

RV Notes

Goose Creek is a relatively RV-friendly campground for those who don't mind driving 11 miles on a dirt road. Medium and long back-ins are available; all

are fairly level. A dump station is near Horse Creek Restaurant on County Road 67, two miles north of Deckers.

Tent Notes

The riverside sites are superb! Showers are available at Horse Creek Restaurant on County Road 67, two miles north of Deckers.

Recreational Opportunities

Goose Creek offers ample fishing for rainbows and brookies, as does the South Platte River. Cheesman Lake (875 acres; no boating) has rainbow, brown, and brook trout, as well as northern pike, sucker, kokanee salmon, and yellow perch. Nighttime fishing is prohibited. Anglers who fish below Cheesman should note that the area is designated as Gold Medal water from the dam to the confluence of the North Fork and South Platte Rivers.

The Goose Creek Trail can be accessed a few miles south of the campground. From there, hikers and equestrians can choose the Goose Creek Trail or Hankins Pass Trail; both lead into the Lost Creek Wilderness. The Goose Creek Trail follows the creek for a couple of miles—with views of spectacular rock formations—eventually leading to the Shafthouse, which makes an interesting destination. Sheep Rock is popular with rock climbers.

Other Nearby Campgrounds

14. Ouzel (13 sites); 5 miles north of Deckers on County Road 67 (S. Platte River Road). Ouzel has a central parking area, tent sites spaced very close together, and poor shade overall. The river is near this tent-only campground, but willows block views of the water. No drinking water is provided. Tents only, no reservations. **(303) 275-5610.**

15. Osprey (10 sites); 7 miles north of Deckers on County Road 67 (S. Platte River Road). You won't find trees, privacy, or drinking water in this tent-only campground. No reservations. **(303) 275-5610.**

16. Kelsey (17 sites); 7.5 miles northwest of Deckers on County Road 126 (S. Deckers Road). Kelsey is close to the Buffalo Creek mountain-bike trails. Paved parking and well-shaded campsites are available. Privacy is good. Accommodates medium-sized RVs. No water. Reservations accepted. **(303) 275-5610.**

17. Lone Rock (19 sites); 0.6 mile west of Deckers on County Road 126 (S. Deckers Road). This is a wildly popular campground along the South Platte River. A paved road leads to many walk-in tent sites and limited spaces for RVs of 20 feet and under. Several sites are near the river, but shade is nonexistent in most sites. Privacy is only a dream. No reservations. **(303) 275-5610.**

NORTH RAMPART RANGE AREA

18. Indian Creek (18 sites); 10 miles southwest of Sedalia on Highway 67. Two smaller loops contain sites best for tents and small RVs. In the center of each loop is a treeless meadow. Shade ranges from poor to adequate. A third loop has 7 equestrian sites and a 15 mile loop horse trail starts from the campground. Maximum RV length is 20 feet. Reservations accepted for equestrian sites only. **(303) 275-5610.**

19. Flat Rocks (19 sites); 14.1 miles southwest of Sedalia. Take Highway 67 southwest for 10 miles to Rampart Range Road. Turn left (south), and go 4 miles. In the heart of motorcycle country, this campground rarely fills due to so many good dispersed camping opportunities in the area. Sites are on either side of a long, narrow road with a small turnaround loop at the end. Most sites provide good shade and privacy, although they're a bit off-level. Maximum RV length is 20 feet. No reservations. **(303) 275-5610.**

20. Devil's Head (21 sites); 19 miles southwest of Sedalia. Take Highway 67 southwest for 10 miles to Rampart Range Road (Forest Road 300). Turn left (south), and go 9 miles. This campground is in a scenic setting with good shade and privacy. Sites are best suited for tents and are not very level. The road through the campground can be difficult for RVs to navigate. No reservations. **(303) 275-5610.**

21. Jackson Creek (9 sites); 25 miles southwest of Sedalia. Take Highway 67 southwest for 10 miles to Rampart Range Road (Forest Road 300). Turn left (south) on Forest Road 300 and go about 13.5 miles to Forest Road 502. Turn left (north) on Forest Road 502, and proceed for 1.5 miles. This is a remote, lightly used campground. The road to the campground is narrow, and the Forest Service discourages RVs from camping here. Five sites are alongside tiny Jackson Creek, and all offer excellent shade and privacy. Maximum RV length is 20 feet. No water. No reservations. **(303) 275-5610.**

WOODLAND PARK AREA

22. Painted Rocks

Location: 8.5 miles north of Woodland Park
Elevation: 7,900 feet
Number of Sites: 18
Recommended RV Length: Up to 21 feet
Season: May through September
Maps: *Colorado Atlas & Gazetteer*, page 50, D2
Colorado Recreational Road Atlas, page 24, A1.5
Phone: 719-636-1602

Scenery: ★★★
RVs: ★★★
Tents: ★★★
Shade: ★★
Privacy: ★★

Directions
From Woodland Park, go 8 miles north on Highway 67 to County Road 78 (Forest Road 340). Turn left (west), and proceed for 0.5 mile.

Distinguishing Features
Painted Rocks has plenty to offer campers who think they've seen it all. Fascinating sculpted red sandstone monoliths and formations are scattered around the edge of the campground. Situated in an open grassy meadow with ponderosa pines providing fair shade, the campground offers a good mix of sun and shade. Two loops in a figure-eight contain sites with fair to good spacing and privacy.

Popularity
From Memorial Day to Labor Day, Painted Rocks fills almost every weekend. Reservations recommended.

Facilities
Facilities include picnic tables, fire grates, firewood for sale, water faucets, and vault toilets.

RV Notes
Medium to long back-ins and one pull-thru characterize the parking spots. Some leveling may be required. The nearest dump station is at the Pike Community Campground about 2 miles back on Highway 67.

Tent Notes
Tents can be easily pitched nearly anywhere in the campsite.

Recreational Opportunities
Nearby 34-acre Manitou Park Lake is a lovely spot where the whole family can enjoy fishing for rainbow and cutthroat trout or hike around the lake. Motorboats and swimming are prohibited. Trout Creek offers stream fishing, and the 4.2-mile paved Manitou Bicycle Trail runs from Manitou Park Lake south to Red Rocks Campground. A short spur from Painted Rocks Campground joins this trail. A maze of OHV and mountain-biking trails lies just a few miles west of the campground. Many campers use Painted Rocks as a base camp to explore the Colorado Springs and Pikes Peak area.

23. Mueller State Park
Location: 7 miles south of Divide
Elevation: 9,500 feet
Number of Sites: 132
Recommended RV Length: Unlimited
Season: Year-round (facilities and campsites limited in winter)
Maps: *Colorado Atlas & Gazetteer*, page 62, B1 *Colorado Recreational Road Atlas*, page 24, A2
Phone: 719-687-2366

Scenery: ★★★
RVs: ★★★★
Tents: ★★★★
Shade: ★★★
Privacy: ★★★

Directions
From Woodland Park, go west about 6.5 miles on Highway 24 to Divide. Turn left (south) onto Highway 67, and proceed 5.5 miles to County Road 61 (Fourmile Road). Turn right (south) on County Road 61, and drive 2 miles.

Distinguishing Features

Visitors love Mueller because it's only 33 miles from Colorado Springs, has ultra-modern facilities and 85 miles of trails, and offers excellent wildlife-watching opportunities. Campsites are in a forested setting of spruce, fir, and aspen. Many sites provide views of Pikes Peak, the Sangre de Cristos, and the Collegiate Peaks. The campground road and parking spaces are all paved. Most sites provide ample shade and privacy.

Mueller State Park

The campground is one long, narrow loop with several spurs splitting off the main loop. The Peak View Loop (all back-ins) is the most popular. Sites have views of Pikes Peak and overlook a pond. Revenuer's Ridge is the main campground loop, with some super-long pull-thrus. Conifer Ridge (sites 23-50) is off the main road and feels a bit more private, with many sites providing views of Pikes Peak. Grouse Mountain (sites 91-132) is the northernmost loop and the second most popular place to camp.

Popularity

Of all the state parks, probably none is more popular than Mueller. From mid-May to mid-October, Mueller fills almost every weekend. From the first week in June through mid-September, this park will fill almost every weekday by noon. Reservations are necessary. The most popular sites are 1-5 and 38-44, all offering views of Pikes Peak. Sites 81 and 82 have views of the Sangre de Cristos and the Collegiate Peaks and are close to the camper services building.

Facilities

Facilities include picnic tables, fire grates, water faucets, flush and vault toilets, showers, laundry facilities, an amphitheater, playground, group camping loop, and livery (bring your own horses).

RV Notes

All sites have electrical hookups, and a dump station is available. Very RV-friendly, campsites offer paved pull-thrus and back-ins. Revenuer's Ridge offers a few super-long pull-thrus.

Tent Notes

The park has 22 great walk-in tent sites with pads. They're heavily wooded and located in Prospector Ridge (sites 55-66) and Turkey Meadow (100-110). Most other sites have pads.

Recreational Opportunities 🚶 🎣 🚴 🐎

The impressive visitor center and the Big View Overlook should be the starting point for learning about adventures to be had in the area. The park offers interpretive programs, exhibits, and ranger-led hikes—keep your eyes open for bighorn sheep, elk, deer, hawks, and eagles. Eighty-five miles of trails are open to hikers, and many are open to mountain bikers; some larger loops are available to horseback riders. No pets are allowed on any of the trails. Anglers can hike to Fourmile Creek and a few stocked trout ponds, but fishing is not a big activity here. Hunting is limited and controlled in the fall, and prohibited during the summer; contact park officials for details. Cross-country skiing and snowshoeing are popular wintertime activities.

Other Nearby Campgrounds

24. South Meadows (64 sites); 6 miles north of Woodland Park on Highway 67. South Meadows is open year-round. Set among tall ponderosa pines, all sites are well-shaded. A paved road leads to spacious sites that provide ample privacy. This RV-friendly campground has many pull-thrus and accommodates large RVs. Reservations accepted. **(719) 636-1602.**

25. Colorado (81 sites); 7 miles north of Woodland Park on Highway 67. Set in a forest of dense ponderosa pines, Colorado provides private sites with little sunlight. A paved road leads to sites with long to extra-long spaces that accommodate large RVs. Many are pull-thrus. Manitou Park Lake is just a half-mile walk away. Reservations accepted. **(719) 636-1602.**

26. Springdale (14 sites); 5 miles east of Woodland Park. From Woodland Park, go north on County Road 22 (a.k.a. Rampart Range Road and Forest Road 300) and go 5 miles. Located 5 miles from Rampart Reservoir, this campground is somewhat primitive and best suited for tents, although a few sites work for RVs. Campers will find adequate shade and privacy. Maximum RV length is 16 feet. No reservations. **(719) 636-1602.**

27. Meadow Ridge (19 sites); 8 miles east of Woodland Park. From Woodland Park, go north on County Road 22 (a.k.a. Rampart Range Road and Forest Road 300) for about 5.5 miles to Forest Road 306. Turn left (northeast) for about 2.5 miles. Set above 500-acre Rampart Reservoir in a forested area, a few sites offer limited lake views. Both the campground road and parking spots are paved. Spruce, ponderosa pine, and aspen trees provide good shade. Maximum RV length is 21 feet. Reservations accepted. **(719) 636-1602.** Due to fires in 2002, this campground might be closed—call first!

28. Thunder Ridge (21 sites); 8 miles east of Woodland Park. From Woodland Park, go north on County Road 22 (a.k.a. Rampart Range Road and Forest Road 300) for about 5.5 miles to Forest Road 306. Turn left (northeast) for about 2.5 miles. Also above Rampart Reservoir, this campground is very similar to its neighbor, Meadow Ridge. A paved road leads to paved parking spaces. Good shade and privacy exist in the campground, although tenters may have a hard time finding a level spot. The lake is just down the hill. Maximum RV length is 21 feet. Reservations accepted. **(719) 636-1602.** Due to fires in 2002, this campground might be closed—call first!

29. Wildhorn
Since the writing of this book, this campground has permanently closed.

30. Wye (21 sites); 13 miles southwest of Colorado Springs. From I-25 in Colorado Springs, go west on Highway 24 about 1.5 miles to 21st Street. Go left (south) on 21st Street for about 1 mile to Gold Camp Road. Turn right (west) and follow the winding Gold Camp Road (Forest Road 370) for about 19 miles. The road and parking spaces in this very primitive campground are in bad shape and are not recommended for RVs. Privacy and shade are fair. No drinking water or trash service is provided. No reservations. **(719) 636-1602.**

31. The Crags (17 sites); 7 miles southeast of Divide. Go south on Highway 67 for 4 miles to Forest Road 383. Turn left (east) on Forest Road 383, and go 3 miles. The Crags is a good alternative to the very popular Mueller State Park. Families who wish to take pets along can bring them here. Many sites are on the creek and shade is ample. Dust can be a problem because of the heavily used trailhead near the end of the campground. A rough, narrow road leading to the campground isn't recommended for larger RVs. No reservations. **(719) 636-1602.**

LAKE GEORGE AREA

32. Spillway

Location: 9 miles southwest of Lake George (see map on p. 291)
Elevation: 8,500 feet
Number of Sites: 23
Recommended RV Length: Up to 25 feet
Season: Early May to early October
Maps: *Colorado Atlas & Gazetteer,* page 61, A6.5
Colorado Recreational Road Atlas, page 23, C2
Phone: 719-836-2031

Scenery: ★★★★
RVs: ★★
Tents: ★★★
Shade: ★★
Privacy: ★★

Directions
From Highway 24 in Lake George, turn southwest onto County Road 96 (Forest Road 245). Go southwest about 9 miles through Elevenmile Canyon; the last 8 miles are on a good dirt road that is a little narrow in spots.

Distinguishing Features
The trip to Spillway is beautiful and half the fun. Solid granite hills form a backdrop to this primitive campground near the end of spectacular Elevenmile Canyon. The campground has two loops on a marginal road, with wonderful views from all sites. Nearly half are on or near the South Platte River, with the Elevenmile Dam only a quarter-mile away. Half the sites are in a relatively flat, open meadow near the river, with tall spruces providing some shade. The rest are around the eastern edges of the two loops and situated in rocky soil with large ponderosa pines providing poor to adequate shade. The boulders are often so huge that they actually shade the sites. Privacy ranges from poor to fair.

Popularity
This campground can fill quickly during busy summer weekends; arriving by noon on Thursday is the best way to find a spot. Reservations accepted.

Facilities

Facilities include picnic tables, fire grates, firewood for sale (from a truck driving through the campground), hand-pumped water, vault toilets, and an amphitheater.

RV Notes

There are short- to medium-sized back-ins and narrow pull-outs for RVs. Five are on the river. Some of these sites are not very level, while others aren't too bad. The road through the campground is rough. The dirt road through the canyon is good, but narrow in spots—be careful. The nearest dump stations are at the private Travel Port Campground in Lake George or at Elevenmile Canyon Reservoir.

Tent Notes

Spots near the river are grassy and fairly level, offering little shade. Sites away from the river are on much harder ground and not always level, but many have good shade. Seven sites are walk-ins. Showers are available at the private Travel Port Campground in Lake George.

Recreational Opportunities

Anglers will find the South Platte River placid and inviting near here. Rainbow, cutthroat, and brown trout await; use artificial flies and lures only. Tubing is very popular, and tubers can float in fairly calm water (normally) for almost 3 miles before some nasty rapids are encountered near Springer Gulch Campground. (Use caution—conditions can change rapidly.) At this point, the trip ends for most tubers. Trail 641 starts from the campground and leads to an overlook 0.5 mile and 500 feet in elevation later, with panoramic views of the canyon and surrounding mountains. Climbers can often be seen scaling the rocky walls of Elevenmile Canyon.

---

33. Spruce Grove

Location: 14 miles north of Lake George
Elevation: 8,600 feet
Number of Sites: 27
Recommended RV Length: Up to 35 feet
Season: Memorial Day to Labor Day
Maps: *Colorado Atlas & Gazetteer*, page 49, C6.5
Colorado Recreational Road Atlas, page 23, C1
Phone: 719-836-2031

Scenery: ★★★
RVs: ★★
Tents: ★★★★
Shade: ★★
Privacy: ★★

Directions

From Lake George, go west 0.75 mile on Highway 24, and then turn right (north) on County Road 77. Go about 13 miles to the campground, which is on your right and poorly marked.

Distinguishing Features

Most of Spruce Grove's sites are clustered in one relatively open loop with minimal shade or privacy. Four sites are on Tarryall Creek. All have good views of the fascinating rock formations jutting out from the surrounding hills.

It's the tent sites that make this a top campground. Eight magical walk-in sites await lucky campers willing to carry all their gear across the creek into a lost world of dinosaur-sized boulders, towering trees, wonderful views, and seclusion. These shady spots rest alongside the creek as it widens while meandering peacefully through a little mini-canyon. You'll wish you could stay lost in there forever.

Popularity

Spruce Grove fills almost every weekend from Memorial Day to Labor Day. Try to arrive before noon on Friday. No reservations.

Facilities

Facilities include picnic tables, fire rings, firewood for sale (from a traveling firewood salesman), hand-pumped water, and wheelchair-accessible vault toilets.

RV Notes

Most sites are fairly level, large back-ins with close spacing and little shade.

Tent Notes
All sites have pads. The walk-in sites are some of the top tent sites in the state.

Recreational Opportunities
Anglers have great luck fishing for brookies (occasionally rainbows and browns) in Tarryall Creek, which is also a popular spot for gold- and garnet-panning. Spruce Grove borders the Lost Creek Wilderness, and several good trails lead into the area from the campground. The campground offers great rock climbing, and good fishing and boating are 11 miles away at Tarryall Reservoir.

This site is also known for an unusual activity: digging for topaz. One fellow camper found a topaz the day I visited, alleging that it was worth nearly $4,000. Your best bet is the privately owned Topaz Mountain Gem Mine, where you can collect topaz for a fee. The mine is located on Forest Road 211 about 7.5 miles south of the campground.

Other Nearby Campgrounds

34. Elevenmile Canyon The five campgrounds in this beautiful area fill almost every summer weekend (especially Spillway). A daily fee station is near the entrance of the canyon. Reservations accepted at all five campgrounds.

Blue Mountain (21 sites) is 1.5 miles south of Lake George. Go south from Lake George on County Road 96 (Forest Road 245) for 1 mile. Turn left (south) onto County Road 61 (Forest Road 240) for 0.5 mile. Of the five campgrounds, Blue Mountain is the only one not in the canyon. This campground consists of large, spacious sites that offer good shade and privacy. Parking spaces for RVs are not very level or long. **Riverside** (19 sites; see map on p. 291) is 2 miles southwest of Lake George. From Lake George, go south on County Road 96 (Forest Road 245) for 2 miles. Set in a flat, grassy meadow, it features 11 good walk-in tent sites with tent pads. The river is just across the road for anglers and tubers, and is easily accessible. Eight RV-friendly sites are also in the campground. Shade ranges from poor to fair. Maximum RV length is 25 feet. No water. **Springer Gulch** (15 sites; see map on p. 291) is 6.8 miles southwest of Lake George. From Lake George, go south on County Road 96 (Forest Road 245) for 6 miles. All but three sites are set back 0.25 mile from the river and the canyon, and are on the outside of a small loop. Shade and privacy vary from poor to good. This is not the best place for RVs, although some spots will work just fine. Maximum RV length is 25 feet. **Cove** (4 sites; see map on p. 291) is 9 miles southwest of Lake George. From Lake George, go south on County Road 96 (Forest Road 245) for 8.5 miles. This is one of the first campgrounds to fill during weekends. All sites are on the outside of a very small loop. Maximum RV length is 16 feet. No water. Reservations are accepted. **(719) 836-2031.**

35. Elevenmile Reservoir State Park (349 sites; see map on p. 291); 11 miles southwest of Lake George. Take Highway 24 northwest about 0.75 mile, and turn left (west) onto County Road 90 (Forest Road 247). This road turns into County Road 92 by the reservoir. Go southwest about 10 miles to the first of eight campgrounds that surround the reservoir. The first three are close together. The fourth is 1.75 miles farther on County Road 92. To get to the others, go another 3.5 miles to County Road 59 and go left (southwest). Follow County Road 59 about 3 miles to the fifth campground. The others are in the next 2 to 4 miles on the left. Eight sparsely shaded campgrounds with little privacy are located around 3,400-acre Elevenmile Reservoir. This is one of the top five fishing areas in the state, especially for salmon. Waterskiing and swimming are prohibited. Many treeless campgrounds offer sites close to the water, where boaters can moor their boats. Most sites have excellent lake and mountain views. The most popular campground is **Rocky Ridge**—away from the lake but offering limited shade and electrical hookups in Loops A, B, and D. The camper services building near Rocky Ridge offers showers and laundry facilities. A dump station is located at the park. Reservations accepted. **(719) 748-3401.**

36. Happy Meadows (10 sites); 3 miles north of Lake George. Take Highway 24 west 1 mile to County Road 77. Turn right (northeast), and go 1.5 miles to County Road 112 (Forest Road 207). Turn right (east), and go 0.5 mile. On the South Platte River in a sparsely shaded meadow, this is an extremely popular campground with anglers. Five sites are on the river, and campers have little privacy. It fills frequently on weekdays and weekends. Maximum RV length is 22 feet. No reservations. **(719) 836-2031.**

37. Round Mountain (16 sites); 6.5 miles northwest of Lake George on Highway 24. Large, RV-friendly sites are widely spaced in one big loop. Trees are not very dense, so shade is fair on average. Traffic noise from the highway is heard at most sites. Reservations accepted. **(719) 836-2031.**

38. Twin Eagles Trailhead (9 sites); 15.25 miles north of Lake George. Take Highway 24 west 1 mile, and turn right (northeast) on County Road 77. Follow the road for 14.25 miles. Few people realize that this trailhead is also a campground. Five wonderful sites are very private walk-in tent sites scattered along the other side of Tarryall Creek. The other four are nothing special and have little shade. No drinking water is provided. Mainly a tent campground, it's not very accommodating for RVs. No reservations. **(719) 836-2031.**

EASTERN PLAINS AREA

39. Bonny State Park (190 sites; see map on p. 290; *Colorado Atlas & Gazetteer*, page 102, B3.5; *Colorado Recreational Road Atlas*, page 20, C2.5); 23 miles north of Burlington. Go north on Highway 385 for 21 miles to County Roads 2 or 3, and turn right (east). Go about 2 miles. Four campgrounds surround 1,900-acre Bonny Reservoir, which offers the full spectrum of water sports, fishing opportunities, and wildlife watching. Willows and cottonwood trees provide shade at this low, 3,700-foot elevation.

    Wagon Wheel (87 sites) is the most central and most developed campground in this parklike setting, offering all sites with electrical hookups. Deluxe amenities include a nearby marina, flush toilets, showers, laundry facilities, and a dump station. Seven paved loops offer campsites all within 25 to 300 yards of the shoreline. Grassy spots are inviting for tents, and those with RVs will find a variety of back-ins and pull-thrus to satisfy their needs. Shade and privacy vary widely. **East Beach** (35 sites) is a primitive campground; the best spots are the shaded walk-in lakeside tent sites 4-13. The rest of the sites have very little shade, but are less than 100 yards from the lake. Vault toilets and water faucets are part of the rustic facilities. **North Cove** (21 sites) is popular with anglers, and all sites are within 50 yards of the water. Fourteen of the sites are lakeside and offer shade, while the rest of the sites are in the open with little shade. Facilities include a boat ramp, vault toilets, and water faucets. **Foster Grove** (42 sites) is the least used campground. About half the sites have wonderful shade, while the rest have very little. The lake is 0.25 mile away, and this quiet setting is said to be a great place for wildlife watching. Thirteen sites have electrical hookups. Flush toilets, water faucets, and a dump station are all available in this location, too. Reservations are accepted at all campgrounds and are highly recommended for summer weekends. **(970) 354-7306.**

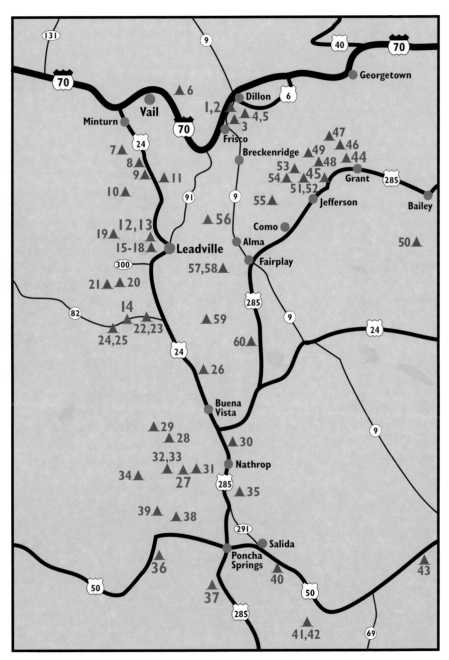

For locations of campgrounds by Dillon Reservoir and Turquoise Lake, see page 292.

This region encompasses some of the most breathtaking scenery in Colorado. The Dillon Reservoir area is a favorite with visitors and locals alike, and just a short drive from Denver. Colorful sailboats dot the lake on hot summer days. Excellent paved bike paths seem to go everywhere—from Dillon to Vail to Breckenridge. Stay on the highway a little longer and you'll reach Leadville, a town known not only for famous historical figures like Baby Doe Tabor and Molly Brown, but for some of the best campgrounds in the state. Lovely Turquoise Lake, surrounded by dense forest, is the perfect setting for a quick getaway, and you'll enjoy views of the beautiful Collegiate Peaks Range. Twin Lakes Reservoir is another outstanding attraction.

Kenosha Pass is one of the best places to enjoy the glittering yellow and gold of Colorado's aspen trees—plan ahead to camp during the peak fall season. The entire South Park area, with its abundant mountain meadows and rich green forests, turns into a spectacular display of autumn color.

Southeast of Buena Vista is America's most heavily rafted stretch of whitewater, the Arkansas River. Commercial river outfitters operating from Buena Vista to Cañon City will be happy to introduce you to the excitement!

▲ 100 BEST

▲1 Heaton Bay
▲2 Peak One
▲12 Baby Doe
▲13 Belle of Colorado
▲14 Whitestar
▲27 Chalk Lake
▲36 Monarch Park
▲37 O'Haver Lake
▲44 Whiteside
▲45 Kenosha Pass
▲56 Kite Lake

▲ All The Rest

▲3 Pine Cove	▲23 Lakeview	▲43 Five Points
▲4 Lowry	▲24 Parry Peak	▲46 Burning Bear
▲5 Prospector	▲25 Twin Peaks	▲47 Geneva Park
▲6 Gore Creek	▲26 Railroad Bridge	▲48 Handcart
▲7 Tigiwon (closed)	▲28 Cottonwood Lake	▲49 Hall Valley
▲8 Hornsilver	▲29 Collegiate Peaks	▲50 Lost Park
▲9 Blodgett (closed)	▲30 Ruby Mountain	▲51 Lodgepole
▲10 Gold Park	▲31 Bootleg	▲52 Aspen
▲11 Camp Hale Memorial	▲32 Mount Princeton	▲53 Jefferson Creek
▲15 Molly Brown	▲33 Cascade	▲54 Michigan Creek
▲16 Tabor	▲34 Iron City	▲55 Selkirk
▲17 Silver Dollar	▲35 Hecla Junction	▲57 Horseshoe
▲18 Father Dyer	▲38 Angel of Shavano	▲58 Fourmile
▲19 May Queen	▲39 North Fork Reservoir	▲59 Weston Pass
▲20 Halfmoon	▲40 Rincon	▲60 Buffalo Springs
▲21 Elbert Creek	▲41 Coaldale	
▲22 Dexter	▲42 Hayden Creek	

DILLON RESERVOIR AREA

1. Heaton Bay

Location: 2 miles northeast of Frisco (see map on p. 292)
Elevation: 9,100 feet
Number of Sites: 81
Recommended RV Length: Up to 90 feet
Season: Late May to mid-October
Maps: *Colorado Atlas & Gazetteer,* page 38, D2
Colorado Recreational Road Atlas, page 14, A1.5
Phone: 970-468-5400

Scenery: ★★★★
RVs: ★★★★
Tents: ★★★
Shade: Varies
Privacy: ★★

Directions

From I-70, take exit 203 (Frisco/Breckenridge), and go south to the first stoplight. Turn left (northeast) onto the Dillon Dam Road (Highway 9), and proceed 1 mile.

Distinguishing Features

Big changes have occurred here recently. In 2005, beetle-infested trees were cut down around Lake Dillon, and many of the campsites have a much more open look, with less privacy and shade than past times. In addition, Heaton Bay is still undergoing renovation, and campsites in Loops C–E have been re-alphabetized and renumbered. Loop C has electrical hook-ups at all sites.

Popularity

Heaton Bay fills every summer weekend, usually by early Friday afternoon. The wisest strategy is to call or go online as far in advance as possible for one of the lakeside campsites in Loops B or E. These sites are in the best position to enjoy the ambience of lakeside camping (although many trees have been cut down now). The most popular sites in Loop B are 18,19, and 21–23 (in that order), and 75, 76, 79, 71, 70, and 78 in Loop E (formerly Loop D).

Facilities
Facilities include picnic tables, fire grates, firewood for sale, water faucets, and accessible toilets. Loop C has lantern posts and electrical hookups.

RV Notes
Fairly level, medium to long, paved back-ins and pull-thrus with fair to good spacing await RVs. Recommended trailer length is 35 feet. Loop C (27–43) now has electrical hookups (and maybe water hookups soon) at every site. The nearest dump station is at Farmer's Corner, close to the intersection of Swan Mountain Road and Highway 9 (going toward Breckenridge).

Tent Notes
Due to recent tree cutting, many campsites now have little or no shade. There will be seven walk-in tent sites in the new Loop D. Pay showers are at nearby recreation centers or the Laundromat in Summit Place. A shopping center is located in Dillon.

Recreational Opportunities
Due to Whirling Disease, the lake hasn't been stocked in several years. The Forest Service reports mainly suckers in the lake to date, but a planned restocking will enable anglers to catch rainbow and brown trout. A special treat for campers is to boat due east for just a few minutes to Sentinel Island, with its own secluded, private cove that makes a great picnic spot. Swimming, jet skiing, and waterskiing are prohibited. The paved Dillon-to-Frisco bike path runs through the campground; bike riders can ride all the way to Vail or Breckenridge on connecting paths.

---

2. Peak One
Location: 2 miles east of Frisco (see map on p. 292)
Elevation: 9,100 feet
Number of Sites: 79
Recommended RV Length: Up to 50 feet
Season: Mid-May through September
Maps: *Colorado Atlas & Gazetteer,* page 38, D2
Colorado Recreational Road Atlas, page 14, A1.5
Phone: 970-468-5400

Scenery: ★★★★
RVs: ★★★
Tents: ★★★
Shade: ★★
Privacy: ★★

Directions
Take exit 203 (Frisco/Breckenridge) off I-70. Proceed south on Highway 9 for 2.5 miles. Turn left (north) at the Peak One Campground sign (Peak One Road), and go about a mile.

Distinguishing Features

The 79 sites are in three paved loops with a mixture of shade and sun. Peak One Campground is on Dillon Reservoir. Campsites are fairly close to the lake, but only a few campers in Loop C have lake views from their sites. A small hill lies between many of the campsites in Loops B and C and the lake. A couple of short steps up and over this hill gets you to the lake. Loop B has mooring spots along the lakeshore available to all campers. A wonderful beach and a trail along the lakeshore are suitable for all types of activities. The Pine Cove boat ramp is conveniently located near the campground. The only drawback to this campground is the sound of cars in the distance and the removal of trees in recent years.

Popularity

Campers can make reservations for sites in Loop B. Peak One usually fills every weekend by early Friday afternoon from Memorial Day to Labor Day; make reservations far in advance. The most popular sites are within 20 to 50 feet of the lake. Sites in order of preference are 45, 46, 49, 51, 43, and 41, all in Loop B.

Facilities

Facilities include picnic tables, fire grates, firewood for sale, water faucets, and bathrooms with sinks and wheelchair-accessible flush toilets.

Peak One

RV Notes

Visitors with RVs will find fairly level, medium to long, paved back-ins and three pull-thrus with tight to satisfactory spacing. The recommended maximum trailer length is 50 feet. The nearest dump station is south of the campground in Farmer's Corner, near the intersection of Swan Mountain Road and Highway 9.

Tent Notes

Try to get a campsite near the little hill for the best views of the lake and mountains. Pitching tents out-of-sight of the campground road is not allowed, preventing camping on the lake. If you're traveling by foot or bicycle, there's always room in the inexpensive hiker/biker sites (private and primitive) just off the main road leading into the campground. Pay showers are available in nearby recreation centers or at the laundromat in Summit Place Shopping Center in Dillon.

Recreational Opportunities

Due to Whirling Disease, the lake hasn't been stocked in years, and the Forest Service reports mainly suckers in the lake. When stocking occurs, anglers can expect to catch rainbow and brown trout. Swimming, waterskiing, and jet skiing are not allowed on Dillon Reservoir. However, the Frisco Marina, where you can rent motorboats, canoes, and sea kayaks, is nearby. Beware of severe afternoon thunderstorms. Single-track mountain-biking trails in the Peninsula Recreation Area near the campground are quite popular. And don't forget your frisbee—one of the few frisbee golf courses in the country is located just a few feet from the southern edge of the campground near the lakeshore.

Other Nearby Campgrounds

3. Pine Cove (55 sites; see map on p. 292); 2.5 miles east of Frisco. From I-70, turn off at exit 203 (Frisco/Breckenridge), and go south on Highway 9 for 2.5 miles. Turn left (north) on Peak One Road, and go about 1.5 miles. With excellent lake and mountain views, Pine Cove is only a few yards from the lake and a boat ramp. However, the campground is nothing more than a paved parking lot for RVs with all sites side by side and no privacy. A narrow, grassy strip along the lakeshore holds a dozen picnic tables; tenters can pitch their tents here. Maximum RV length is 50 feet. No reservations. **(970) 468-5400.**

4. Lowry (24 sites; see map on p. 292); 6.5 miles southeast of Dillon. From I-70, take exit 205 (Dillon/Silverthorne) and go southeast on Highway 6 for 4.5 miles to Swan Mountain Road. Turn right (west), go 2 miles to the Lowry Campground sign, and turn left. This former military campground sits about a mile east of Dillon Reservoir. Although tenting (three walk-in sites) is okay, electrical hookups for RVs are the main draw. Sites are well-shaded, tightly spaced, and have little privacy. Maximum RV length is 50 feet. Reservations accepted. **(970) 468-5400.**

5. Prospector (107 sites; see map on p. 292); 6 miles southeast of Dillon. From I-70, take exit 205 (Dillon/Silverthorne) and go southeast on Highway 6 for 4.5 miles to Swan Mountain Road. Turn right (west), go 2 miles to the Prospector Campground sign, and turn right. Go about 0.5 mile. This is a basic campground near Dillon Reservoir (with all the campsites set away from the lake) in a lodgepole pine forest. Shade is decent, privacy ranges from poor to fair, and site size varies tremendously. Sites 55-66 in the D loop are the most popular spots. Maximum RV length is 32 feet. Reservations are accepted. **(970) 468-5400.**

VAIL—MINTURN AREA

6. Gore Creek (25 sites); 2.3 miles east of East Vail. Take exit 180 off of I-70, and go east for 2.3 miles on South Frontage Road. Located in a forested, V-shaped canyon along Gore Creek, this campground is the only one close to Vail and is full almost every night. The lower loop has 17 sites, with seven along the creek. Some campsites can handle large RVs. For tents only is the upper loop, which contains sites 18-25. No reservations. **(970) 827-5715.**

7. Tigiwon
Since the writing of this book, this campground has been permanently closed.

8. Hornsilver (6 sites); 9 miles south of Minturn. From I-70, go south on Highway 24 (exit 171) about 11 miles. Set near the side of a busy highway, this can be a noisy place. This small campground has sites offering ample shade but little privacy. No reservations. **(970) 827-5715.**

9. Blodgett
Since the writing of this book, this campground has been permanently closed.

10. Gold Park (11 sites); 18 miles south of Minturn. From I-70, go south on Highway 24 (exit 171) for about 12.5 miles to Forest Road 703. Turn right (southwest), and go about 7 miles. Located along Homestake Creek, this is a pleasant, popular campground. Sites are well-shaded, provide poor to fair privacy, and offer medium to long RV parking spaces. Maximum RV length is 40 feet. Four sites are on the creek. No reservations. **(970) 827-5715.**

11. Camp Hale Memorial (21 sites); 14 miles south of Minturn. From I-70, go south on Highway 24 (exit 171) about 16 miles. Set in a wide, flat mountain valley at the edge of what was Camp Hale (home of the World War II Tenth Mountain Division), this campground rarely fills. A paved road leads to a mix of open and shaded sites that offer pretty views of the surrounding hills. Sites will handle large RVs, and privacy ranges from poor to adequate. Maximum RV length is 60 feet. Reservations accepted. **(970) 827-5715.**

LEADVILLE—TWIN LAKES AREA

photo by Gil Folsom

12. Baby Doe

Location: 5 miles west of Leadville (see map on p. 292)
Elevation: 9,900 feet
Number of Sites: 50
Recommended RV Length: Up to 32 feet
Season: Memorial Day to Labor Day
Maps: *Colorado Atlas & Gazetteer,* page 47, B6.5
Colorado Recreational Road Atlas, page 13, B3.5
Phone: 719-486-0749

Scenery: ★★★★
RVs: ★★★
Tents: ★★★
Shade: ★★★
Privacy: ★★

Directions

Several roads lead to the Turquoise Lake Recreation Area, which can be confusing. Heading south on Highway 24, turn right (west) onto Mountain View Drive, just past the Safeway at the north side of Leadville. Go west for about 2.7 miles to a "T" intersection. Turn right, go 0.6 mile, then left across the railroad tracks. Go west for about 0.5 mile to County Road 9 (another "T" intersection). Turn right (north), go 0.8 mile, then left to the campground.

Distinguishing Features

Baby Doe is only a few feet from 7,780-acre Turquoise Lake. This large, beautiful mountain lake has dense forest along its shoreline. The paved road leads through the campground and through two heavily forested loops. The lower loop (sites 1-26) is closest to the lake, with almost all campers in this loop getting some kind of a lake view. The upper loop (sites 28-50) also allows most campers to see the lake, although their views are generally a bit more obstructed by the trees. It's just a short walk to the shore from every site. Afternoon winds can be quite strong here, so make sure everything is securely tied down.

Popularity
Every site is reservable. Tied with Molly Brown as the most popular of the seven campgrounds at Turquoise Lake, this campground becomes booked far in advance for summer weekends. If you want to arrive on a Friday or Saturday, make reservations as early as possible. The most requested sites within a few feet of the lake are 4, 8, 2, 6, 10, 11, 13, and 14.

Facilities
Facilities include picnic tables, fire grates, and water faucets. In the bathrooms are flush toilets, sinks, mirrors, and electrical outlets.

RV Notes
Medium to long back-ins and one pull-thru characterize the parking spots. Some leveling may be required. The nearest dump stations are at the Molly Brown and Printer Boy campgrounds.

Tent Notes
Many of the sites here are in a gravel area, which encompasses a picnic table, and can double as tent pads.

Recreational Opportunities
Turquoise Lake is stocked with brown trout, cutthroat trout, mackinaws, and kokanee salmon. The water in the lake is very cold, so swimming and water-skiing are not advised (see Belle of Colorado for more recreational opportunities).

---

13. Belle of Colorado
Location: 4 miles west of Leadville (see map p. 292)
Elevation: 9,900 feet
Number of Sites: 19
Season: Memorial Day to Labor Day
Maps: *Colorado Atlas & Gazetteer,* page 47, B6.5
Colorado Recreational Road Atlas, page 13, B3.5
Phone: 719-486-0749

Scenery: ★★★★
RVs: No
Tents: ★★★★
Shade: ★★★★
Privacy: ★★

Directions
Several access roads lead to the Turquoise Lake Recreation Area, which can be confusing. Heading south on Highway 24, turn right (west) onto Mountain View Drive, just past the Safeway as you enter the northern outskirts of

photo by Gil Folsom

Belle of Colorado

Leadville. Go west for about 2.7 miles to a "T" intersection. Turn right, go 0.6 mile, then left across the railroad tracks. Go west for about 0.5 mile to County Road 9 (another "T" intersection). Turn right (north), then left (west) after 0.1 mile.

Distinguishing Features
Belle of Colorado is a walk-in, tent-only campground on the shore of 7,780-acre Turquoise Lake. Campsites are scattered among skinny pines, with some sites as close as 50 to 100 feet from the water. Everyone has an excellent lake view. With the cars marooned in the parking lot, you'll have a real feeling of camping in the woods. Bring warm clothes, as it can get very cold.

Popularity
Reservations are not taken, and during summer weekends the sites can fill quickly. Arrive early on Thursday to be sure of getting a space. If you do arrive from Sunday afternoon through Thursday morning, you should usually be able to find a spot.

Facilities
Facilities include picnic tables, fire grates, and water faucets. Bathrooms have flush toilets, sinks, mirrors, and electrical outlets.

Tent Notes
Pitch your tent securely, as the wind can get fierce in the afternoon.

Recreational Opportunities
The possibilities are endless. The lake is stocked with trout, and all types of watercraft are permitted. The 6.4-mile Turquoise Lake Trail is suitable for

both hikers and mountain bikers. It runs the entire length of the lake along the north shore, passing through the campground. Nearby Mount Elbert (14,433 feet) is the tallest mountain in Colorado and an exceptionally popular day hike. Hagerman Pass (easy) and Mosquito Pass (moderate) are great for four-wheeling (see also Baby Doe).

14. Whitestar

Location: 22 miles southwest of Leadville
Elevation: 9,300 feet
Number of Sites: 68
Recommended RV Length: Up to 32 feet
Season: Mid-May through September
Maps: *Colorado Atlas & Gazetteer*, page 47, D6.5
Colorado Recreational Road Atlas, page 23, A1.5
Phone: 719-486-0749

Scenery: ★★★★★
RVs: ★★★
Tents: ★★★
Shade: ★★
Privacy: ★★

Directions
From Leadville, go south on Highway 24 for about 15 miles, and turn right (west) on Highway 82; proceed about 7 miles.

Distinguishing Features
This lakeside campground has a breathtaking mountain backdrop. Whitestar is composed of three loops near the Twin Lakes Reservoir (2,700 acres). The views across the lake of the Collegiate Peaks Range are breathtaking. The Sage Loop (sites 1-28) is newly remodeled, is the closest to the lake, and is more open with less shade and less privacy. From this loop, the lake is a five-minute walk away. Overlooking Sage Loop, the Ridge Loop (sites 30-45) includes campsites with fantastic views of the lake and mountains. Heavily forested, the Valley Loop (sites 46-66) contains campsites that are the farthest from the lake and have the least impressive views.

Popularity
From July 4 through Labor Day, this campground fills during most weekends. Reservations are accepted. Try to arrive before 4:00 p.m. on Friday if you're planning to visit without a reservation. The most popular reservable sites are those closest to the lake: 10, 8, 13, 15, and 17.

Facilities
Facilities include picnic tables, fire grates, firewood for sale, hand-pumped water and faucets, and vault toilets.

RV Notes
Mostly medium back-ins with four medium to large pull-thrus are available. The Sage Loop now has many larger RV sites. A little leveling may be required. A dump station (fee charged) is near the entrance.

photo by Gil Folsom

Whitestar

Tent Notes

Not only do many of the sites have tent pads, but folks with tents have the best seats in the house. The popular sites mentioned above have tent pads placed strategically on top of a little knoll. You'll also find a few walk-ins, and sites 37-39 are on top of the Ridge Loop with fantastic views.

Recreational Opportunities

Anglers will find trout in Twin Lakes, and all water sports and watercraft are permitted. The Colorado Trail runs along the lake edge. The Continental Divide Trail and the trail to Colorado's highest mountain, Mount Elbert (14,433 feet), are nearby.

Other Nearby Campgrounds

15. Molly Brown (49 sites; see map on p. 292); in the Turquoise Lake Recreation Area, 4 miles west of Leadville. From Highway 24 in Leadville, go west on Mountain View Drive, and proceed for 4 miles. Follow the signs. Molly Brown is almost a virtual clone of Baby Doe and also deserves a spot in the "Top 100." Consisting of two paved loops providing sites close to the lake, this campground earned its name from the famed Margaret Brown, who survived the sinking of the *Titanic*. All sites provide good shade. Maximum RV length is 32 feet. Reservations are accepted; try reserving lakeside sites 3, 4, 6, 8, 10, 12, or 13. **(719) 486-0749.**

16. Tabor (44 sites; see map on p. 292); in the Turquoise Lake Recreation Area, 4 miles west of Leadville. From Highway 24 in Leadville, go west on Mountain View Drive, and proceed for 4 miles. Follow the signs. This campground is basically two gravel parking lots very close to the lake, next to the boat ramp. The upper lot has 19 shaded sites that work for tents, but only 12 picnic tables. The rest of the sites in the upper loop and all of those in the lower loop are strictly for RVs. None of the RV sites have shade, and you'll find little privacy, but sites do offer excellent views. Maximum RV length is 37 feet. No reservations. **(719) 486-0749.**

17. Silver Dollar (43 sites; see map on p. 292); in the Turquoise Lake Recreation Area, 4 miles west of Leadville. From Highway 24 in Leadville, go west on Mountain View Drive, and proceed for 4 miles. Follow the signs. The lake is a five- to 10-minute walk from here on a nature trail. Trees are so dense in this campground that campers may feel a little boxed in. Sites offer no views and fair to adequate privacy. Sites offer formal tent pads and excellent wind protection. Maximum RV length is 22 feet. Reservations are accepted. **(719) 486-0749.**

18. Father Dyer (25 sites; see map on p. 292); in the Turquoise Lake Recreation Area, 4 miles west of Leadville. From Highway 24 in Leadville, go west on Mountain View Drive, and proceed for 4 miles. Follow the signs. A quarter mile from Turquoise Lake and heavily wooded, these campsites offer satisfactory spacing and privacy, little sun, and no views. Facilities include flush toilets. Maximum RV length is 32 feet. Reservations accepted. **(719) 486-0749.**

19. May Queen (27 sites; see map on p. 292); in the Turquoise Lake Recreation Area, 9 miles west of Leadville. Go west from Leadville on Turquoise Lake Road (Forest Road 105) for 9 miles. This campground on the western edge of Turquoise Lake is the most remote of this area's campgrounds. Campsites range in shade and privacy. Eleven sites are long pull-thrus. Maximum RV length is 32 feet. Reservations accepted. **(719) 486-0749.**

20. Halfmoon (22 sites); 9.5 miles southwest of Leadville. From Leadville, take Highway 24 southwest for 3 miles to Highway 300. Turn right (west), go about a mile, and turn left (south) onto Forest Road 110. Go 5.5 miles. Halfmoon East is on the right side of the road and offers a beautiful setting by the creek. Sites are tightly spaced, have little privacy, and offer adequate shade and fair RV spaces. Halfmoon West is on the left side of the road and offers widely varying campsites; all have adequate shade. Maximum RV length is 16 feet. No reservations. **(719) 486-0749.**

21. Elbert Creek (17 sites); 10 miles southwest of Leadville. From Leadville, take Highway 24 southwest for 3 miles to Highway 300. Turn right (west), go about a mile, and turn left (south) onto Forest Road 110. Go 6 miles. Set near the Mount Elbert trailhead, this popular campground attracts peak-baggers hoping to summit Colorado's tallest mountain. Sites have excellent spacing and privacy and adequate shade. Although many are near the creek, only a few are prime creekside spots. RVers will find medium to long back-ins. No reservations. **(719) 486-0749.**

22. Dexter (24 sites); 19 miles southwest of Leadville. From Leadville, take Highway 24 for 14 miles and turn right (west) onto Highway 82. Go about 5 miles. Loved by anglers and boaters, this is a treeless campground on Twin Lakes that amounts to nothing more than a side-by-side gravel parking lot for RVs. Tenters will find spots with picnic tables scattered around the hillside that offer superb lake views. Maximum RV length is 37 feet. No reservations. **(719) 486-0749.**

23. Lakeview (59 sites); 23 miles southwest of Leadville. From Leadville, take Highway 24 for 14 miles and turn right (west) onto Highway 82. Go 4.5 miles, and turn right (north) onto County Road 24. Go about 4 miles. This large campground sits well above Twin Lakes in eight terraced loops with very few lake views. Sites are generally RV-friendly and have good shade and some tent pads. A paved road leads through the campground. This is a busy place every weekend. Maximum RV length is 35 feet. Reservations accepted. **(719) 486-0749.**

24. Parry Peak (26 sites); 24 miles southwest of Leadville. From Leadville, take Highway 24 southwest for 14 miles to Highway 82. Turn right (west), and go 9.25 miles. This campground has two distinct loops. The upper, remodeled loop has tent pads in all sites and is RV-friendly. Most of these upper sites have good shade and offer some privacy. The lower loop offers two dynamite walk-in sites (25 and 26). By the creek, this loop provides more seclusion from the highway. Many sites have tent pads and offer good spacing. Maximum RV length is 32 feet. No reservations. **(719) 486-0749.**

25. Twin Peaks (39 sites); 25 miles southwest of Leadville. From Leadville, take Highway 24 southwest for 14 miles to Highway 82. Turn right (west), and go 10 miles. This is a pleasant, RV-friendly campground offering great mountain views and adequate privacy and shade. Twenty-five feet down from the main campground are four fantastic, secluded walk-in tent sites on the water (34-37). Maximum RV length is 32 feet. No reservations. **(719) 486-0749.**

26. Railroad Bridge (14 sites); 28 miles south of Leadville. Go west on Highway 24 from Leadville for about 24 miles to County Road 371 (between milemarkers 201 and 202). Turn left (east) across the bridge, turn right (south), and go about 4.5 miles. Near the Arkansas River and a put-in/take-out point for rafters, campers will find a mix of sites suitable for both RVs and tents. Good views of the Collegiate Peaks abound and the river is less than a two-minute walk from most sites. However, shade is sparse and so are the facilities. No drinking water or trash service. Reservations accepted. **(719) 539-7289.**

BUENA VISTA AREA

27. Chalk Lake

Location: 16 miles southwest of Buena Vista
Elevation: 8,700 feet
Number of Sites: 21
Recommended RV Length: Up to 35 feet
Season: Memorial Day through September
Maps: *Colorado Atlas & Gazetteer*, page 60, C1
Colorado Recreational Road Atlas, page 23, A2.5
Phone: 719-539-3591

Scenery: ★★★★★
RVs: ★★★
Tents: ★★★★★
Shade: ★★★
Privacy: ★

Directions
Go about 7.5 miles south of Buena Vista on Highway 285 to just south of
Nathrop. Turn right (west) onto paved County Road 162, and go 8 miles.

Distinguishing Features
Chalk Lake Campground is located by Chalk Creek and is only a few feet
away from 3-acre Chalk Lake. This campground is a magical place. Mountain
views are exceptional and include Mount Antero and Mount Princeton as
well as the Chalk Cliffs. Chalk Creek becomes a mellow shadow of itself as
it meanders through the campground and is quiet enough for children to
wade in. Aspens, cedars, and ponderosa pines provide shade. Thirteen sites
are creekside, and nine of those are tent-only sites. Be mindful of bears.

Popularity

This campground fills almost every night from late June until Labor Day, so reservations are strongly recommended. The best RV sites are 2 or 10. The best tent sites are 2, 6, 9, 7, and 8. Sites 1-14 are creekside.

Facilities

Facilities include picnic tables, fire grates, firewood for sale, hand-pumped water, and wheelchair-accessible vault toilets.

RV Notes

Ten sites are suitable for RVs. Medium to long, fairly level back-ins available. All but one of these are 35 feet or longer. If making reservations, try for sites 2 or 10. The nearest dump stations are at the Amoco gas station in Buena Vista if heading north, or next to the Salida Chamber of Commerce (no fee) on Highway 50 if southbound.

Tent Notes

This is tent heaven! The nine sites designated for tents have tent pads and are all close to the creek. Sites are close together, but making friends with neighbors can make up for the lack of privacy.

Recreational Opportunities

Anglers can try their luck in Chalk Creek or in Chalk Lake, which is stocked. Chalk Lake is a lovely little pond surrounded by trees but not big enough for boats. The many four-wheel-drive roads nearby attract all types of off-road enthusiasts. Hiking trails include Agnes Vaille Falls Trail, the Colorado Trail, and Poplar Gulch Trail. Peak-baggers have a choice of two 14,000-foot peaks, Mount Antero and Mount Princeton. Horseback riding and hot-spring soaking are available at Mount Princeton Hot Springs, which is just 5 miles away.

Other Nearby Campgrounds

28. Cottonwood Lake (28 sites); 11 miles southwest of Buena Vista. Take County Road 306 west about 7 miles to Forest Road 344. Turn left on Forest Road 344, and proceed for 4 miles. Set in the aspens a mile from Cottonwood Lake (37 acres), most sites have impressive views of steep, rugged mountain peaks. Sites provide adequate privacy. RV parking spots are medium-sized and generally not level. Maximum RV length is 40 feet. No reservations. **(719) 539-3591.**

29. Collegiate Peaks (56 sites); 11 miles west of Buena Vista on County Road 306. This large campground has four loops, with sites that offer privacy and picturesque views. Most sites have decent shade, provided mainly by aspens. Ten spots close to Middle Cottonwood Creek are the most sought-after. Try for sites G, E, J, 19, 20, 15, or 16. Maximum RV length is 35 feet. Reservations are recommended. **(719) 539-3591.**

30. Ruby Mountain (20 sites); 8.5 miles south of Buena Vista. Go south on Highway 285 for 5.5 miles to County Road 301, go left (north), and continue for about 3 miles. Set along the Arkansas River, this is a popular place for rafters, kayakers, anglers, and rock hounds. Six excellent walk-in tent sites are only a few feet from the river. Sites 18, 15, and 10 have adequate shade, and the rest are fairly open with little shade. Privacy is poor in all campsites, and there is no drinking water. Maximum RV length is 35 feet. Reservations accepted. **(719) 539-7289.**

31. Bootleg (6 sites); 13 miles southwest of Buena Vista. Go 7.5 miles south on Highway 285, and turn right (west) on County Road 162. Go for 5.5 miles to the Chalk Creek Trailhead. The only way to get to this tent-only campground —used primarily by Colorado Trail hikers—is by hiking the quarter mile to it. No drinking water or trash service provided. No reservations. **(719) 539-3591.**

32. Mount Princeton (19 sites); 14 miles southwest of Buena Vista. Go 7.5 miles south on Highway 285, and turn right (west) on County Road 162. Go for 6.5 miles. Recently renovated, Mount Princeton can now accommodate large RVs in most sites. The ground is very rocky, but all sites have tent pads. Sites have good privacy and spacing, and eight are creekside. Watch for bears. The campground fills every weekend. Reservations accepted. **(719) 539-3591.**

33. Cascade (21 sites); 16 miles southwest of Buena Vista. Go 7.5 miles south on Highway 285, and turn right (west) on County Road 162. Go for 8.5 miles. The mountains shoot straight up near Cascade, providing spectacular views. Sites offer good shade and fair to good privacy. Most sites are suitable for medium-sized RVs. Make reservations or arrive early, as the campground fills almost every night. Watch for bears. **(719) 539-3591.**

34. Iron City (15 sites); 22 miles southwest of Buena Vista. Go 7.5 miles south on Highway 285, and turn right (west) on County Road 162. Go for 14.5 miles. Heavily wooded, this long, narrow campground offers several sites by the creek. Parking spots are typically double-wide, short, not level, and suitable for small RVs. Privacy ranges from poor to excellent. Bears are frequently spotted in the area. No reservations. **(719) 539-3591.**

35. Hecla Junction (22 sites); 12 miles north of Salida. Take Highway 291 northwest for 7 miles to Highway 285, and turn right (north). Go 1.75 miles, and turn right (east) onto County Road 194. Continue for about 2.5 miles. Set two miles off the main road, this campground is popular with anglers and rafters. Sitting above the Arkansas River with a commanding view, it features sparsely shaded sites spaced close together. Sites have tent pads, and there is no drinking water. Maximum RV length is 35 feet. Reservations accepted. **(719) 539-7289.**

PONCHA SPRINGS—SALIDA AREA

36. Monarch Park

Location: 17 miles west of Poncha Springs
Elevation: 10,500 feet
Number of Sites: 38
Recommended RV Length: Up to 40 feet
Season: Memorial Day through September
Maps: *Colorado Atlas & Gazetteer,* page 59, D7
Colorado Recreational Road Atlas, page 23, A3
Phone: 877-444-6777

Scenery: ★★★★
RVs: ★★★
Tents: ★★★
Shade: ★★★
Privacy: ★★★

Directions
From Poncha Springs, go west on Highway 50 about 15 miles, then left (south) on Forest Road 231 (dirt) about 1.5 miles.

Distinguishing Features
Monarch Park Campground is in a large, flat, wooded area of Douglas fir and ponderosa pine, and a stream meanders through the sites. Monarch Park's charm is enough to lure many campers back every year. Lovely mountain views add to the park's allure. Two large loops with good spacing between sites provide campers with plenty of peace and quiet.

Popularity
Monarch Park rarely fills—even on weekends. Many sites are close to the

stream. Campers can make reservations, and the most popular sites are 34, 4, and 5.

Facilities
Facilities include picnic tables, fire grates, firewood for sale, hand-pumped water, and vault toilets.

RV Notes
Back-ins range from short to long. A few pull-thrus are available as well. Some may require leveling. The nearest dump station is 20 miles east on Highway 50, next to the Salida Chamber of Commerce (no fee).

Tent Notes
Large, flat campsites mean plenty of excellent tent-pitching options. The mercury often dips into the mid-30s at night.

Recreational Opportunities
Fishing is poor in the portion of the South Arkansas River running through the campground. However, good fishing opportunities for cutthroat trout await in the beaver ponds close to the campground. Among the more popular hiking trails in the area are the Colorado and Continental Divide. A ride called "Crest" at the top of Monarch Pass is extremely popular with mountain bikers. Four-wheel-drive roads in the vicinity include Old Monarch Pass, County Road 235 to Boss Lake, and County Road 231 near the beaver ponds. The Salida Hot Springs Pool, 20 miles away, is a great place to relax.

---

37. O'Haver Lake
Location: 9 miles southwest of Poncha Springs
Elevation: 9,200 feet
Number of Sites: 29
Recommended RV Length: Up to 35 feet
Season: Memorial Day through September
Maps: *Colorado Atlas & Gazetteer*, page 70, A1
Colorado Recreational Road Atlas, page 23, B3
Phone: 877-444-6777

Scenery: ★★★★
RVs: ★★
Tents: ★★★
Shade: ★★
Privacy: ★

Directions
From Poncha Springs, go south about 5 miles on Highway 285. Go right (southwest) on dirt Forest Road 243 (County Road 200) for 2.3 miles. Turn right (west) onto Forest Road 200 (County Road 202), and proceed for 1.5 miles (this is a curvy dirt road that can get a little rough).

Distinguishing Features
O'Haver Lake is the most popular campground in the area. Above this gorgeous 15-acre lake towers 13,955-foot Mount Ouray. Tall ponderosa pines and aspens surround the lake, providing fair shade. Fifteen of the sites

photo by Gil Folsom

O'Haver Lake

are lakeside or very near the lake, which attracts many anglers up for the day. Most campsites are spaced fairly close to one another.

Popularity
The campground fills almost every day from mid-June through Labor Day. Campers are strongly urged to make reservations. Of the reservable spots, the most popular are sites 10 and 11, close to the lake across from the fishing dock, and 25 and 20, which are lakeside. Other reservable lakeside sites are 16, 19, 22, and 24.

Facilities
Facilities include picnic tables, fire grates, firewood for sale, hand-pumped water, and wheelchair-accessible vault toilets.

RV Notes
On average, campers will find medium back-ins that require some leveling. Most sites are spaced close together. The nearest dump station (no fee) is next to the Salida Chamber of Commerce on Highway 50, 10 miles from the campground.

Tent Notes
There are no restrictions on tent placement, so campers can pitch their tents just a few feet from the lake.

Recreational Opportunities
Fishing is by far the biggest attraction here. O'Haver Lake is heavily stocked with trout. An excellent wheelchair-accessible pier provides fishing access for all, and boats without motors are permitted. Anglers might try nearby Poncha Creek and Silver Creek, too. Hikers and mountain bikers can access the Colorado Trail and Continental Divide Trail at Marshall Pass, or try the Rainbow Trail.

Other Nearby Campgrounds

38. Angel of Shavano (20 sites); 10 miles northwest of Poncha Springs. Take Highway 50 west for 6 miles. Turn right (north) on Forest Road 240, and go 4 miles. A favorite of many campers, this was a wintering spot for the Utes. The campground offers beautiful views of Mount Shavano. A river and the Colorado Trail are nearby; beaver ponds stretch along the river. Sites range widely in privacy and shade, with many medium-sized RV spots. Reservations accepted. **(719) 539-3591.**

39. North Fork Reservoir (8 sites); 16 miles northwest of Poncha Springs. Go west for 6 miles on Highway 50, and turn right (north) on Forest Road 240. Proceed for 12.5 miles. Campers here enjoy one of the most spectacular settings in the area by a pristine alpine lake. However, a rough, steep, 6-mile stretch of bad road leading to the campground limits access to high-clearance vehicles and is not recommended for RVs. No drinking water is provided. No reservations. **(719) 539-3591.**

40. Rincon (8 sites); 8 miles southeast of Salida on Highway 50. This riverside campground has all its sites on the Arkansas River, next to the busy highway. Sites have little shade, are closely spaced, and lack privacy. This campground works best for tents and small RVs. No drinking water or trash service is provided. Reservations accepted. **(719) 539-7289.**

41. Coaldale (11 sites); 23 miles southeast of Salida. Take Highway 50 southeast for 19 miles to County Road 6. Turn right (southwest), and go about 4 miles. Here's a little-known campground with many fine tent sites on Hayden Creek. Four sites are across the creek. Oaks and pines provide good shade. Most sites are not good for RVs, and no drinking water is provided. Maximum RV length is 20 feet. No reservations. **(719) 539-3591.**

42. Hayden Creek (11 sites); 24 miles southeast of Salida. Take Highway 50 southeast for 19 miles to County Road 6. Turn right (southwest), and go about 5 miles. Lightly used by campers, Hayden Creek works best for tents and is passable for small RVs. Half the sites are on or near the creek. Privacy and shade are fair. No reservations. **(719) 539-3591.**

43. Five Points (20 sites); 16 miles west of Cañon City on Highway 50. Five Points is just a place to spend the night. On a busy road across from the Arkansas River, 90 percent of its tightly spaced sites are in the open with no shade or privacy. Sites have tent pads and are RV-friendly, but no drinking water is provided. Maximum RV length is 35 feet. Reservations accepted. **(719) 539-7289.**

GRANT—KENOSHA PASS —SOUTH PARK AREA

44. Whiteside
Location: 2.5 miles northwest of Grant
Elevation: 8,900 feet
Number of Sites: 5
Season: Mid-May to mid-October
Maps: *Colorado Atlas & Gazetteer,* page 39, D5
Colorado Recreational Road Atlas, page 14, B2
Phone: 303-275-5610

Scenery: ★★★
RVs: No
Tents: ★★★★
Shade: ★★★
Privacy: ★★

Directions
From Bailey, go west about 11.5 miles on Highway 285 to Grant, then turn right (north) on Forest Road 118 (Guanella Pass Scenic Byway or County Road 62), and go about 2.5 miles.

Distinguishing Features
Whiteside is a lovely tent campground set beside Geneva Creek, with all campsites on or very close to the water. Two sites are on one side of the creek, while the others are all within a two-minute walk across the creek via a footbridge. Most are closely spaced, offering little privacy from fellow campers. Mature spruce and some aspen trees provide fair to adequate shade. Next to the road, this campground can be noisy at times. A sign warns of

bears; since the campground has no trash receptacles, it's imperative that campers store trash in their vehicles and not leave food or coolers out.

Popularity
Whiteside fills almost every weekend from Memorial Day to Labor Day. Arriving by 2:00 p.m. on Friday is the best way to get a spot. No reservations.

Facilities
Facilities include picnic tables, fire grates, hand-pumped water, and vault toilets with wheelchair access. No trash service is available—pack it in, pack it out.

Tent Notes
All spots are fairly flat and work well for tents.

Recreational Opportunities
The creek offers limited trout fishing. The Threemile Trail is only 0.8 mile north of the campground, and the Burning Bear Trailhead is 2.1 miles farther. The Threemile Trail gains 2,600 feet as it follows a creek for 6 miles before joining the Rosalie Trail. A horse trail runs near the campground as well.

The Guanella Pass Scenic Byway, a 22-mile route to Georgetown, is unbelievably popular for fall drives when the aspens are turning. You can access the Webster Pass four-wheel-drive road via County Road 60, which begins several miles west of Grant on Highway 285 and links with many other four-wheel-drive roads.

45. Kenosha Pass
Location: 8 miles southwest of Grant
Elevation: 10,000 feet
Number of Sites: 25
Recommended RV Length: Up to 20 feet
Season: Mid-May to mid-October
Maps: *Colorado Atlas and Gazetteer*, page 49, A5.5
Colorado Recreational Road Atlas, page 14, B3
Phone: 303-275-5610

Scenery: ★★★
RVs: ★★
Tents: ★★★
Shade: ★★★
Privacy: ★★★

Directions
From Grant, go about 8 miles southwest on Highway 285.

Distinguishing Features
Set near the top of Kenosha Pass, this campground takes on a golden aura in the fall as the aspens turn. The Kenosha Pass and South Park area is one of the best places near Denver to take advantage of this short but brilliant time, and Kenosha Pass is in a strategic location for enjoying the fall foliage to its fullest. Aspens and lodgepole pines provide adequate shade for most campers, with aspens comprising 60 to 70 percent of the trees. Sites are located

around one flat loop, with ample spacing and privacy. A short walk leads to spectacular vistas of the surrounding mountains, and South Park.

Popularity

On summer weekends, the campground often fills. If you arrive before 3:00 p.m. on Friday afternoon, obtaining a spot is usually not too difficult. Also check out Kenosha East Camping Area on the opposite side of the road. No reservations.

Facilities

Facilities include picnic tables, fire grates, firewood for sale, hand-pumped water, and wheelchair-accessible vault toilets.

RV Notes

RV visitors will find the sites are all back-ins, except for one pull-thru. The road and parking spots are a little run-down, and leveling will be required in many spaces. Parking spaces range from short to very long, and if the campground isn't full, campers with medium rigs should find an available spot.

Tent Notes

Campers can pitch their tents in flat, shady sites.

Recreational Opportunities

For both mountain bikers and hikers, the Colorado Trail is the biggest draw. From the campground, the trail heads west through a beautiful aspen forest.

Across the road from Kenosha Pass Campground

Hikers are treated to delightful views of the South Park area below. The trail leads down through open meadows into South Park before re-entering the forest, eventually climbing to the top of Georgia Pass. Across the road to the east, the Colorado Trail continues for several miles before entering the Lost Park Wilderness Area (no bikes).

Four-wheel-drive roads are plentiful. A popular but difficult road leads to the top of North Twin Cone Peak (12,319 feet). From the top, you'll enjoy exquisite views of Guanella Pass and South Park.

Other Nearby Campgrounds

46. Burning Bear (13 sites); 5.5 miles north of Grant on Forest Road 118 (Guanella Pass Scenic Byway or County Road 62). This ho-hum campground offers little privacy. Parking spots are not level, and shade ranges from poor to fair. All sites are in a single loop. Maximum RV length is 20 feet. No water. No reservations. **(303) 275-5610.**

47. Geneva Park (26 sites); 7.5 miles north of Grant. Take Forest Road 118 (Guanella Pass Scenic Byway or County Road 62) about 7.5 miles, and then turn left (west) onto Forest Road 119. This campground is set in the forest near Geneva Creek. The road through it is reminiscent of a minefield, with rocks and huge potholes to dodge. Sites work for tents, and offer medium to long back-ins for RVs; many require leveling. Maximum RV length is 20 feet. Shade is good on average, and privacy ranges from fair to good. Reservations accepted. **(303) 275-5610.**

48. Handcart (10 sites); 7.5 miles west of Grant. Take Highway 285 west for 3.5 miles to Forest Road 120 (County Road 60). Turn right (west), and go 4 miles. This is a tent-only campground with good shade. Sites have setups for tents and offer satisfactory privacy. A few are very close to a brown, mineral-polluted creek (no fish), and five are less than a minute's walk from the creek. Some sites have good views of the surrounding mountains. The campground rarely fills. No reservations. **(303) 275-5610.**

49. Hall Valley (9 sites); 8 miles west of Grant. Take Highway 285 west for 3.5 miles to Forest Road 120 (County Road 60). Turn right (west), and go 4.5 miles. Hall Valley is just beyond Handcart, but the road is high-clearance only for this stretch. Six sites are set in the trees, with four close to the same creek that Handcart is adjacent to. The other three are in a grassy, open meadow offering beautiful views, especially in the fall. Maximum RV length is 20 feet. No reservations. **(303) 275-5610.**

50. Lost Park (13 sites); 21 miles southeast of Jefferson. Go north on Highway 285 about 1.5 miles, and turn right on Forest Road 127 (County Road 56).

Proceed for 19 miles. At the end of a gravel road, Lost Park is on the edge of the Lost Creek Wilderness and is popular with hikers. Upper and lower loops lead to very primitive sites with good shade and privacy. Maximum RV length is 22 feet. No reservations. **(719) 836-2031.**

51. Lodgepole (35 sites); 4.5 miles northwest of Jefferson. Take County Road 35 about 2 miles to Forest Road 401 (County Road 37), and turn right (north). Go about 2.5 miles. Campsites are all in one big loop in a thin stand of lodgepole pines. Shade and privacy range from fair to good. Sites are fine for tents and medium-sized RVs. Reservations accepted. **(719) 836-2031.**

52. Aspen (12 sites); 4.5 miles northwest of Jefferson. Take County Road 35 about 2 miles to Forest Road 401 (County Road 37), and turn right (north). Go about 3 miles. This open, cheery campground is set in an aspen grove by a large mountain meadow. With good views of Jefferson Hill and the surrounding scenery, this is an especially beautiful fall campground. Shade ranges from poor to good. Maximum RV length is 25 feet. Reservations are accepted. **(719) 836-2031.**

53. Jefferson Creek (17 sites); 6 miles northwest of Jefferson. Take County Road 35 about 2 miles to Forest Road 401 (County Road 37), and turn right (north). Go about 4.5 miles. Set near Jefferson Creek and Jefferson Lake, this shaded, RV-friendly campground is a good spot for anglers. Maximum RV length is 25 feet. Reservations accepted. **(719) 836-2031.**

54. Michigan Creek (13 sites); 6 miles northwest of Jefferson. Take County Road 35 about 3 miles to Forest Road 400 (County Road 54), and turn right (northwest). Go about 3 miles. This open, sunny campground offers wonderful views from most sites. Half are unshaded, while aspens provide fair shade to others. Most spots can accommodate larger RVs, and the campground rarely fills. No reservations. **(719) 836-2031.**

55. Selkirk (15 sites); 8 miles north of Como. From Como, take Forest Road 404 (County Roads 50 and 33 or Boreas Pass Road) for about 7 miles. The campground is off the road 1 mile to the left. Located in a thick spruce forest, this spot offers adequate shade, and privacy is fair to good. No drinking water or trash service. Maximum RV length is 25 feet. No reservations. **(719) 836-2031.**

FAIRPLAY AREA

56. Kite Lake

Location: 11 miles northwest of Fairplay
Elevation: 12,000 feet
Number of Sites: 7
Recommended RV Length: Not recommended for RVs
Season: Mid-June to mid-October
Maps: *Colorado Atlas & Gazetteer,* page 48, B1.5
Colorado Recreational Road Atlas, page 13, C3
Phone: 719-836-2031

Scenery: ★★★★
RVs: ★
Tents: ★★★
Shade: No
Privacy: ★★

Directions
From Fairplay, take Highway 9 north 5 miles to Alma. Make a left (west) on gravel Forest Road 416 (County Road 8) in the middle of town. (Look closely for a little street sign that reads "Buckskin" and "Kite Lake.") Proceed for 5.5 miles.

The Forest Service recommends a four-wheel-drive vehicle, although on a beautiful September day I found only the last 1.3 miles to be a little rough; most vehicles can make the trip, assuming the road is in good condition. However, flat tires are frequent, so beware!

Distinguishing Features
Kite Lake has seven sites, of which only two are suitable for small RVs. At a lofty 12,000 feet, this is indeed the "top campground" in the country. Kite

Lake is nestled in a high mountain basin above timberline near the Continental Divide. Primarily a tent-camping area, the seven sites are scattered throughout a high meadow, with four sites very close to the tiny lake. This campground has no trees, but plenty of wildflowers delight the eye. Campers are treated to outstanding views of Mount Lincoln (14,286 feet), Mount Bross (14,169 feet), and Mount Democrat (14,148 feet).

Popularity
Kite Lake fills with peak-baggers most weekends from Memorial Day (if the road is plowed) to Labor Day. Boy Scout troops also frequent this campground. Show up no later than Friday morning to be sure of getting a spot. No reservations.

Facilities
Somewhat primitive facilities include picnic tables, fire grates, and a vault toilet. Water is not available.

RV Notes
Two large, uneven back-ins could work for RVs with high clearance. Few RVs ever get up here, and it's probably best not to try.

Tent Notes
Campers who like to pitch their tent away from RVs should check out this campground. Kite Lake is at an elevation of 12,000 feet and campers are unprotected from the elements. Bring warm clothes and a weatherproof tent. Violent weather changes can occur at any moment.

Recreational Opportunities
An enterprising hiker/climber can scale the three relatively easy, nearby fourteeners (four if you count the "unofficial" 14,238-foot Mount Cameron) on a weekend visit. The best climbing weather is from 6:00 a.m. until 2:00 p.m.; hikers should be off the peaks by early afternoon to avoid severe weather—including intense lightning—that can pop up.

   The area has a rich mining history, and there's much to explore. The trees in the Bristlecone Pine Scenic Area to the east are among the oldest in the country, some approaching 2,500 years. The trip over nearby Mosquito Pass takes you over the highest pass in the country at 13,188 feet and is a moderate, 17-mile four-wheel-drive adventure. This little lake hasn't been stocked in years, so don't bother trying your luck fishing.

Other Nearby Campgrounds

57. Horseshoe (19 sites); 8 miles west of Fairplay. Take Highway 285 south for 1.25 miles, and turn right (west) on County Road 18. Follow County Road 18 (which becomes Forest Road 421) for 7 miles. Set along Fourmile Creek, with two trails starting from the campground, sites have adequate shade and poor to fair privacy. Maximum RV length is 25 feet. Reservations accepted. **(719) 836-2031.**

58. Fourmile (14 sites); 9 miles west of Fairplay. Take Highway 285 south for 1.25 miles, and turn right (west) on County Road 18. Follow County Road 18 (which becomes Forest Road 421) for 8 miles. Fourmile Creek is a short walk down from the campground. The ground is extremely rocky, and is not the best place for pitching a tent. Sites have adequate shade with fair to satisfactory privacy. Nearby Horseshoe Campground is somewhat nicer. Maximum RV length is 22 feet. No reservations. **(719) 836-2031.**

59. Weston Pass (14 sites); 16 miles southwest of Fairplay. Take Highway 285 south for 4.75 miles, and turn right (west) on County Road 5. Go about 7 miles, turn right (southwest) on Forest Road 425 (County Road 22), and follow it for 4.5 miles. Set near the summit of Weston Pass, this campground offers good shade and large back-in sites for RVs. All sites are on the outside of one long loop. The South Platte River (just a creek here) is 200 to 300 yards down a hill. Maximum RV length is 25 feet. No water. No reservations. **(719) 836-2031.**

60. Buffalo Springs (18 sites); 12.5 miles south of Fairplay. Take Highway 285 for 13 miles to Forest Road 431. Turn right (west) onto Forest Road 431, and go about 0.75 mile. This little-used campground is convenient for travelers. Sites are well-spaced in one large loop, with plenty of shade and privacy. Maximum RV length is 25 feet. Reservations accepted. **(719) 836-2031.**

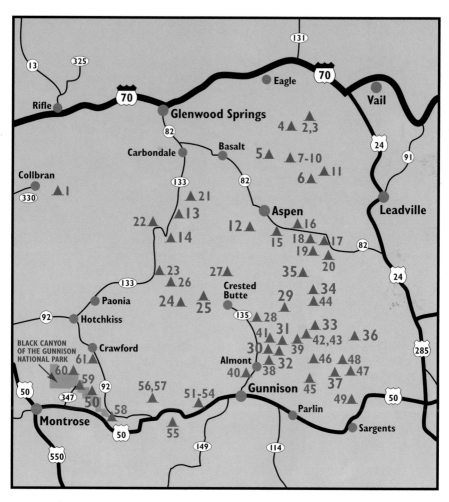

For locations of campgrounds by Blue Mesa Reservoir and Ruedi Reservoir, see page 293.

A Photographer's Paradise

This area lends itself to superlatives. The Black Canyon of the Gunnison National Park contains one of the steepest, narrowest, and most impressive canyons in the country. Blue Mesa Reservoir is Colorado's largest lake, with 96 miles of shoreline. The Maroon Bells near Aspen are Colorado's most photographed spot, and the Crystal River Mill near Marble is probably the second.

You'll find world-class mountain biking near Crested Butte. Superb hiking and backpacking abound both there and in the Maroon Bells/Snowmass Wilderness Area. Challenging four-wheel-drive opportunities await near Crested Butte, Marble, Taylor Park, Tincup, and Pitkin. OHV riding is wildly popular around Tincup and Taylor Park, and Ruedi Reservoir near Basalt is a favorite of boaters and anglers. The fishing in the Taylor Canyon and Taylor Park Reservoir is matched only by the magnificent scenery.

Campgrounds are especially busy in the Aspen, Crested Butte, Marble, Redstone, Taylor Canyon, and Taylor Park areas.

▲▲100 BEST

- ▲5 Mollie B
- ▲6 Chapman
- ▲12 Silver Bar, Silver Bell, and Silver Queen
- ▲13 Redstone
- ▲14 Bogan Flats
- ▲24 Lost Lake
- ▲25 Lake Irwin
- ▲29 Mosca
- ▲30 North Bank
- ▲31 Rosy Lane
- ▲32 One Mile
- ▲33 Lakeview
- ▲34 Dinner Station
- ▲35 Dorchester
- ▲36 Mirror Lake
- ▲37 Pitkin
- ▲50 East Portal

▲ All The Rest

- ▲1 Vega State Park
- ▲2 Yeoman Park
- ▲3 Fulford Cave
- ▲4 Sylvan Lake State Park
- ▲7 Ruedi Marina
- ▲8 Little Maud
- ▲9 Little Mattie
- ▲10 Dearhamer
- ▲11 Elk Wallow
- ▲15 Difficult
- ▲16 Weller
- ▲17 Lost Man
- ▲18 Lincoln Gulch
- ▲19 Lincoln Creek Dispersed
- ▲20 Portal
- ▲21 Avalanche

- ▲22 McClure
- ▲23 Paonia State Park
- ▲26 Erickson Springs
- ▲27 Gothic
- ▲28 Cement Creek
- ▲38 Granite
- ▲39 Lodgepole
- ▲40 Almont
- ▲41 Spring Creek
- ▲42 Cold Springs
- ▲43 Lottis Creek
- ▲44 Rivers End
- ▲45 Comanche
- ▲46 Gold Creek
- ▲47 Middle Quartz
- ▲48 Quartz

- ▲49 Snowblind
- ▲51 Stevens Creek
- ▲52 Elk Creek
- ▲53 Dry Gulch
- ▲54 Red Creek
- ▲55 Lake Fork
- ▲56 Ponderosa
- ▲57 Soap Creek
- ▲58 Cimarron
- ▲59 South Rim
- ▲60 North Rim
- ▲61 Crawford State Park

COLLBRAN—EAGLE AREA

1. Vega State Park (108 sites, 5 cabins); 11 miles east of Collbran. Take County Road 330E 6.75 miles east to County Road 64.60. Turn right (south), and go about 4 miles. Almost 2 miles long and covering 900 acres, Vega Reservoir is open to all water sports except swimming. Four campgrounds are situated around the lake, with only **Aspen Grove** (the best place for tents) offering much shade or privacy. **Oak Point** is popular for RVs. Many sites are near the water, and facilities include a dump station, vault toilets, and a boat ramp. **Early Settlers** offers many pull-thru sites with water and electrical hookups. About 10 sites are lakeside, and most other sites are less than 100 yards from the lake. Campers will find flush toilets, showers, and a playground here. **Pioneer** has 10 walk-in tent sites and 5 cabins. Maximum RV length is 50 feet. Reservations accepted. **(970) 487-3407.**

2. Yeoman Park (24 sites); 16 miles southeast of Eagle (I-70 exit 147). From Eagle, head south on Brush Creek Road (Forest Road 400) for 10.25 miles to Forest Road 415. Turn left (east) on Forest Road 415, and go about 5.75 miles. In this campground near Brush Creek, campers enjoy enchanting views of Craig Peak (11,902 feet) and aspen-covered hills across a wetland meadow. Most sites have adequate shade. Six can handle any RV, while others work best for medium RVs. Two sites are wheelchair-accessible, and a wheelchair-accessible creekside fishing platform is provided. Maximum RV length is 36 feet. No water. No reservations. **(970) 328-6388.**

3. Fulford Cave (7 sites); 17 miles southeast of Eagle (I-70 exit 147). From Eagle, head south on Brush Creek Road (Forest Road 400) for 10.25 miles to Forest Road 415. Turn left (east) on Forest Road 415, and go about 6.75 miles. Popular with spelunkers and hikers, this small campground is in a picturesque spot surrounded by mountains. Campers enjoy a mix of sun and shade, with aspens providing most of the shade. The campground is suitable for tents and pickup campers only. No water. No reservations. **(970) 328-6388.**

4. Sylvan Lake State Park (46 sites, 11 cabins); 16 miles south of Eagle (I-70 exit 147). From Eagle, head south on Brush Creek Road (Forest Road 400) for 16 miles. Visitors here enjoy panoramic views of alpine scenery in one of the most beautiful mountain settings of all the state parks. Fifty-acre Sylvan Lake offers superb trout fishing and is open to non-gas motorized boats. The two grassy and predominantly treeless campgrounds are filled most summer weekends. **Elk Run Campground** lies a short distance from the lake in two loops, with large back-in and pull-thru spaces. West Brush Creek flows by five of the sites, and one of the loops boasts a few trees. All sites in **Fisherman's Paradise** are side by side and just a few feet from the lake. Amenities in the park include flush toilets, showers, a dump station, and nine rental cabins. Maximum RV length is 35 feet. Reservations accepted. **(970) 328-2021.**

BASALT—RUEDI RESERVOIR AREA

photo by Gil Folsom

5. Mollie B

Location: 16 miles east of Basalt (see map on p. 293)
Elevation: 7,800 feet
Number of Sites: 26
Recommended RV Length: Up to 35 feet
Season: Memorial Day to September 3
Maps: *Colorado Atlas & Gazetteer,* page 46, B3.5
Colorado Recreational Road Atlas, page 4, C2.5
Phone: 970-963-2266

Scenery: ★★★★
RVs: ★★★
Tents: ★★★
Shade: ★
Privacy: ★

Directions

From Highway 82 in Basalt, go east on Frying Pan Road (Forest Road 105) for about 16 miles.

Distinguishing Features

Ruedi Reservoir is a 4.5-mile-long, 1,000-acre reservoir surrounded by steep hills. Some sites are less than 100 feet from the water. Mollie B Campground offers impressive views of the steep, forested hills rising above the other side of the reservoir. The campground consists of one paved loop in an open, grassy meadow. Aspens and other trees border the campground but provide little shade. Most sites are open and offer fair to good spacing. Campers should never leave food or coolers out, as bears do wander into this campground.

Popularity

On holiday weekends and on weekends when summer temperatures soar, Mollie B can fill. Sites 36, 35, 33, and 37 are within 25 to 100 feet of the reservoir. Reservations accepted.

Facilities

The many facilities include picnic tables, fire grates, firewood for sale, water faucets, lighted flush toilets, sinks with hot and cold running water, mirrors, and electrical outlets in bathrooms.

RV Notes

Campers will typically find short to medium-sized back-ins and four pull-thru sites. While some sites are fairly level, the amount of effort needed for leveling varies considerably from site to site. The nearest dump station is between Little Maud and Mollie B campgrounds.

Tent Notes

Twelve sites are rated for two or more tents, so finding a decent spot to pitch tents shouldn't be a problem.

Recreational Opportunities

Ruedi Reservoir offers the full menu of water-related activities. A large boat ramp allows easy access for any size boat. Status seekers should head down to the Aspen Sailing and Yacht Club at Benedict Bay to hobnob with the rich and famous! Anglers will find bluehead suckers, mackinaws, kokanee salmon, and any number of trout varieties, and the Fryingpan River provides additional fishing opportunities. Hikers should check out the Ruedi Trail or one of the many other trails near the campground.

---

6. Chapman

Location: 30 miles east of Basalt
Elevation: 8,800 feet
Number of Sites: 84
Recommended RV Length: Up to 50 feet
Season: Mid-May to November 15
Maps: *Colorado Atlas & Gazetteer*, page 47, B4
Colorado Recreational Road Atlas, page 4, C3
Phone: 970-963-2266

Scenery: ★★★
RVs: ★★★
Tents: ★★★
Shade: ★★★
Privacy: ★★★

Directions

From Highway 82 in Basalt, go east on Frying Pan Road (Forest Road 105) for about 30 miles.

Distinguishing Features

Chapman is an intriguing campground. Set at the base of a wide valley with pleasant mountain views, it has much to offer. Although large, the loops (or "areas") lie far enough apart from each other that the campground never feels big or crowded. Lodgepole pines provide ample shade, and aspen groves are also prominent in certain areas.

The eight areas have eight very distinct personalities. Nineteen sites are on the Fryingpan River, and about seven are on a small lake (Chapman Dam Reservoir). A small, man-made spillway cascades into a pond in the campground. Areas A, B, and E are closest to the lake, and most sites in C and D are on the river. A few sites in areas F, G, and H are on the river as well.

Popularity

Sites 15-22 and 42-83 can be reserved. Chapman can fill on busy holiday weekends and occasionally at other times. The most popular reservable sites are 17-20, 62, 64, 66, and 75-78; all are near the river.

Facilities

Facilities include picnic tables, fire grates, firewood for sale, and water faucets. Some of the vault toilets are wheelchair-accessible.

RV Notes

Such a large campground offers a wide variety of sites. The popular sites listed above are 25- and 30-foot back-ins. One of the best sites for RVs is number 64, a large pull-thru right on the river. Overall, areas F, G, and H are the best places for RVs; medium to long back-ins and a few pull-thrus, with varying degrees of leveling required, are the norm. The nearest dump station is about 12 miles west, between Mollie B and Little Maud campgrounds at the western edge of Ruedi Reservoir.

Tent Notes

Areas A (0-6) and B (7-9) are walk-in-only tent sites. Although every spot in this campground is fine for tents, lakeside sites 28-30 are the nicest.

photo by Gil Folsom

Recreational Opportunities

The lower Fryingpan River is classified as Gold Medal water for anglers, and the little lake in the campground also provides fishing possibilities for rainbows and brookies. Only boats without motors are allowed on the lake. Hikers will find a number of trails from which to choose, and mountain bikers and off-road enthusiasts will find a variety of dirt roads and easy four-wheel-drive roads—such as Hagerman Pass—to explore (see also Mollie B).

Other Nearby Campgrounds

7. Ruedi Marina (8 sites; see map on p. 293); 15 miles east of Basalt. From Highway 82, go left (east) on Frying Pan Road (Forest Road 105). Next to the marina and boat ramp, this is primarily a side-by-side parking area for large, self-contained RVs. There is no shade or privacy. No reservations. **(970) 963-2266.**

8. Little Maud (22 sites; see map on p. 293); 15 miles east of Basalt. From Highway 82, go left (east) on Frying Pan Road (Forest Road 105). Next to Mollie B, Little Maud sits a little farther above the reservoir. Sparsely shaded sites (four with adequate shade) are well-spaced around one paved loop. The lake is a five- to 10-minute walk away, and many sites have decent lake views. Lighted bathrooms offer flush toilets, sinks, and electrical outlets. Some sites handle large RVs, and a dump station is provided. Maximum RV length is 40 feet. No reservations. **(970) 963-2266.**

9. Little Mattie (20 sites; see map on p. 293); 15 miles east of Basalt. From Highway 82, go left (east) on Frying Pan Road (Forest Road 105). Of the campgrounds around Ruedi Reservoir, this one is the farthest from the water (although some sites are only a two-minute walk away). Most sites have adequate privacy and decent shade, provided mainly by aspens. A paved road goes through the campground. Maximum RV length is 40 feet. No reservations. **(970) 963-2266.**

10. Dearhamer (13 sites; see map on p. 293); 23 miles east of Basalt. From Highway 82, go left (east) on Frying Pan Road (Forest Road 105). At the far eastern end of Ruedi Reservoir and alongside the Fryingpan River, this campground is a favorite of anglers and families. Sites are tightly spaced in one loop, with fair to good shade and little privacy; four are on the river. A boat ramp is nearby. It's often very windy between 11:00 a.m. and 2:00 p.m. Maximum RV length is 35 feet. No reservations. **(970) 963-2266.**

11. Elk Wallow (7 sites); 29 miles east of Basalt. From Highway 82, go left (east) on Frying Pan Road (Forest Road 105) for 26 miles. Turn left (east) on Forest Road 501, and continue for 3.5 miles. This attractive and forested rustic campground is set on the Fryingpan River in a secluded location. Privacy is fair. Medium to large spaces are available for RVs. Sites are close to the river. No drinking water or trash service is provided. Maximum RV length is 30 feet. No reservations. **(970) 963-2266.**

ASPEN AREA

12. Silver Bar, Silver Bell, and Silver Queen

Location: 5 to 6 miles southwest of Aspen
Elevation: 8,460, 8,490, and 8,680 feet
Number of Sites: 4, 9, and 6
Recommended RV Length: Up to 20 feet
(pickup and pop-up campers only; not allowed
in Silver Bar)
Season: Memorial Day through September
Maps: *Colorado Atlas & Gazetteer*, page 46, C2
Colorado Recreational Road Atlas, page 4, C3
Phone: 970-925-3445

Scenery: ★★★★★
RVs: ★
Tents: ★★★★
Shade: ★★
Privacy: ★★

Directions

From Aspen, go west on Highway 82 about 0.5 mile to the second light
out of town. Turn left (west) onto Maroon Creek Road (County Road 13).
Proceed for about 5 miles to Silver Bar, 5.2 miles to Silver Bell, or 5.5 miles
to Silver Queen (the road becomes Forest Road 125). Campground passes
are required during summer; pick them up at the entrance station just across
from Silver Bar.

Distinguishing Features

These three, very small, tent-oriented campgrounds are within 1.5 miles of each other along Maroon Creek. Stunningly set in a narrow valley surrounded by aspen- and evergreen-cloaked mountains, this terrific trio is the gateway to the most photographed spot in Colorado—the Maroon Bells—and to the spectacular hiking, backpacking, and climbing that await in the Maroon Bells–Snowmass Wilderness.

Silver Bar's four sites are all on the creek in an open meadow. Evergreens and aspens border the campground, providing limited shade and privacy. Silver Bell's sites are on the creek side of a small loop; sites are medium-sized, with aspens providing ample shade. Silver Queen is the closest of the three to the Maroon Bells. Sites are medium-sized, with fair to good spacing and privacy, and aspens provide fair shade. This is the best campground for pickup campers or pop-up trailers.

Popularity

Reservations are accepted, and don't arrive without them. These three campgrounds are full every night during summer. All have a five-day stay limit. The most popular sites are 2 and 3 in Silver Bar, 1-4 in Silver Bell, and 2 and 3 in Silver Queen.

Facilities

Facilities include picnic tables, fire grates, firewood for sale, hand-pumped water (no water in Silver Bell), and vault toilets.

RV Notes

The Forest Service says RVs are a no-no, except for pickup campers and pop-up trailers. These vehicles are not allowed in Silver Bar, but Silver Bell has two spots that will work for them, as will all sites in Silver Queen (which has one pull-thru).

Tent Notes

Every site is great for tents, and several are on the creek.

Recreational Opportunities

Rainbows and brookies are plentiful in the creek running beside the campgrounds and at 25-acre Maroon Lake. Hikers, backpackers, and climbers will find excellent opportunities in and around the Maroon Bells–Snowmass Wilderness; these exceptional backcountry experiences all start from either the East Maroon trailhead or the trailhead at Maroon Lake.

The sight of the Maroon Bells reflecting off Maroon Lake is a breathtaking and unforgettable experience, and many feel strongly that it is Colorado's signature mountain scene. Even the most casual visitor should take the easy one-hour Maroon Lake scenic trail. For more ambitious mountaineers, several trails of varying lengths provide a lot of options. Buckskin, Willow, West Maroon, and Frigid Air Passes are all accessible from this starting point, and cycling is popular up and down Maroon Creek Road.

13. Redstone

Location: 16 miles south of Carbondale
Elevation: 7,200 feet
Number of Sites: 32
Recommended RV Length: Up to 40 feet
Season: Memorial Day to mid-November
Maps: *Colorado Atlas & Gazetteer*, page 45, C7
Colorado Recreational Road Atlas, page 4, B3
Phone: 970-963-2266

Scenery: ★★★★★
RVs: ★★★★★
Tents: ★★★★
Shade: ★
Privacy: ★★

Directions

From Carbondale, go south on Highway 133 for about 14.5 miles to just past the campground sign. Turn left (east) at the "Redstone North" entrance, and cross the bridge over the Crystal River. Turn left.

Distinguishing Features

Welcome to the Redstone Hilton! Stunning scenery, thoroughly modern amenities, and complete wheelchair accessibility are just some of Redstone's charms. The views from this campground—set close to the Crystal River with near-vertical red cliffs rising in the background—are inspiring. This renovated facility offers the ultimate in amenities compared to 99 percent of other Forest Service campgrounds.

Upon entering the campground, a right turn leads to the less expensive Mechau Loop (a.k.a. Redstone 2; 13 sites), with large, level, gravel sites. No hookups are available. Turning left leads to the more expensive Allgier and Osgood Loops (a.k.a. Redstone 1; 19 sites), which feature electrical and water hook-ups. These two loops offer large, level, RV-oriented gravel sites.

Most sites are in the open and are surrounded by wildflower-covered meadows and aspens. Several sites are doubles.

Popularity
On weekends, it's a good idea to make reservations. No sites are on the river. The most requested sites are 17, 4, 3, and 15 in Redstone 1, and 7, 10, and 11 in Redstone 2.

Facilities
Facilities include picnic tables, fire grates, firewood for sale, wheelchair-accessible water hydrants, and composting and flush toilets. Solar-powered showers, lantern posts, and tent pads are also available. The bathroom at Redstone 1 has hot and cold running water, electrical outlets, and mirrors.

RV Notes
Wide, long to extra-long, fairly level gravel back-ins and pull-thrus can accommodate any modern rig. Many sites exceed 50 feet in length, and several of the pull-thrus are 100 feet long. Head left upon entering the campground for electrical and water hookups. The nearest dump station is at the Conoco gas station near the Wal-Mart in Glenwood Springs, or in the fairgrounds in Hotchkiss if you're heading over McClure Pass.

Tent Notes
Tent pads, lantern posts, and hot showers make for the ultimate in camping comfort. Unless you need hookups, turn right after entering the campground to the Mechau Loop, and save some money. Be careful with the hydrants: water shoots out quite forcefully! The bathrooms on the left side of the campground (Redstone 1) have sinks, mirrors, and electrical outlets.

Recreational Opportunities
The campground has horseshoe pits and a children's sandbox. The scenic Crystal River is only a 100- to 200-foot walk from many campsites and offers so-so fishing for rainbow and brown trout. The area contains excellent hiking trails. A mile from the campground is the charming community of Redstone, with its arts and craft shops and the historic Redstone Castle.

The natural, unmarked Penny Hot Springs are only 1 mile away as well. Drive north toward Carbondale on Highway 133, and look for a pull-out on the right just past mile marker 55 and the County Road 11 sign. Head down toward the river, and follow your nose to the springs! (Also see Bogan Flats.)

14. Bogan Flats

Location: 22 miles south
of Carbondale
Elevation: 7,600 feet
Number of Sites: 37
Recommended RV Length:
Up to 40 feet
Season: Memorial Day
to mid-October
Maps: *Colorado Atlas & Gazetteer,*
page 45, D7
Colorado Recreational Road Atlas,
page 4, B3.5
Phone: 970-963-2266

Scenery: ★★★★★
RVs: ★★★★
Tents: ★★★★
Shade: ★★
Privacy: ★★

Directions
From Carbondale, go south on Highway 133 for about 20 miles. Turn left (southeast) at the bottom of McClure Pass onto Forest Road 314 (County Road 3), which goes to Marble. Proceed about 1.5 miles, and turn left.

Distinguishing Features
Bogan Flats offers 19 riverside sites along the Crystal River. As if that weren't enough, it also provides close-up views of gorgeous aspen- and evergreen-covered slopes. Designed to take maximum advantage of its riverfront property, this long campground has two distinct personalities. Sites 1-17 are generally large, fairly private, and well-shaded by tall spruce, pine, cottonwood, and aspen trees. Sites 18-37 are in an open meadow, spaced closer together with less privacy and hardly any shade; these sites do, however, have excellent mountain views.

Popularity
From mid-June to Labor Day, Bogan Flats typically fills every weekend and occasionally on weekdays. Campers should reserve ahead! If that isn't possible, arrive Thursday or early Friday. Of the reservable sites, the most popular are 15-18, 8, 9, 12, 13, and 24-26 (all of these are riverside sites). Other reservable riverside sites are 19, 21, and 23.

Facilities
Facilities include picnic tables, fire grates, firewood for sale, water faucets, and vault toilets.

RV Notes

Long back-in spaces and seven long pull-thrus make this an RV-friendly place. In fact, 27 sites are 40 feet or more in length. Try reserving the super-long back-in river sites (15 or 16) and you won't be sorry. Some leveling might be required. The nearest dump stations are in the fairgrounds in Hotchkiss if you're heading over McClure Pass, or at the Conoco gas station next to the Wal-Mart in Glenwood Springs on the way to I-70.

Tent Notes

Campers should try to reserve the riverside campsites numbered below 19. Redstone Campground, about 6 miles away, has pay showers for campers wishing to clean up.

Recreational Opportunities 👯 🐾 🚙 🚵

Anglers should try their luck for brown and brook trout just a few feet away in Crystal River or at nearby 25-acre Beaver Lake, just past Marble. The most popular activity in this area is taking the four-wheel-drive road or hiking to the world-famous Crystal Mill, about 5 miles beyond Marble. Along with the Maroon Bells, it's probably the most photographed spot in Colorado. Another interesting drive/hike leads you to the Yule Marble Quarry just above Marble. The Lead King Basin and the dangerous Schofield Pass four-wheel-drive roads are favorites with off-road enthusiasts and mountain bikers. Several hiking trails are nearby. Look for the unmarked Penny Hot Springs along the Crystal River on Highway 133 between mile markers 55 and 56, just past Redstone. (Also see Redstone Campground.)

Other Nearby Campgrounds

15. Difficult (47 sites); 4.5 miles southeast of Aspen on Highway 82. It is indeed "difficult" to find a spot here, as it fills every day—reserve now! A paved road leads through two loops in this large campground. Aspens and underbrush provide good shade and excellent privacy. Sites are RV-friendly. Maximum RV length is 60 feet. Reservations accepted. **(970) 925-3445.**

16. Weller (11 sites); 8 miles southeast of Aspen on Highway 82. This charming campground is located in one paved loop just off the highway. Towering aspens provide a wonderful ambiance. Large back-in spaces are available for RVs. Shade and privacy are fair, but road noise can be a problem. Maximum RV length is 40 feet. No reservations. **(970) 925-3445.**

17. Lost Man (10 sites); 13.4 miles southeast of Aspen on Highway 82. Lost Man Campground is set next to a trailhead alongside the highway. On the outside of one small loop, all but two sites are shaded. Two spots are on the river. Privacy ranges from fair to good, and several sites will hold larger RVs. No reservations. **(970) 925-3445.**

18. Lincoln Gulch (7 sites); 9.5 miles southeast of Aspen. From Highway 82, turn right (south) on Forest Road 106. Set about 200 feet below the highway, this campground's sites are located on the outside of one small loop. Several are on the river. Shade ranges from poor to fair. Sites have fair to good spacing and fair privacy. The short road leading to the campground is not easy for RVs to maneuver. Maximum RV length is 30 feet. No reservations. **(970) 925-3445.**

19. Lincoln Creek Dispersed (22 sites); 10-13 miles southeast of Aspen. Go south on Highway 82 for 9.5 miles to Forest Road 106, and turn right (south). The sites are scattered along the first 3 miles of a rough, bumpy, high-clearance road. These free campsites have only fire rings as an amenity. They are only suitable for tents or pickup campers, as the road is quite rough. No reservations. **(970) 925-3445.**

20. Portal (7 sites); 15 miles southeast of Aspen. Go south on Highway 82 for 9.5 miles to Forest Road 106. Turn right (south), and go 5.5 miles. In a lovely location on Grizzly Reservoir, this campground offers medium-sized sites that provide fair to adequate privacy. All but three are shaded. The 6-mile trek to the campground is over one of the roughest and bumpiest dirt roads you've ever seen; it's not advisable for RVs. No water. No reservations. **(970) 925-3445.**

21. Avalanche (13 sites); 14 miles south of Carbondale. Take Highway 133 south for 11 miles to County Road 30 (Forest Road 310). Turn left (east), and go about 3 miles. Set at the edge of the Maroon Bells–Snowmass Wilderness, this is a popular spot for backpackers and equestrians. The campground is near Avalanche Creek, with three sites on the creek. Shade and privacy range from fair to good. The 2.5-mile County Road 30 (Forest Road 310) is bumpy and narrow, so it limits the campground to tents and pickup campers. No reservations. **(970) 963-2266.**

PAONIA AREA

22. McClure (19 sites); about 26 miles south of Carbondale, near the top of McClure Pass (between Paonia and Carbondale) on Highway 133. Sites are located in a pretty aspen grove. Towering aspens provide adequate shade and privacy, but block views of the mountains. Maximum RV length is 35 feet. No reservations. **(970) 527-4131.**

23. Paonia State Park (15 sites); 16 miles northeast of Paonia on Highway 133. Paonia Reservoir (334 acres) offers all water sports. Two separate campgrounds near the north end of the reservoir accommodate small to medium-sized RVs. **Spruce Campground** lies just a few feet off the highway and has eight tightly spaced sites under tall spruce trees. A small stream runs near the sites. **Hawsapple Campground** is across the river and away from traffic noise. Popular with waterskiers, these sites are set in a mix of sun and shade with little privacy (except site 7). There is no drinking water available. Reservations accepted. **(970) 921-5721.**

CRESTED BUTTE AREA

24. Lost Lake

Location: 18 miles west of Crested Butte
Elevation: 9,600 feet
Number of Sites: 11
Recommended RV Length: Up to 21 feet
Season: Mid-June through September
Maps: *Colorado Atlas & Gazetteer*, page 57, B7
Colorado Recreational Road Atlas, page 22, B2
Phone: 970-527-4131

Scenery: ★★★★★
RVs: ★★★
Tents: ★★★
Shade: ★★★
Privacy: ★★★

Directions

From Crested Butte, take County Road 12 (Whiterock Avenue) west for about 16 miles. The well-graded gravel road travels over Kebler Pass. Turn left (south) onto Forest Road 706, and proceed south for 2.3 miles.

Distinguishing Features

Lost Lake is worth finding. The campground is adjacent to Lost Lake Slough, with East Beckwith Mountain forming a magnificent backdrop across the lake. Wildflowers are abundant and beautiful! This is one of those special spots where you might find yourself so mesmerized by the view that you won't do anything but sit transfixed and try to absorb it all. About seven sites are on or just across from the lake; the rest are in a small loop (still near the lake) at the end of the campground. Excellent spacing equates to good privacy.

Popularity
Campers cannot make reservations, and from Memorial Day to Labor Day this campground fills almost every weekend. But during the week, you can usually get a spot. If the campground is full, a few dispersed campsites dot the road leading up to the lake; the best ones are the closest to County Road 12.

Facilities
Facilities include picnic tables, fire grates, wheelchair-accessible vault toilets, and firewood for sale. No water.

RV Notes
Sites are medium to long back-ins with one small pull-thru. Some leveling is required. RV dump stations can be found in Crested Butte or Paonia.

Tent Notes
Campers will find good and spacious sites in which to pitch their tents.

Recreational Opportunities
Try your luck fishing for trout in the lake or in Middle Creek. Enjoy motorless boating in Lost Lake Slough. Three Lakes Trail starts here; this terrific 2.1-mile loop leads past Lost Lake, Dollar Lake, Lost Lake Slough, and a small waterfall. Another easy hike that splits off from Three Lakes Trail leads to Beckwith Pass in 2 miles or down into Horseback Park a little farther. The Beckwith Pass Trail gets heavy use from horseback riders.

---

25. Lake Irwin
Location: 9 miles west of Crested Butte
Elevation: 10,200 feet
Number of Sites: 32
Recommended RV Length: Up to 35 feet
Season: Late June through September
Maps: *Colorado Atlas & Gazetteer*, page 58, A1
Colorado Recreational Road Atlas, page 22, B2
Phone: 970-641-0471

Scenery: ★★★★★
RVs: ★★
Tents: ★★★
Shade: ★★
Privacy: ★★

Directions
From Crested Butte, go west on County Road 12 (Whiterock Avenue), for 6.5 miles. Turn right (north) on Forest Road 826, and proceed 2.3 miles north.

Distinguishing Features

This is one of the most gorgeous settings in Colorado! Ruby Peak, Mount Owen, and Purple Peak form a breathtaking backdrop. Lake Irwin and mesmerizing wildflowers add to the beauty. Campsites are in one big loop above the lake, with eight sites on the lake or just above it. Sites 1-10 are nearest to the lake and have the best views. Sites 11-32 are mostly higher, with many great mountain views.

Popularity

From late June through mid-August, Lake Irwin is full almost every weekend. Weekdays around this time are also quite busy. Reservations are highly recommended. If you don't have a reservation, try to arrive before 4:00 p.m. The most requested reservable sites—3 and 6—are lakeside. For family reunions, reserve sites 27 and 28.

Facilities

Facilities include picnic tables, fire grates, firewood for sale, hand-pumped water, and vault toilets as well as a picnic area.

Lake Irwin

RV Notes

Five sites are pull-thrus. Lengths vary tremendously, but enough choices are available that campers shouldn't have a problem finding a spot for most medium-sized RVs. Some leveling may be required. Sites 2, 10, 15-17, 27, and 30 have gray water dumps. Crested Butte offers a free dump station, behind the Phillips 66 gas station at the corner of Highway 135 and County Road 12 (Whiterock Avenue).

Tent Notes

All spots should be fine for tents, and site 3 is in a great spot overlooking the lake. Temperatures dip into the low 40s most summer nights, so come prepared. Showers and laundry facilities are available in Crested Butte at the Youth Hostel at 500 East Teocalli.

Recreational Opportunities

Anglers can fish for rainbow and brook trout in the lake and in Anthracite Creek. Motorless boating is permitted on the lake. Mountain bikers and off-road enthusiasts can take off from the campground for many exciting adventures. The Raggeds Wilderness area borders Lake Irwin and offers great possibilities for day-hikers and backpackers alike. An unforgettable horseback ride can be arranged at Lake Irwin Lodge: horses quickly take you to the tops of the mountains just above the campground.

Other Nearby Campgrounds

26. Erickson Springs (18 sites); about 24 miles west of Crested Butte on County Road 12 (Whiterock Avenue). This campground is at the relatively low elevation of 6,800 feet—opening up early and late-season camping opportunities. Sites are well-shaded, with heavy brush providing good privacy to most. Maximum RV length is 35 feet. No reservations. **(970) 527-4131.**

27. Gothic (4 sites); 10 miles north of Crested Butte on County Road 317 (Gothic Road). This tiny, tent-oriented campground has no drinking water. Just a few steps away, some of the most spectacular mountain scenery in the state awaits. Sites are small, tightly spaced, and well-shaded. No reservations. **(970) 641-0471.**

28. Cement Creek (13 sites); 11 miles southeast of Crested Butte. Take Highway 135 southeast for about 7 miles to Forest Road 740. Go left (east), and proceed for about 4 miles. Seven sites are situated along a creek with promising trout fishing. Most have adequate shade. This can be a busy campground, and it's especially popular with hunters in the fall. Maximum RV length is 32 feet. No reservations. **(970) 641-0471.**

GUNNISON AREA

29. Mosca

Location: 29 miles northeast of Gunnison
Elevation: 10,000 feet
Number of Sites: 20
Recommended RV Length: Up to 35 feet
Season: Memorial Day to mid-October
Maps: *Colorado Atlas & Gazetteer,* page 59, B4
Colorado Recreational Road Atlas, page 22, C2
Phone: 970-641-0471

Scenery: ★★★
RVs: ★★
Tents: ★★★
Shade: ★★★
Privacy: ★★

Directions
From Gunnison, drive 10 miles north on Highway 135 to Almont. Turn right (northeast) onto Forest Road 742 (Taylor Canyon Road), and go 7.2 miles to the junction of Forest Road 744. Turn left (north) on Forest Road 744, and proceed 12 miles (the last 10 are gravel). The entrance will be on your right.

Distinguishing Features
Mosca—in a lovely, high alpine setting by 86-acre Spring Creek Reservoir—has a loyal following of campers who return year after year. Civilization and other campgrounds seem far away. Most sites are well-spaced and situated in a single, wooded loop. Four sites are almost on the lake, with two of these tent-only sites. Several others offer views of the lake through the trees.

Popularity

From July 4 through early August, Mosca often fills—but if you ask the hosts politely, they can usually find you a site! You'll also find good dispersed camping sites along the road near the campground. No reservations.

Facilities

Mosca offers picnic tables, fire grates, firewood for sale, and vault toilets. No water.

RV Notes

There is a mix of short-to-medium pull-thrus (seven) and back-ins. Most sites are not level. Six can reportedly accommodate vehicles up to 40 feet in length.

Tent Notes

Try to get spots 8 or 9: they're side by side but provide fantastic views of the reservoir. These sites rank as some of the best in the entire state!

Recreational Opportunities

Anglers will find trout fishing in both the lake and the stream. Campers can take motorless boats on the reservoir, which is a wonderful way to spend a warm, sunny afternoon. Also possible near the campground are dirt biking, ATV riding, and jeeping. Campers routinely spot elk and deer.

30. North Bank

Location: 18 miles northeast of Gunnison
Elevation: 8,600 feet
Number of Sites: 17
Recommended RV Length: Up to 35 feet
Season: Memorial Day through September
Maps: *Colorado Atlas & Gazetteer*, page 58, C3
Colorado Recreational Road Atlas, page 22, C2.5
Phone: 970-641-0471

Scenery: ★★★
RVs: ★★
Tents: ★★★
Shade: ★★
Privacy: ★★

Directions

From Gunnison, drive 10 miles north on Highway 135 to Almont. Turn right (northeast) onto Forest Road 742 (Taylor Canyon Road), and go 7.8 miles. The entrance will be on your left.

Distinguishing Features

North Bank sits just above the Taylor River and is the only campground in the canyon located on the north side of the river. Situated well away from the road, North Bank offers a little more peace and quiet than other campgrounds in Taylor Canyon. During the daytime, however, vehicle traffic accessing the

North Bank

nearby trailhead can kick up dust clouds. Six sites are just above the river and provide easy access to it. A resident bat population keeps the mosquito population much lower than in other nearby campgrounds.

Popularity

From mid-July through mid-August, North Bank fills most of the time, especially on weekends. Campers should arrive early in the afternoon to be sure to get a spot. No reservations.

Facilities

Facilities include picnic tables, fire grates, firewood for sale, hand-pumped water, and a vault toilet.

RV Notes

Eight medium to long pull-thrus and several back-ins are available; most are a little off-level. The pull-thrus are in the open without much privacy, but they're near the river.

Tent Notes

Aside from site 8—the best spot in this campground—tent campers might be happier in the small, nine-site loop that lies just to the left of the main road leading through the campground. It's more secluded, has better shade, and offers great views of the rock formations.

Recreational Opportunities

Fly-fishing is just a few steps away from many sites. The nearby Doctor Park Trail eventually connects up with the Colorado Trail and is popular with hikers, mountain bikers, and horseback riders (see Rosy Lane and One Mile).

31. Rosy Lane

Location: 19 miles northeast of Gunnison
Elevation: 8,600 feet
Number of Sites: 20
Recommended RV Length: Up to 35 feet
Season: Memorial Day through September
Maps: *Colorado Atlas & Gazetteer,* page 58, C3 *Colorado Recreational Road Atlas,* page 22, C2.5
Phone: 970-641-0471

Scenery: ★★★★
RVs: ★★★
Tents: ★★★
Shade: ★★
Privacy: ★★

photo by Gil Folsom

Directions
From Gunnison, take Highway 135 north 10 miles to Almont. Turn right (northeast) onto Forest Road 742 (Taylor Canyon Road), and proceed 9.1 miles. The entrance is on the left side of the road.

Distinguishing Features
Here's a gorgeous riverside campground, with the steep Taylor Canyon walls forming an impressive backdrop. Rosy Lane may quickly win a special place in your heart. Ten of the sites are next to the Taylor River. All but two sites are on the outside of a single, paved loop. A wheelchair-accessible paved path runs along the river, with pull-outs for fishing or viewing. Rafters and kayakers pass by as they negotiate the rapids.

Popularity
From mid-June until mid-August, this extremely popular campground fills almost every night. Reservations are accepted; if you're arriving without one, try to get there on a weekday morning, go straight to the host, and ask if anyone is leaving. The most popular reservable sites are 6, 8, 13, 4, and 5; all are on the river.

Facilities
Facilities include picnic tables, fire grates, firewood for sale, water faucets, and wheelchair-accessible vault toilets (with exhaust fans!).

RV Notes

Rosy Lane is very RV-friendly, with level sites of which 10 are long pull-thrus and the rest are medium to long back-ins. Site 8 has electricity available for a small fee.

Tent Notes

The ground is fairly level, and several sites have tent pads.

Recreational Opportunities

Fantastic fishing, rafting, and kayaking are all just a few feet away from your campsite. Three Rivers Outfitting in Almont offers Class II to III and III to IV whitewater trips on the Taylor River, or easy Class I to II trips on the nearby Gunnison River. Taylor Canyon is a rock climber's mecca as well (see North Bank and One Mile).

---

32. One Mile

Location: 18 miles northeast of Gunnison
Elevation: 8,600 feet
Number of Sites: 26
Recommended RV Length: Up to 35 feet
Season: Memorial Day through September
Maps: *Colorado Atlas & Gazetteer*, page 58, C3
Colorado Recreational Road Atlas, page 22, C2.5
Phone: 970-641-0471

Scenery: ★★★
RVs: ★★★★★
Tents: ★★
Shade: ★★
Privacy: ★★

Directions

From Gunnison, take Highway 135 north 10 miles to Almont. Turn right (northeast) onto Forest Road 742 (Taylor Canyon Road), and proceed 8.2 miles. The entrance is on the right side of the road.

Distinguishing Features

Welcome to RV heaven! One Mile offers those with RVs a wonderful place in which to relax. Views of rocky hills and the Taylor River greet campers as they step out into the campground, which is set above the river and road among lodgepole pines and aspens. One Mile is a long, narrow campground with a single paved road leading through it; extra-large campsites are situated along the sides of the campground road.

Popularity

From June through August, this campground is booked almost every night. Fifteen sites are reservable, and it's tough to find a spot without a reservation. If you don't have one, get here early in the day and check with the hosts.

Facilities

Facilities include wheelchair-accessible picnic tables, fire grates, firewood for sale, water faucets, lantern posts (a rarity!), and wheelchair-accessible vault toilets with lights and fans.

RV Notes

Thirteen extra-long, fairly level pull-thrus and several back-ins should accommodate any rig. Electrical hookups, direct connection to faucets (for filling only), and two gray water dump facilities round out this exceptionally RV-friendly campground.

Tent Notes

A few sites have pads. Tent campers may feel a bit overwhelmed by all the RVs.

Recreational Opportunities

The myriad recreational opportunities include fly-fishing, hiking, rock climbing, rafting, kayaking, and mountain biking (see North Bank and Rosy Lane).

33. Lakeview

Location: 33 miles northeast of Gunnison
Elevation: 9,400 feet
Number of Sites: 68
Recommended RV Length: Up to 35 feet
Season: Mid-May to mid-September
(a few sites open to hunters until November)
Maps: *Colorado Atlas & Gazetteer*, page 59, B5
Colorado Recreational Road Atlas, page 22, C2
Phone: 970-641-0471

Scenery: ★★★★★
RVs: ★★★
Tents: ★★★
Shade: ★★
Privacy: ★★

Directions

From Gunnison, take Highway 135 north 10 miles to Almont. Turn right (northeast) onto Forest Road 742 (Taylor Canyon Road), and proceed about 23 miles. The entrance is on the right side of the road.

Distinguishing Features

Lakeview is perched on the side of a hill about 100 feet above the south end of Taylor Park Reservoir, providing most campers with million-dollar views! The Ute referred to Taylor Park as "The Valley of the Gods." Visitors won't disagree, judging by the expansive views of Taylor Park Reservoir, Taylor

Park, and the Collegiate Peaks. A new lower loop (sites 47-68) offers large, spacious sites with electrical hookups. These are choice RV spots. The middle loop (sites 11-29) features open sites with better views, but with little privacy or shade. The long upper loop (sites 30-46) offers larger sites, more trees and shade, and ample privacy. Sites 45 and 46 have it all: trees, views, and privacy.

Popularity

Campers can make reservations for about half the sites. From mid-June until mid-August, and on holiday weekends, a reservation is a must. Of the reservable sites, the most popular ones are 45, 46, 11, 2, 3, 32, and 34. The most popular sites on the new lower loop are 55, 54, 56 and 57.

Facilities

Facilities include picnic tables, fire grates, firewood for sale, water faucets, and vault toilets, two with wheelchair access.

RV Notes

A mix of back-in, pull-out, and pull-thru sites are available. They're generally long, with a bit of leveling required. Sites 47-68 have electrical hookups.

Tent Notes

Most sites have tent pads.

Recreational Opportunities

The 2,000-acre Taylor Park Reservoir is a beautiful spot for boating or for snagging a nice-sized trout or kokanee salmon. Non-motorized and motorized boats and all the fishing gear you'll need are available for rent at the Trading Post—if you rent their deep-water fishing gear and use it as instructed, you probably won't leave disappointed. The reservoir is a 5- to 10-minute walk down the hill from the campground. Plenty of hiking trails and four-wheel-drive roads are nearby.

---

34. Dinner Station

Location: 43 miles northeast of Gunnison
Elevation: 9,600 feet
Number of Sites: 22
Recommended RV Length: Up to 35 feet
Season: Memorial Day to late September
Maps: *Colorado Atlas & Gazetteer*, page 59, A5
Colorado Recreational Road Atlas, page 22, C2
Phone: 970-641-0471

Scenery: ★★★★
RVs: ★★★
Tents: ★★★
Shade: ★★★
Privacy: ★★★

Directions

From Gunnison, take Highway 135 north 10 miles to Almont. Turn right (northeast) onto Forest Road 742 (Taylor Canyon Road), and proceed for about 33 miles. The entrance is on the left side of the road.

Dinner Station

Distinguishing Features

At one time, this was a noontime stop on the stagecoach line from Tincup to Aspen. Eleven prime sites are set along the banks of the Taylor River. A typical site is relatively large with adequate spacing between it and the next site. Most campers are never far from the water. Many campsites have magnificent 180-degree vistas of the jagged mountains rising across the valley floor. Lodgepole pines provide ample shade to some sites. Sites 00 and 17-22 are in the open sagebrush without shade but give campers breathtaking mountain views.

Popularity

You'll want to make reservations. From July 4 through the first week of August, Dinner Station often fills on weekends, but usually not on weekdays. The most popular reservable spots are riverside sites 13, 12, 11, and 17. Site 14 is also popular, although it isn't on the river.

Facilities

Facilities include picnic tables, fire grates, firewood for sale, hand-pumped water, and vault toilets.

RV Notes
RV-friendly sites are in good supply. Nine fairly level, medium to long pull-thrus and some back-ins will accommodate most rigs. Sites 17-22 offer long pull-thru spaces, but no shade. A dump station is just southwest of Taylor Park Reservoir down Forest Road 765 (Cumberland Pass Road).

Tent Notes
You can pitch your tent on good, level ground by the river. The Taylor Park Trading Post in Taylor Park offers pay showers and a laundromat.

Recreational Opportunities
Anglers can fly-fish or bait-fish in the river for pan-sized brown trout. The fishing is better at the small, rainbow-stocked Pothole Reservoirs 1 and 2, just a few miles north along the road. These reservoirs are excellent places for children to try fishing. The numerous jeep roads are this area's biggest draw. Mountain biking is becoming increasingly popular in Taylor Park, and only 0.5 mile away is the Gunnison loop of the Colorado Trail—although the campground host reports that little hiking is done in the vicinity.

---

35. Dorchester
Location: 50 miles northeast of Gunnison
Elevation: 9,800 feet
Number of Sites: 10
Recommended RV Length: Up to 28 feet
Season: Memorial Day through September
Maps: *Colorado Atlas & Gazetteer*, page 59, A4
Colorado Recreational Road Atlas, page 22, C2
Phone: 970-641-0471

Scenery: ★★★★
RVs: ★★
Tents: ★★★
Shade: ★★★
Privacy: ★★★

Directions
From Gunnison, take Highway 135 north 10 miles to Almont. Turn right (northeast) onto Forest Road 742 (Taylor Canyon Road), and proceed 40 miles. The entrance is on the left side of the road.

Distinguishing Features
This campground is isolated, peaceful, and quiet. All sites are in a well-spaced row against a small, forested hill. Every camper enjoys a very scenic view of the Collegiate Peaks and Taylor Park as they gaze out across the open meadows where the town of Dorchester once stood. Historical markers by an old cabin near the campground give history buffs a wealth of information about Dorchester and the area's mining activities.

Popularity
Dorchester occasionally fills from July 4 through early August, but you can usually find a spot. No reservations. Ample dispersed camping opportunities are also near the road for about the next 5 miles.

Facilities
Facilities include picnic tables, fire grates, firewood for sale, hand-pumped water, and vault toilets.

RV Notes
The gravel road leading to the campground can be rough at times, so not many RVs come here. The sites—short to medium back-ins—are just a little off-level.

Tent Notes
This is a great campground for tents, with plenty of shady spots.

Recreational Opportunities
The Taylor River offers stream fishing just a few hundred yards southwest of the campground in an open, marshy meadow, or try the Pothole Reservoirs just a few miles to the south. Many jeep roads lead past old mines as they head up into the mountains. The hosts report that the wildlife viewing is good and that campers often hear elk bugling and coyotes howling in the evening.

Dorchester

36. Mirror Lake

Location: 45 miles northeast of Gunnison
Elevation: 11,000
Number of Sites: 9
Recommended RV Length: Up to 16 feet
Season: Late June through September
Maps: *Colorado Atlas & Gazetteer*, page 59, B6
Colorado Recreational Road Atlas, page 23, A2.5
Phone: 970-641-0471

Scenery: ★★★★★
RVs: ★★
Tents: ★★
Shade: ★
Privacy: ★★

Directions
From Gunnison, go 10 miles north on Highway 135 to Almont. Turn right (northeast) on Forest Road 742 (Taylor Canyon Road), and go about 24 miles to Forest Road 765 (just past the southern end of Taylor Park Reservoir). Turn right (east) on Forest Road 765, and go 8 miles to Tincup. Turn left (east) onto Forest Road 267, and go 3 miles

Distinguishing Features
Very few campgrounds in Colorado can rival this scenery. Situated just above Mirror Lake (27 acres) in a single paved loop, all 10 sites have spectacular views. Campers in four of the sites have unobstructed lake views, and those who camp in the other sites are treated to great mountain and partial lake views. Sites are on the small side, without much privacy. Shade is fair at best— but you'll be so busy enjoying the sunshine that you won't notice. Only two other campgrounds in Colorado are in loftier spots. Daytime temperatures rarely exceed 65 degrees and can dip into the 30s at night.

Popularity

From July through mid-August, Mirror Lake fills up three to four days of the week (but not always on weekends). During this period, try to arrive before noon to secure a spot, as reservations aren't taken. If the campground is full, you'll find good, free spots along the side of the road leading to the campground.

Facilities

Facilities include picnic tables, fire grates, firewood for sale, a water faucet, and a vault toilet. Please conserve water here: it has to be hauled up every week!

RV Notes

Mirror Lake is best suited for smaller RVs. Sites are small to medium back-ins, with one pull-thru. About half the sites are fairly level. You might be better off trying one of the dispersed camping spots on the road leading to the campground. A dump station is located on Forest Road 765 near the Taylor Park Reservoir.

Tent Notes

All sites are fine for tents, but you won't find much protection from the weather if it turns nasty. Temperatures can drop at night, so come prepared.

Recreational Opportunities

Mirror Lake provides good trout fishing and nonmotorized boating opportunities. The Timberline trailhead, about half a mile away, gives hikers access to the Timberline and Continental Divide Trails. Forest Road 267 (Tincup Pass Jeep Road) runs parallel to Mirror Lake and offers excellent alpine scenery on its journey over the Continental Divide and down to the well-preserved ghost town of St. Elmo. The road is also suitable for well-conditioned mountain bikers.

---

37. Pitkin

Location: 28 miles northeast of Gunnison
Elevation: 9,300 feet
Number of Sites: 24
Recommended RV Length: Up to 35 feet
Season: Memorial Day through September
Maps: *Colorado Atlas & Gazetteer*, page 59, D5.5
Colorado Recreational Road Atlas, page 23, A3
Phone: 970-641-0471

Scenery: ★★★
RVs: ★★★★
Tents: ★★★
Shade: ★★★★
Privacy: ★★★

Directions

From Gunnison, drive east on Highway 50 for 12 miles to Parlin. Turn left (northeast) on County Road 76 for 15 miles to Pitkin. From Pitkin, go east for 1 mile on Forest Road 765 (the last 0.5 mile is a well-maintained gravel road).

Distinguishing Features
This modern, renovated campground caters to all campers' needs. Conveniently located just a mile east of the small community of Pitkin (supplies available), it's set near Quartz Creek in a dense forest. Most sites are large, with good spacing and privacy.

Popularity
Pitkin is very popular, especially from July through mid-August. Try to get here early in the day to secure a spot. No reservations.

Facilities
Facilities include picnic tables, fire grates, firewood for sale, lantern posts, water faucets, and vault toilets. The picnic tables and vault toilets are wheelchair-accessible.

RV Notes
Most sites are extremely RV-friendly, except sites 10-14. About 10 of the sites are large, level pull-thrus; the rest are back-ins. Direct connection to water faucets is available for filling purposes only, and a gray water disposal station is available as well.

Tent Notes
More than half the sites have tent pads, but almost all are fine for tents. Sites 10-14 are set below the rest of the campground along Quartz Creek. These absolutely delightful sites are the best in the campground.

photo by Gil Folsom

Recreational Opportunities 🏃 ⛴ 🚙 🏍 🚵

Fishing for medium-sized trout in Quartz Creek is good, with additional fishing possibilities in nearby beaver ponds. Hikers will find several trails leading from nearby Gold Creek Campground and the end of the Alpine Tunnel Road. Off-road enthusiasts will find jeep and OHV possibilities not far away. Mountain bikers should check out nearby riding possibilities on trails leading from Forest Road 767 (Middle Quartz Creek Road).

Other Nearby Campgrounds

38. Granite (7 sites); 17.5 miles northeast of Gunnison. Follow Highway 135 for 10 miles north to Almont. Turn right (northeast) onto Forest Road 742 (Taylor Canyon Road), and go 7.5 miles. This is a walk-in, tent-only campground, with all sites set on a steep bank overlooking the Taylor River. Most sites are fairly open with good views of Taylor Canyon. No water. No reservations. **(970) 641-0471.**

39. Lodgepole (15 sites); 25 miles northeast of Gunnison. Follow Highway 135 for 10 miles north to Almont. Turn right (northeast) onto Forest Road 742 (Taylor Canyon Road), and go 15 miles. Set in a dense stand of lodgepole pines across the road from the river (but still providing river access), Lodgepole is workable, but not great, for RVs. Maximum RV length is 25 feet. Reservations accepted. **(970) 641-0471.**

40. Almont (10 sites); 9 miles north of Gunnison on Highway 135. All but one site in this tent-oriented campground are set in cottonwood trees on the Gunnison River. A favorite among anglers and hunters, Almont is the first campground to open in the spring and the last to close in the fall. It's a poor choice for RVs. Maximum RV length is 28 feet. No reservations. **(970) 641-0471.**

41. Spring Creek (12 sites); 19 miles northeast of Gunnison. Take Highway 135 north for 10 miles to Almont. Turn right (northeast) onto Forest Road 742 (Taylor Canyon Road), and go 7.2 miles to Forest Road 744. Turn left (north) onto Forest Road 744, and go 2 miles. Only 2 miles from Taylor Canyon, this peaceful spot rarely fills. Spring Creek is a pleasant place in a lightly shaded, relatively open area with about half its sites on the creek. Maximum RV length is 35 feet. No reservations. **(970) 641-0471.**

42. Cold Springs (6 sites); 26 miles northeast of Gunnison. Take Highway 135 north for 10 miles to Almont. Turn right (northeast) onto Forest Road 742 (Taylor Canyon Road), and go 16 miles. This small, tent-oriented campground is also set in the lodgepole pines across the road from the river. Sites have excellent separation and privacy. No drinking water is available. No reservations. **(970) 641-0471.**

43. Lottis Creek (27 sites, 8 group sites); 27 miles northeast of Gunnison. Take Highway 135 north for 10 miles to Almont. Turn right (northeast) onto Forest Road 742 (Taylor Canyon Road), and go 17 miles. This very pleasant campground is well-suited for both tents and RVs. Most sites are level and spacious, and have decent shade provided by a mix of pines and aspens. Six sites are on the creek. Maximum RV length is 35 feet. No reservations. **(970) 641-0471.**

44. Rivers End (18 sites); 29 miles northeast of Gunnison. Take Highway 135 north for 10 miles to Almont. Turn right (northeast) onto Forest Road 742 (Taylor Canyon Road), and go 29 miles. Rivers End has many large pull-thrus and is strategically located in an open sagebrush area near both Taylor Park Reservoir and the Taylor River. It has wonderful views and is a favorite of anglers and the OHV crowd. Maximum RV length is 35 feet. No reservations. **(970) 641-0471.**

45. Comanche (4 sites); 23 miles east of Gunnison. Take Highway 50 east from Gunnison for 12 miles to Parlin. Turn left (east) onto County Road 76, and go 8.75 miles to Forest Road 771. Go left (north) for 2 miles. Four lovely sites, best suited for tents, are sheltered almost entirely in an aspen grove. A creek is just across the road. Comanche has no drinking water. No reservations. **(970) 641-0471.**

46. Gold Creek (6 sites); 28 miles northeast of Gunnison. Take Highway 50 east for 12 miles to Parlin. Turn left (east) onto County Road 76. Go about 8.75 miles to Forest Road 771. Turn left (north), and go about 6.5 miles. This is a small, tent-oriented campground. Sites are close to a creek, with several hiking trails nearby. No water. No reservations. **(970) 641-0471.**

47. Middle Quartz (7 sites); 33 miles northeast of Gunnison. Take Highway 50 east for 12 miles to Parlin. Turn left (east) onto County Road 76. Go about 15 miles to Pitkin. From Pitkin, go east 1 mile on Forest Road 765 to bumpy Forest Road 767. Turn right (southeast) on Forest Road 767, and go about 5 miles. This tent-oriented campground has good mountain views, privacy, and shade. Two sites are on a creek. No water. No reservations. **(970) 641-0471.**

48. Quartz (10 sites); 31 miles northeast of Gunnison. Take Highway 50 east for 12 miles to Parlin. Turn left (east) onto County Road 76. Go about 15 miles to Pitkin. From Pitkin, go east 4 miles on Forest Road 765. This is a quiet little campground with a mix of open and shaded sites suitable for smaller RVs. No reservations. **(970) 641-0471.**

49. Snowblind (23 sites); 45 miles east of Gunnison. Take Highway 50 east for about 35 miles to Forest Road 888 (about 1.5 miles northeast of Sargents). Turn left (north) on Forest Road 888, and go about 8 miles. A pleasant spot, Snowblind offers 11 spacious sites on Tomichi Creek. With both open and shaded sites among the aspens and evergreens, campers will easily find a place to relax. Snowblind works well for small to medium RVs. No reservations. **(970) 641-0471.**

BLACK CANYON OF THE GUNNISON NATIONAL PARK

50. East Portal

Location: 19 miles northeast of Montrose
Elevation: 7,500 feet
Number of Sites: 15
Recommended RV Length: Up to 22 feet
Season: May through October
Maps: *Colorado Atlas & Gazetteer*, page 57, D5
Colorado Recreational Road Atlas, page 22, A3
Phone: 970-641-2337

Scenery: ★★★★★
RVs: ★
Tents: ★★★★
Shade: ★★★★
Privacy: ★★

Directions

From Montrose, take Highway 50 east for 7 miles. Turn left (north) on Highway 347, and proceed for 6 miles. Just past the Black Canyon of the Gunnison National Park visitors' entrance, turn right (southeast) on County Road 175 (East Portal/River Access Road). Go 5.5 miles down this steep, paved, winding road to the bottom of the canyon.

Distinguishing Features

Some campers think of this campground as the deep, dark secret of a deep, dark canyon. This place is almost too good to be true. While the masses camp above on the canyon rim with no views, wise campers stay at the bottom.

Ten walk-in sites are set down about 12 feet from the parking lot level in a hollow under a canopy of hackberry and box elders. These wonderfully shaded sites are compact and tightly spaced. Campers in these sites have limited canyon views but no river views. The other five sites are arranged on the edges of a very small loop on the main level of the campground. They are also small, spaced close together, and have only fair shade—which isn't much of an issue, since the canyon is so steep and narrow that little sunshine penetrates it. The difference with these sites is that they all have magnificent views of the Gunnison River and the Black Canyon. The host says that the only biting insects are ticks, which you should watch out for from March until about July 4.

Popularity

On busy weekends this campground can fill, but spots are usually available. To be safe, get here by 3:00 p.m. on Friday if you're coming for a summer weekend. No reservations.

Facilities

Facilities include picnic tables, fire grates, water faucets, and lighted, wheelchair-accessible vault toilets.

RV Notes

The river access road is restricted to vehicles under 22 feet in total length, which eliminates most RVs. For those who do venture down the hill, there are five small back-in sites.

Tent Notes

This is the place to camp when visiting the Black Canyon of the Gunnison— don't even think about camping up above!

Recreational Opportunities

Anglers can catch rainbow and brown trout in the river. Expert kayakers sometimes use this as a put-in for an 11-mile, Class IV to V run with several difficult portages. Kayakers must register, as this is a very dangerous stretch of water even for experts.

A beautiful 1.5-mile drive along the base of the canyon leads to the Crystal Dam; picnic tables are scattered along the way. Most visitors explore the Black Canyon of the Gunnison from above, but seeing it from below is a wonderful way to experience it.

Other Nearby Campgrounds

51. Stevens Creek (54 sites; see map on p. 293); 12 miles southwest of Gunnison on Highway 50. Three paved loops and large paved back-ins are very near the lake in a treeless, sagebrush environment with little privacy. Popular with RVers, it is not a good campground for tents. Maximum RV length is 45 feet. Reservations accepted. **(970) 641-2337.**

52. Elk Creek (179 sites; see map on p. 293); 16 miles west of Gunnison on Highway 50. This campground is near the marina, restaurant, and lake. Most sites are RV-friendly and have excellent lake views, but the scattered trees provide little shade or privacy. Sixteen walk-in tent sites are very close to the lake. Twenty-eight sites in Loop D now have electric hookups. Deluxe facilities include flush toilets, showers, and a dump station. Maximum RV length is 45 feet. Reservations accepted. **(970) 641-2337.**

53. Dry Gulch (10 sites; see map on p. 293); 17 miles west of Gunnison on Highway 50. Situated in a sheltered dry gulch area under tall cottonwoods (good shade), this is a decent choice for tents or RVs. Sites are not close to the lake. Maximum RV length is 30 feet. No reservations. **(970) 641-2337.**

54. Red Creek (7 sites; see map on p. 293); 19 miles west of Gunnison on Highway 50. Set along small Red Creek, with shady cottonwoods and aspens and great views of the pinnacle rock formations. Two sites work well for RVs; the other five are walk-in tent sites. Sites are close together. Maximum RV length is 25 feet. Reservations accepted. **(970) 641-2337.**

55. Lake Fork (87 sites; see map on p. 293); 27 miles west of Gunnison on Highway 50. Perched well above the lake in an RV parking lot by the marina, Lake Fork provides views of the lake and the West Elk Wilderness, with no trees or privacy. Five walk-in tent sites are available, as well as flush toilets, showers, laundry facilities, and a dump station. Maximum RV length is 45 feet. Reservations accepted. **(970) 641-2337.**

56. Ponderosa (29 sites; see map on p. 293); 36 miles west of Gunnison. Take Highway 50 27 miles west to Highway 92. Turn right (northwest) on Highway 92, and go about 1.5 miles to County Road 721 (Soap Creek Road). Turn right (east) on County Road 721, and go about 7.5 miles. Located among scattered pines near the reservoir, this primitive campground gets you away from the hustle and bustle of Highway 50. Sites are large and well-spaced, with little shade. The campground has a boat ramp and horse corral. Maximum RV length is 45 feet. No reservations. **(970) 641-2337.**

57. Soap Creek (21 sites; see map on p. 293); 38 miles west of Gunnison. Take Highway 50 for 27 miles west to Highway 92. Turn right (northwest) on

Highway 92, and go about 1.5 miles to County Road 721 (Soap Creek Road). Turn right (east) on County Road 721, and go about 9.5 miles (the last 2 miles are very washboardy). Two miles north of Blue Mesa Reservoir, this is a pleasant spot with striking views of the West Elks. Sites are large and spacious and offer adequate shade. Five walk-in tent sites are available. Maximum RV length is 35 feet. No reservations. **(970) 641-0471.**

58. Cimarron (22 sites; see map on p. 293); 20 miles east of Montrose. From Montrose, take Highway 50 for 20 miles east to Cimarron. Then turn left (north) on County Road Q83, and proceed for 1 mile. This lightly used, RV-friendly campground is just west of Morrow Point Reservoir. Some large cottonwood trees shade some sites. A dump station is available, and bathrooms have flush toilets, sinks, mirrors, and outlets. Maximum RV length is 45 feet. No reservations. **(970) 641-2337.**

59. South Rim (103 sites); 13.4 miles east of Montrose. Take Highway 50 for 7 miles to Highway 347. Turn left (north) on Highway 347, and go 6 miles. This serves as the main campground for Black Canyon of the Gunnison visitors. Generally small, tightly spaced campsites are located in three loops. Twenty-two sites in Loop B now have electric hookups and have been elarged for RVs. A thick concentration of short Gambel oaks and serviceberry bushes provide some shielding from other campers. Maximum RV length is 36 feet in Loop B, shorter elsewhere. Reservations accepted. **(970) 641-2337.**

60. North Rim (13 sites); 23 miles south of Hotchkiss. From Hotchkiss, go southeast on Highway 92 for 11 miles to Crawford. From Crawford, go southwest on County Road 38.50 for about 4.5 miles to County Road 77.50. Turn right (south), and then take the first right (west) on Amber Road. Go about 0.75 mile to Black Canyon Road, and turn left (south). Proceed for about 6.5 miles to Rim Drive North, turn right, and go about 0.75 mile. Very inaccessible and hidden, North Rim is in a dense, tall piñon pine forest with great shade and small sites. Some of the most beautiful canyon views in the park are just a short walk away. Maximum RV length is 25 feet. No reservations. **(970) 641-2337.**

61. Crawford State Park (66 sites); 12 miles southeast of Hotchkiss. Go southeast on Highway 92 for 11 miles to Crawford. Continue 1 mile south. In two sparsely shaded campgrounds on Crawford Reservoir (400 acres) are many sites within 100 to 200 feet from shore. Some have shade shelters to provide relief from the sun. **Iron Creek** (sites 1-44) is RV-friendly with electrical hookups. **Clear Fork** (sites 45-66) offers a mix of sites, including five walk-in tent sites. Both campgrounds have flush toilets, pay showers, RV hookups, and a dump station. Neither campground offers much shade. The fishing is superb, and this is an excellent spot for teaching kids how to fish. Reservations accepted. **(970) 921-5721.**

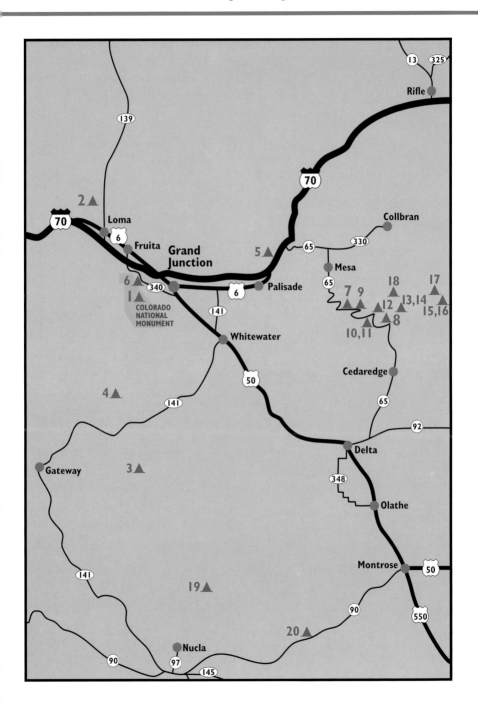

Colorado National Monument—just a few miles west of Grand Junction—offers spectacular scenery and is a must-see for every visitor to this area. Southeast of Grand Junction is the Grand Mesa—a delightful treat for water lovers. As the world's largest flattop mountain, the mesa is also Colorado's own "Land of Lakes," with an average elevation of over 10,000 feet. The small hills scattered around the mesa top almost make you forget that you're on the top of a huge, flat mountain. (Think of yourself as an ant on top of a card table. You're up high, but you don't know it until you walk to the edge of the table.)

Here in this mini-Minnesota is a concentration of more than 300 stream-fed lakes and reservoirs in a flat, forested setting. Most of the lakes are small, with the largest—Island Lake—covering only 179 acres. Several have boat launch ramps. The bottom line: this is a trout-fishing paradise.

The campgrounds on Grand Mesa are some of the least used in the state. Campers will, however, find a friendly little critter sharing this water paradise with them: the mosquito. July is the worst month for mosquitoes, and August can also be bad—so plan accordingly.

More than 300 miles of trails await hikers, horseback riders, mountain bikers, and OHV enthusiasts. The most popular hiking trail is the Crag Crest National Recreation Trail, a 10-mile loop with a spectacular view from its crest. The area hosts many hunters in the fall as well.

The Grand Mesa Scenic Byway crosses the mesa along its 55-mile journey on Highway 65 from I-70 to Cedaredge. The Lands End Road (mile marker 29 on Highway 65) forms part of the byway. This good gravel road goes west 12 miles, following the rim of the mesa to an overlook and the Lands End Observatory.

▲100 BEST

▲1 Saddlehorn
  (Colorado National Monument)
▲2 Highline State Park/Bookcliff
▲7 Jumbo
▲8 Ward Lake

▲ All The Rest

▲3 Divide Fork
▲4 Hay Press
▲5 Island Acres State Park
▲6 Colorado River State Park – Fruita
▲9 Spruce Grove
▲10 Island Lake
▲11 Little Bear
▲12 Cobbett Lake
▲13 Kiser Creek
▲14 Crag Crest
▲15 Twin Lake (closed)
▲16 Weir and Johnson
▲17 Big Creek
▲18 Cottonwood Lake
▲19 Columbine (closed)
▲20 Iron Springs (closed)

GRAND JUNCTION AREA

1. Saddlehorn (Colorado National Monument)

Location: About 12 miles west of Grand Junction
Elevation: 5,787 feet
Number of Sites: 80
Recommended RV Length: Up to 35 feet
Season: Year-round
Maps: *Colorado Atlas & Gazetteer*, page 42, D2.5
Colorado Recreational Road Atlas, page 21, A1.5
Phone: 970-858-3617

Scenery: ★★★★
RVs: ★★
Tents: ★★★
Shade: ★
Privacy: ★

Directions
From Grand Junction, go west on I-70 about 10 miles to Highway 340 (exit 19). Go left (south) on Highway 340 for about 2.5 miles, and turn right (south) onto Rim Rock Drive at the sign for Colorado National Monument. Go 4.3 miles on a steep, winding road.

Distinguishing Features
Situated on a high plateau above the Grand Valley, Saddlehorn is in a semiarid piñon-juniper forest with sagebrush, red sandstone rock formations, and red sandy soil. An easy walk from the campground leads to spectacular overlooks of the valley 2,000 feet below, the Book Cliffs, and the imposing rock monoliths of Colorado National Monument. Wildflowers bloom from mid-April to June, with cacti usually starting to bloom in May. The campground consists of three paved loops, with sites that are generally small and spaced closely together. Some sites in the B loop have views of the Grand Valley, but getting a good overlook view from most sites requires a short walk.

Popularity
Reservations are not taken, but this campground rarely fills. On a typical summer night, only 20 to 40 sites are occupied. A fee is charged.

Facilities
Facilities include picnic tables, fire grates, water faucets, flush toilets, sinks and mirrors in the bathrooms, and drinking fountains.

RV Notes
A mix of short to long gravel back-ins, pull-thrus, and pull-outs await intrepid RVers. Many sites require some leveling. The nearest dump station is at the Colorado Welcome Center off I-70 at Highway 340 (exit 19).

Tent Notes
All sites are great for tents; a freestanding tent works best in the sandy soil. Showers are available for a small fee at the Fruita RV Park and at Colorado River State Park off I-70 at Highway 340 (exit 19).

Recreational Opportunities
The 23-mile Rim Rock Drive leads to breathtaking overlooks of towering rock monoliths, balanced rocks, massive domes, sheer-walled canyons, the Grand Valley, the Book Cliffs, and distant mountains. If you go cycling on the road, be on the lookout for inattentive drivers. Backpackers, hikers, and equestrians interested in more extended exploring should ask at the visitor center for suggestions. Backcountry camping is permitted, but you must register at the visitor center. Pets are prohibited in the backcountry.

2. Highline State Park/Bookcliff

Location: About 23 miles northwest of Grand Junction
Elevation: 4,700 feet
Number of Sites: 28
Recommended RV Length: Up to 35 feet
Season: Year-round
Maps: *Colorado Atlas & Gazetteer*, page 42, B2
Colorado Recreational Road Atlas, page 21, A1
Phone: 970-858-7208

Scenery: ★★★
RVs: ★★★
Tents: ★★★★
Shade: ★★
Privacy: ★★

Directions

From Grand Junction, go west on I-70 about 15 miles to Highway 139 (exit 15). Go right (north) on Highway 139 for 5 miles to County Road Q.00. Turn left (west), and go about 1.5 miles to County Road 11.8. Turn right (north), and go 1 mile to the park entrance.

Distinguishing Features

Highline Lake Campground is a gem. It's surrounded by farms, and most campers pass it by as they drive along I-70. But it's the top pick of many visitors, especially those to the Grand Junction area. With its manicured lawn and large, mature trees, the campground has a parklike quality. Next to Highline Lake (160 acres) and Mack Mesa Lake (30 acres), it provides access to any number of activities to while away the warm summer days. Campsites are in grassy areas, and many are shaded by cottonwood, ash, ponderosa pine, and willow trees. Sites are medium-sized and spaced fairly well apart. A few even have limited views of the lakes. Enjoy!

Popularity

Highline Lake fills frequently on weekends from March through Labor Day. If you show up without a reservation on a spring or summer weekend, try to be there by 3:00 p.m. on Friday. The most requested sites are 10, 3, 14, and 30. Reservations are taken from April through Labor Day.

Facilities

The many facilities include picnic tables, fire grates, water faucets, a laundry room, a picnic area, a snack shack, and a boat ramp. Bathrooms supply wheelchair-accessible flush toilets, showers, sinks, mirrors, and outlets.

RV Notes

Sites are fairly level, medium to long pull-thru/pull-out spaces (25) and back-ins. A dump station is available in the campground.

Tent Notes

The manicured lawn and large shade trees give tent campers a wonderful setting to relax in. The low elevation (for Colorado) results in pleasant nighttime temperatures.

Recreational Opportunities

Mack Mesa Lake is a great early-season trout-fishing spot, with boating limited to hand-propelled craft. Next-door-neighbor Highline Lake is a much busier place, where the catfish and crappie are in good supply. All boating is allowed, and jet skis, paddleboats, and inflatables are available for rental. During busy summer weekends the number of boats allowed on the lake may be limited, and visitors will have to wait for another boat to leave before venturing out. There's a swim beach, and summer water temperatures reach into the 70s.

Informative signs at the Watchable Wildlife Overlook and Kiosk describe the 150 species of birds that have been spotted in the park. The Highline Lake Trail is a 3.5-mile loop around the lake on a gravel surface that works well for both hikers and mountain bikers. Ask at the park about a new mountain-bike trail connection, which enables rides to adjacent BLM land.

Other Nearby Campgrounds

3. Divide Fork (11 sites); 38 miles south of Grand Junction. Take Highway 50 south for 9.25 miles to Highway 141. Turn right (southwest), go about 13.5 miles to County Road 26.10 (it becomes Forest Road 402, a.k.a. Divide Road), and turn left (southwest). Follow this road for about 15.5 miles. Just a place to camp, this spot offers a mix of open and shaded sites. Maximum RV length is 22 feet. No reservations. **(970) 242-8211.**

4. Hay Press (11 sites); 21 miles southwest of Grand Junction. Take Highway 340 southwest from Grand Junction for 1 mile, and turn left (southwest) onto County Road D5.00 (which becomes Rim Rock Drive), and go about 7 miles. Where County Road D5.00 goes to the left (south) off of Rim Rock Drive, follow County Road D5.00 for about 5.75 miles to County Road 16.50 at Glade Park. Turn left (south) on County Road 16.50, and go about 7 miles. Near a small reservoir and extremely isolated, this campground offers little shade or privacy. Drinking water at picnic area. Maximum RV length is 16 feet. No reservations. **(970) 242-8211.**

5. Island Acres State Park (80 sites); 15 miles northeast of Grand Junction on I-70 (exit 47). Close to four small lakes and the Colorado River in the scenic De Beque Canyon, this is a popular, deluxe campground. Shade, privacy, and facilities vary in the four loops. Flush toilets, showers, electrical hookups, a laundry, a dump station, an amphitheater, and a playground are all available. Maximum RV length is 50 feet. Reservations accepted. **(970) 434-3388.**

6. Colorado River State Park–Fruita (63 sites); 11 miles northwest of Grand Junction. Take I-70 west from Grand Junction about 10 miles to Highway 340 (exit 19 in Fruita). Go left (south) on Highway 340 about 0.25 mile. This campground is built on a reclaimed gravel pit and is close to the Colorado River and a small 23-acre lake. Forty-four RV-friendly pull-thrus and back-ins all include hookups. Thirteen sites are walk-in tent sites. Very little natural shade exists. Amenities include flush toilets, showers, a laundry, a dump station, and a boat ramp. Reservations accepted. **(970) 434-3388.**

GRAND MESA AREA

7. Jumbo

Location: 43 miles east of Grand Junction
Elevation: 9,800 feet
Number of Sites: 26
Recommended RV Length: Up to 55 feet
Season: Mid-June to late September
Maps: *Colorado Atlas & Gazetteer*, page 44, D1
Colorado Recreational Road Atlas, page 21, C1.5
Phone: 970-242-8211

Scenery: ★★★
RVs: ★★★★
Tents: ★★★
Shade: ★★★
Privacy: ★★★

Directions

From Grand Junction, go east on I-70 about 17 miles to Highway 65 (exit 49). Turn right (east) on Highway 65, and continue for about 26 miles. Turn right on Forest Road 252, and go about 100 yards.

Distinguishing Features

A fisherman's haven, Jumbo also draws visitors viewing the aspens in the fall. Set between Jumbo Reservoir and Sunset Lake on the northern edge of Grand Mesa, Jumbo is one of the prettiest campgrounds on the mesa. Aspen, spruce, and fir trees provide decent shade for most sites. Two sites have good views of Jumbo Reservoir, and two others have lovely views of Sunset Reservoir. Sites are generally spacious and well-separated, allowing ample privacy. Recent renovations have made this campground RV friendly. By Sunset Lake is a lodge offering a restaurant, supplies, and rowboat rentals.

Popularity

During busy summer weekends the campground may fill to 90 percent of capacity, and it may be completely full on holidays. No reservations.

Facilities

Facilities include picnic tables, fire grates, firewood for sale, water faucets, and vault toilets.

RV Notes

Recently renovated, this campground is now RV friendly, with electrical hookups at all sites.

Tent Notes

Campers will enjoy the recreational opportunities available to them during the day and find their campsite a wonderful place to spend an evening.

Recreational Opportunities

This is a fishing paradise. Anglers can choose from eight small lakes known collectively as Mesa Lakes. Jumbo Reservoir (7 acres) and Sunset Lake (18 acres) are adjacent to the campground, while Mesa Lake (26 acres), Beaver Lake (6.5 acres), Glacier Springs Lake (3 acres), and Water Dog Reservoir (24 acres) are all within 1 mile of the campground. Ambitious fishermen will hardly have a chance to limber up before reaching South Mesa Lake (10 acres) at 0.5 mile or Lost Lake (4 acres) at 1 mile via a very well maintained hiking trail. Stream-fishing just below the dam of Sunset Lake in Mesa Creek provides a little variety. Several of the lakes prohibit motorized watercraft. Anglers will find rainbow (heavily stocked), brook, and cutthroat trout as well as white suckers.

Non-anglers can partake in hiking along the West Bench Trail starting near the ranger station. This scenic 5-mile (one way) easy to moderate trail is suitable for hikers and mountain bikers. Across the road from the campground are some ATV trails.

8. Ward Lake

Location: 52 miles east of Grand Junction
Elevation: 10,200 feet
Number of Sites: 27
Recommended RV Length: Up to 35 feet
Season: Late June through September
Maps: *Colorado Atlas & Gazetteer*, page 44, D2
Colorado Recreational Road Atlas, page 21, C1.5
Phone: 970-242-8211

Scenery: ★★★
RVs: ★★★
Tents: ★★★
Shade: ★★
Privacy: ★★

Directions

From Grand Junction, go east on I-70 about 17 miles to Highway 65 (exit 49). Turn right (east) and go about 35 miles. Turn left (east) on Forest Road 121, and go just a short distance.

Distinguishing Features

This campground is in a lovely spot adjacent to Ward Lake (85 acres). The

upper loop (sites 1-13) consists of medium-sized sites, with great shade provided by spruce and fir trees. Two sites offer scenic lake views and are only about 100 feet from the water. Most campers head for the lower loop. Almost all sites on this loop are spread out along the shore in a meadow, with scattered trees providing some shade. Campers have fairly unobstructed lake views and are never more than a few yards from the water. Sites are large and open, but provide little privacy. Beware: the mosquitoes are vicious in July.

Popularity

Ward Lake fills only a few nights per season. But to get a prime lakeside site, it wouldn't hurt to arrive a little early in the week, as the best spots often get snatched up by Friday morning. No reservations.

Facilities

Facilities include picnic tables, fire grates, firewood for sale, water faucets, vault toilets, and a boat ramp.

RV Notes

Large pull-thru sites in the lower loop provide wonderful lakeside camping. Most of the sites in this loop are long pull-thrus.

Tent Notes

Sites 1-13 in the upper loop offer plenty of shade and privacy.

Recreational Opportunities

You can catch rainbows, brookies, white suckers, and splake in Ward Lake. Rainbow trout are stocked several times a season, and splake are stocked periodically. Boating is popular as well.

The nearby Crag Crest National Recreation Trail is a 10-mile circular trail. The spectacular crest portion (6.5 miles) runs along a ridge at the edge of Grand Mesa—and at the top of the world—with breathtaking views of sparkling lakes on one side and distant mountain ranges on the other. The loop portion (3.5 miles) is easier. Certain sections of the Crag Crest Trail are suitable for horses and mountain bikes. The area has many ATV trails, but not at Ward Lake.

Other Nearby Campgrounds

9. Spruce Grove (16 sites); 44 miles east of Grand Junction. Take I-70 east about 17 miles to Highway 65 (exit 49), and go right (east) for about 27 miles. A mile or so east of Jumbo is this campground near the popular Mesa Lakes. Set about 100 yards off the road in a stand of large spruce trees, Spruce Grove offers solitude and is RV-friendly, with most sites medium to long pull-thrus. No reservations. **(970) 242-8211.**

10. Island Lake (41 sites); 52 miles east of Grand Junction. Take I-70 east about 17 miles to Highway 65 (exit 49). Turn right (east) on Highway 65, and go about 35 miles. Positioned near Island Lake (179 acres), the largest reservoir on the Grand Mesa, this campground offers well-shaded sites with adequate spacing. A few will accommodate large RVs, with a maximum length of 45 feet. One toilet facility has flush toilets, sinks, and an electrical outlet. No reservations. **(970) 242-8211.**

11. Little Bear (36 sites); 52 miles east of Grand Junction. Take I-70 east about 17 miles to Highway 65 (exit 49). Turn right (east) on Highway 65, and go about 35 miles. Nine sites are either on Island Lake or very close to it. Offering a bathroom with a flush toilet, sink, and outlet, this campground accommodates RVs up to 40 feet in length in a few sites. Most sites accommodate RVs up to 22 feet long. Privacy ranges from poor to fair, but it's the second-best lakeside campground on Grand Mesa. No reservations. **(970) 242-8211.**

12. Cobbett Lake (a.k.a. Carp Lake, 20 sites); 53 miles east of Grand Junction. Take I-70 east about 17 miles to Highway 65 (exit 49). Turn right (east) on Highway 65, and go about 36 miles. This campground is by a 12-acre lake with several sites either right on the lake or offering good views of it. Spacing is good, and sites range from shady to open. Maximum RV length is 30 feet. Reservations accepted. **(970) 242-8211.**

13. Kiser Creek (12 sites); 54 miles east of Grand Junction. Take I-70 east about 17 miles to Highway 65 (exit 49). Turn right (east) on Highway 65, and go about 35 miles to Forest Road 121. Turn left (east) on Forest Road 121, and go about 2 miles. This campground is best suited for small RVs and tents. Campers can hear, but not see, the creek from the campsites. Sites offer good shade and fair privacy. Maximum RV length is 16 feet. No reservations. **(970) 242-8211.**

14. Crag Crest (11 sites); 57.5 miles east of Grand Junction. Take I-70 east about 17 miles to Highway 65 (exit 49). Turn right (east) on Highway 65, and go about 35 miles to Forest Road 121. Turn left (east) on Forest Road 121, and go about 5.5 miles. This campground is also on the side of a hill and overlooks Eggleston Lake. The Crag Crest Trail runs near it. Tents are the best choice for this campground. Campsites are clustered around the edge of one loop, with several others at the end of a dead-end spur. No reservations. **(970) 242-8211.**

15. Twin Lake
Since the writing of this book, this campground has been permanently closed.

16. Weir and Johnson (12 sites); 16.5 miles southeast of Collbran. Go south from Collbran on County Road 58.50 for 2 miles to County Road 59.00 (it becomes Forest Road 121), turn left (east), and go about 12.5 miles to Forest Road 126. Turn left (east), and go about 2 miles. This is a forested, tent-oriented campground with a few sites able to handle small RVs (up to 22 feet). Set above two small reservoirs (47-acre Weir and Johnson Reservoir and 10-acre Sackett Reservoir), several sites have excellent lake views. Sites are tightly spaced with little privacy. No reservations. **(970) 242-8211.**

17. Big Creek (26 sites); 12 miles south of Collbran. From Collbran, go south on County Road 58.50 for 2 miles to County Road 59.00 (it becomes Forest Road 121), turn left (east) and go about 11.5 miles. Most sites are either on Big Creek Reservoir Number 1 (63 acres) or offer a view of it. Sites are generally very close to the road and are small, spaced close together, and offer little privacy. A few sites can handle larger RVs up to 30 feet. No reservations. **(970) 487-3534.**

Other Nearby Campgrounds

18. Cottonwood Lake (36 sites); 16.5 miles south of Collbran. Go south from Collbran on County Road 58.50 for 2 miles to County Road 59.00 (it becomes Forest Road 121), turn left (east), and go about 9.5 miles to Forest Road 257. Turn right (west), and go about 5 miles. Rustic and primitive and one of the most remote campgrounds on Grand Mesa, this is a very lightly used facility near Cottonwood Lake Number 1 (77 acres). Parts of the road to this primitive campground can be washboardy. Maximum RV length is 30 feet. No reservations. **(970) 242-8211.**

19. Columbine
Since the writing of this book, this campground has been permanently closed.

20. Iron Springs
Since the writing of this book, this campground has been permanently closed.

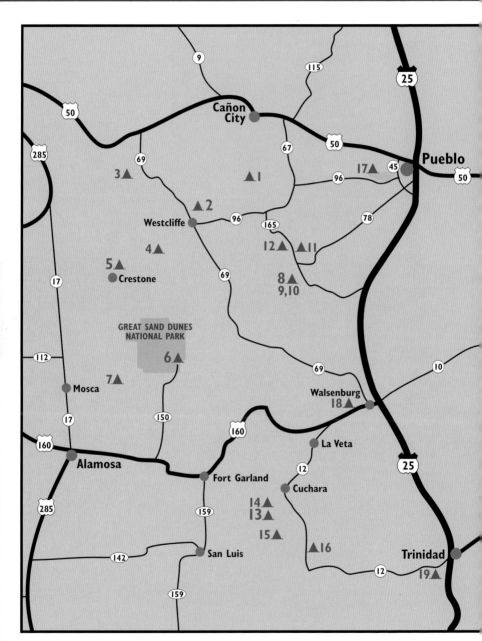

▲ 20 is not visible on the map above. Consult the maps in DeLorme's *Colorado Atlas & Gazetteer* or Pierson Guides' *Colorado Recreational Road Atlas* for the location of this campground on the Eastern Plains. For locations of campgrounds around Pueblo Reservoir, see map on p. 294.

In the western half of this region is a high-altitude desert, the San Luis Valley. Backing up to the Sangre de Cristo Range at the edge of the valley, the Great Sand Dunes National Park attracts more than 300,000 visitors a year—where else can you find a 700-foot-high sandpile? On the other side of the mountains, the peaceful community of Westcliffe offers scenic De Weese Reservoir, along with four-wheeling, camping, and hiking in the Sangre de Cristos.

Lake Isabel is a perfect weekend escape for Pueblo and Colorado Springs families. This idyllic mountain lake offers a peaceful setting for just enjoying the great outdoors. The zany Bishops Castle a few miles away is a very cute roadside attraction. Eleven-mile-long Pueblo Reservoir is another popular weekend escape for Front Range residents, and farther south are two additional water playgrounds along I-25: Lathrop State Park near Walsenburg and Trinidad State Park near Trinidad.

Several campgrounds are located southwest of Walsenburg near Cuchara in an attractive, little-known alpine setting. The Spanish Peaks provide a wonderful backdrop for these facilities.

▲ 100 BEST

▲ **2** De Weese Reservoir
▲ **5** North Crestone
▲ **6** Great Sand Dunes
▲ **8** Lake Isabel—St. Charles
▲ **13** Blue Lake

▲ All The Rest

▲ **1** Oak Creek
▲ **3** Lake Creek
▲ **4** Alvarado
▲ **7** San Luis Lakes State Park
▲ **9** Lake Isabel—South Side
▲ **10** Lake Isabel—La Vista
▲ **11** Davenport
▲ **12** Ophir Creek
▲ **14** Bear Lake
▲ **15** Purgatoire
▲ **16** Monument Lake
▲ **17** Lake Pueblo State Park
▲ **18** Lathrop State Park
▲ **19** Trinidad State Park
▲ **20** John Martin Reservoir State Park

CAÑON CITY AREA

1. Oak Creek (15 sites); about 13 miles south of Cañon City on County Road 143 (Oak Creek Grade Road). Oak Creek is a free, very rustic, rarely used campground in a remote location. The road leading to it is steep and narrow, and not recommended for RVs. Sites have fair to adequate shade; no drinking water or trash service are provided. Maximum RV length is 25 feet. No reservations. **(719) 269-8500.**

WESTCLIFFE AREA

2. De Weese Reservoir

Location: About 5 miles northwest of Westcliffe
Elevation: 7,700 feet
Number of Sites: No designated sites
Recommended RV Length: Unlimited
Season: Year-round
Maps: *Colorado Atlas & Gazetteer*, page 71, C6.5
Colorado Recreational Road Atlas, page 23, C4
Phone: 719-561-5300

Scenery: ★★★★
RVs: ★★
Tents: ★★
Shade: ★★
Privacy: ★★

Directions
From Westcliffe, go northwest on Highway 69 about 0.25 mile to County Road 241. Turn right (north) on County Road 241, and proceed about 4 miles (the last mile is a well-graded gravel road) until you see the "Welcome—Lake De Weese Resort/Camping" sign. Bear right, and drive 1 mile to the reservoir.

Distinguishing Features
This campground is a truly magical place. On a cloudless summer night, as the moonlight shimmers on the reservoir and the peaks of the Sangre de Cristos rise majestically above the valley floor, a camper's spirit is resurrected. De Weese attracts a loyal following of devoted campers who consider this place their personal secret. All sites provide wonderful, unobstructed views of the reservoir and mountains. There are no designated campsites, giving campers freedom from the restriction of conventional sites. Shade varies from poor on the reservoir to adequate up the hill. The town of Westcliffe is about five miles away.

Popularity
This is a busy place, but finding an available site should be easy. No reservations.

Facilities

Facilities are primitive. A few picnic tables, some fire rings, and vault toilets (bring your own toilet paper) are available. No drinking water is available.

RV Notes

Most RVers park along the shore of the treeless reservoir, and the spaces are as large as you want them to be. The more daring head up the hill on a so-so dirt road that wanders through the ponderosa pines, splitting off in several directions.

Tent Notes

Campers wanting more shade should bypass the sites along the reservoir and head up the dirt road through the pines until they find a spot that catches their fancy.

Recreational Opportunities

Anglers can cast their lines for smallmouth bass, tiger muskies, rainbow, brown, and lake trout. Fishing is good in the reservoir and also permitted in the first 0.25 mile of the river below the dam. Technically, the only boating allowed is that which is connected to fishing, but jet skiing and waterskiing happens frequently. A boat ramp is available.

Other Nearby Campgrounds

3. Lake Creek (12 sites); 15 miles northwest of Westcliffe. Take Highway 69 northwest for about 13 miles, turn left (west) on County Road 198 (becomes Forest Road 300), and go 3 miles. This is a long, narrow campground with six creekside sites. Sites are small to medium in size, and aspens provide satisfactory shade. Most sites offer a lot of privacy. Maximum RV length is 30 feet. No reservations. **(719) 269-8500.**

4. Alvarado (47 sites); 10 miles southwest of Westcliffe. Take Highway 69 south for 3 miles, and go right (west) onto County Road 140. Go for 7 miles. Alvarado is a somewhat primitive campground that works best for tents and smaller RVs; many sites require leveling. There are three equestrian sites. Some sites have scenic views of the valley and surrounding hills. Shade is good, and privacy ranges from poor to excellent. No drinking water. Reservations accepted. **(719) 269-8500.**

North Crestone

photo by Gil Folsom

CRESTONE AREA

5. North Crestone

Location: 1.2 miles north of Crestone
Elevation: 8,800 feet
Number of Sites: 13
Recommended RV Length: Up to 25 feet
Season: Memorial Day through September
Maps: *Colorado Atlas & Gazetteer*, page 71, D5
Colorado Recreational Road Atlas, page 29, C1
Phone: 719-655-2547

Scenery: ★★★★
RVs: ★★
Tents: ★★★★
Shade: ★★★★
Privacy: ★★★★

Directions
From Crestone, go north on Alder Street (which becomes Forest Road 950), and go 1.2 miles.

Distinguishing Features
Nestled in North Crestone Canyon—with jagged formations and trees holding on precariously to the steep slopes—North Crestone Creek roars gloriously as it races downhill. What a sound! All but one of the sites allow campers to pitch their tents near this powerful creek, and all but one are tucked between the creek and the campground road. A nice mix of deciduous trees and evergreens provides wonderful shade, and most sites offer excellent privacy, too.

Popularity
Plan to arrive early in the day, as most sites fill quickly (especially during busy summer weekends). No reservations.

Facilities
Facilities include picnic tables, fire grates, hand-pumped water, and vault toilets (one offers wheelchair access).

RV Notes
Alas, this place isn't really meant for larger RVs. Most spots are short back-ins suitable only for small pop-ups and pickup campers. An advanced degree in leveling wouldn't hurt.

Tent Notes
Among the sea of campgrounds overrun by RVs, this is a tenting oasis. Supplies and grub are only a mile away in Crestone.

Recreational Opportunities
Lucky anglers might snag a brookie or a cutthroat as they go speeding by—hold on tightly to your pole! Hikers, backpackers, and climbers need only to throw on the backpack and walk to the end of the campground to start their way up the North Crestone Trail.

GREAT SAND DUNES AREA

6. Great Sand Dunes

Location: 34 miles northeast of Alamosa
Elevation: 8,175 feet
Number of Sites: 88
Recommended RV Length: Up to 25 feet
Season: Year-round (some services limited in winter)
Maps: *Colorado Atlas & Gazetteer*, page 81, C6.5
Colorado Recreational Road Atlas, page 29, C2
Phone: 719-378-2312

Scenery: ★★★★★
RVs: ★★
Tents: ★★★
Shade: ★★
Privacy: ★

Directions

From Alamosa, drive 14 miles east on Highway 160. Go left (north) on Highway 150, and proceed 20 miles. If you're coming from the Front Range, take I-25 south to Walsenburg, then Highway 160 west about 60 miles to Highway 150.

Distinguishing Features

The Great Sand Dunes cover 39 square miles and are up to 750 feet tall, making them North America's tallest dunes. Campers flock here to share a one-of-a-kind view and enjoy a truly unique camping experience. The road through the campground is paved, as are the parking spaces. Campsites are small and tightly spaced, with little privacy. Beautiful piñons and junipers provide some shade, and wildflowers dot the campground. Incredible vistas of the sand dunes and surrounding mountains are visible from almost every site. If you want to escape the crowds, a short walk into the backcountry offers peace and quiet.

Popularity

During summer, this campground fills almost every night (especially on weekends), and reservations aren't taken. Showing up early in the day is the best strategy, and if you're coming for the weekend you should arrive on Thursday.

Facilities

This campground provides nearly everything a camper needs—including a visitor center, seasonal mini-store, and amphitheater. You'll find picnic tables, fire grates, firewood for sale, and water faucets, and the bathrooms have flush toilets and sinks. Cold showers (no soap permitted) are located in the day use area. A group camping area is available by reservation only. Several sites are wheelchair-accessible.

RV Notes

The small to medium paved parking spaces work best for smaller RVs. A few sites can accommodate larger rigs, but it's hard to predict their availability. Many sites require some leveling. A dump station is near the campground entrance (open May through September).

Tent Notes

Campers can pitch tents on pads under the trees located in many of the sites. Pay showers are 3 miles away at the Great Sand Dunes Oasis RV park.

Recreational Opportunities 🚶 🚙

Guided walks, interpretative programs, and campfire programs are all available —check at the visitor center for ideas. Hiking in the sand dunes at 8,000 feet can be strenuous, and temperatures in the sand can reach up to 140 degrees Fahrenheit in the summer. There are no designated trails in the dunes area, and remember to take a hat, sunscreen, sturdy shoes, and plenty of water on any excursion. Medano Pass is popular with four-wheelers. An excursion to the San Luis Lakes gives you a view of its bird wetlands area. Also nearby is the Colorado Gator Farm which raises alligators.

Nearby Campground

7. San Luis Lakes State Park (51 sites); 22 miles northeast of Alamosa. Take Highway 17 north for 13.5 miles to County Road 6N (Six Mile Road). Turn right (east), and go 7.5 miles. A combination of wetlands, lakes, and the dry valley draws visitors to this park. The campground consists of three treeless loops, but many sites have covered picnic tables for a little shade. Privacy often is lacking, but the views of the lake, mountains, and sand dunes are appealing. Sites are RV-friendly with many long pull-thrus that can accommodate any RV, electrical hookups at all sites, and a dump station. Amenities include flush toilets, showers, and laundry facilities. Reservations accepted. **(719) 378-2020.**

LAKE ISABEL AREA

8. Lake Isabel–St. Charles

Location: 39 miles southwest of Pueblo
Elevation: 8,800 feet
Number of Sites: 15
Recommended RV Length: Up to 35 feet
Season: Mid-May to early October
Maps: *Colorado Atlas & Gazetteer*, page 82, A2
Colorado Recreational Road Atlas, page 30, A1
Phone: 719-269-8500

Scenery: ★★★
RVs: ★★★
Tents: ★★★
Shade: ★★★
Privacy: ★★★

Directions
From Pueblo, go south on I-25 for about 23 miles to Highway 165 (exit 74). Go west on Highway 165 for about 16 miles to the Lake Isabel Recreation Area. Follow the signs.

Distinguishing Features
Campers, kick off your shoes, pull out the lawn chair, stick your toes in the creek, close your eyes, and listen to the water while relaxing with a cold one (rootbeer, of course!). Lake Isabel–St. Charles is a homey little campground in the aspens beside a gurgling creek. About 10 sites border the creek, and campers are less than a mile from picturesque Lake Isabel (40 acres). The sites here are good sized, with excellent separation.

Popularity

Of all the campgrounds in the area, Lake Isabel–St. Charles is the most popular. Campers, make your reservations now, as this place fills almost every night, seven days a week. The most popular reservable sites are all creekside, so try for sites 5, 7, 2, 3, or 10.

Facilities

Facilities include picnic tables, fire grates, firewood for sale, hand-pumped water, and a vault toilet.

RV Notes

Most sites are medium to long back-ins with two pull-thrus and one pull-out. A little leveling may be required. If you need an electrical hookup, camp just up the road at La Vista Campground (above the lake, but not nearly as pleasant).

Tent Notes

Good tent-pitching options await campers.

Recreational Opportunities

Anglers can warm up by catching a few brookies in St. Charles River, and finish off by landing the big one (rainbow or cutthroat) at Lake Isabel. After that, why not rent a paddleboat or "yacht" (rowboat), and admire the lovely mountain views. Or bring your own watercraft, as long as it's motorless. The 10.4-mile multi-use Cisneros Trail is near the campground and links to several other trails. Great little swimming holes are just up the trail.

Other Nearby Campgrounds

9. Lake Isabel–South Side (8 sites); 40 miles southwest of Pueblo. Take I-25 south for 21 miles, and then go right (west) on Highway 165 for 19 miles. Popular with anglers because it offers the best lake access, this is really just a parking lot with RV pull-thru sites side by side, very little separation, no privacy, no shade, and no views. Maximum RV length is 40 feet. Reservations accepted. **(719) 269-8500.**

10. Lake Isabel–La Vista (29 sites); 40 miles southwest of Pueblo. Take I-25 south for 21 miles, and then go right (west) on Highway 165 for 19 miles. La Vista is set above the lake, and is about a five- to 10-minute walk from it. Unfortunately, the lake views are somewhat obscured. The campground features 19 extremely popular RV/tent sites with electrical hookups and little shade. Ten additional walk-in tent sites offer shade. Maximum RV length is 50 feet. Reservations accepted. **(719) 269-8500.**

11. Davenport (12 sites); 44 miles southwest of Pueblo. Take I-25 south for 21 miles, and then go right (west) on Highway 165 for 25 miles to Forest Road 382. Turn right (east) on Forest Road 382, and go 1.5 miles. Davenport is a quiet little campground with walk-in tent sites and two sites for RVs. Most sites are close to Squirrel Creek. Shade is satisfactory. Maximum RV length is 25 feet. No water. No reservations. **(719) 269-8500.**

12. Ophir Creek (31 sites); 48 miles southwest of Pueblo. Take I-25 south for 21 miles, and then go right (west) on Highway 165 for 26.5 miles to Forest Road 400 (a.k.a. Forest Roads 360, 361), and go left (west) about 0.5 mile. Ophir Creek often fills on weekends, and has a mix of walk-in tent sites and back-in sites suitable for RVs. Twenty-three sites are on the creek. Some have sparse shade; others offer great shade. Maximum RV length is 40 feet. No reservations. **(719) 269-8500.**

Near the North Crestone Campground

LA VETA AREA

13. Blue Lake

Location: 18.5 miles southwest of La Veta
Elevation: 10,500 feet
Number of Sites: 15
Recommended RV Length: Up to 40 feet
Season: Memorial Day to Labor Day
Map: *Colorado Atlas & Gazetteer*, page 92, B1
Colorado Recreational Road Atlas, page 30, A3
Phone: 719-269-8500

Scenery: ★★★
RVs: ★★★★
Tents: ★★★
Shade: ★★★
Privacy: ★★★

Directions
From La Veta, go 14.5 miles south on Highway 12 (south of Cuchara about 3.5 miles). Turn right (west) on Forest Road 413 (also Forest Road 422), a good dirt road, and proceed for 4 miles.

Distinguishing Features
Blue Lake is a beautiful campground bisected by a stream. Many happy campers can be found relaxing beside the stream. Sites are generally large, with good separation and excellent shade.

Popularity
No reservations are taken, and this place is popular. Campers should arrive Thursday or early Friday to secure a weekend spot, especially in mid-summer. The Cuchara Music and Arts Festival in July and August impacts the campground, with sites filling up during this time.

Facilities
Facilities include picnic tables, fire grates, hand-pumped water, and vault toilets. One of the toilets is wheelchair-accessible.

RV Notes
Parking spurs have been modernized. As a result, you'll find long, level, back-in spaces that should accommodate most RVs.

Tent Notes
Hurry up and pitch the tent by the stream, and start enjoying yourself. It's high up here, so don't forget to bring something warm to wear at night, or snuggle up with a loved one.

Recreational Opportunities
Anglers can try their luck in the stream, or hike or drive to the brown and rainbow trout-stocked ponds: Blue Lake (3 acres) or Bear Lake (5 acres). The 15.5-mile Indian Trail, which starts at the edge of the campground, is a multi-use trail for hikers, mountain bikers, motorcyclists, and ATVers. The trail connects to the multipurpose Baker and Dodgeton Trails. Four-wheel-drive roads are here for the exploring as well.

Other Nearby Campgrounds

14. Bear Lake (14 sites); 19.5 miles southwest of La Veta. Take Highway 12 south from La Veta for 14.5 miles to Forest Road 413 (also Forest Road 422). Turn right (west), and go 5 miles. This is a popular campground near pretty little Bear Lake. No sites are on the lake, but a few are creekside. Half the sites are in an open meadow without shade, and the other half have fair to good shade. Maximum RV length is 40 feet. No reservations. **(719) 269-8500.**

15. Purgatoire (23 sites); 29 miles southwest of La Veta. Go south on Highway 12 for 24 miles, and turn right (west) on County Road 34.5 (North Fork Road) which becomes Forest Road 411. Follow the road for 4.5 miles. Purgatoire is a primitive, overgrown, lightly used campground up a rough dirt road. Surrounded by aspens and impressive views, it's a great choice in the fall. Three-quarters of the sites are in an open, wildflower-filled meadow, and the rest have decent shade. Reservations accepted. **(719) 269-8500.**

16. Monument Lake (150 sites); about 26 miles south of La Veta on Highway 12. A cross between a commercial and a public campground, it has all the amenities and activities a tent or RV camper could ask for. With a magnificent mountain background and a lovely 100-acre lake, it's no surprise that this is a popular camping destination. The lake is stocked with rainbow trout and kokanee salmon. Campers will find a variety of sites. For RVs (45 sites) there are designated campsites with partial and full hookups away from the lake. Shade and privacy range from poor to good. A dump station is on the premises. RVers should make reservations if arriving on the weekends. The most requested sites are 19, 18, and 12. There are designated lakeside camping areas for tents at the northwest and southwest corners of Monument Lake. There are also sites by a stream up in the woods and also in the RV-oriented camping sites. If you want to skip camping altogether, the resort offers lodge rooms, kitchenettes, or cabins. A restaurant, lounge, laundromat, bath house, boat rentals, and other amenities are also available. Open April through September. **(719) 868-2226** or **www.monumentlake.com.**

Blue Lake Campground

PUEBLO AREA

17. Lake Pueblo State Park (401 sites; see map on p. 294); 14 miles west of Pueblo. Go west 2.5 miles on Highway 50, turn left (south) on Highway 45, and go 4 miles to Highway 96 (Thatcher Avenue). Turn right (west), go 3.5 miles to the reservoir turnoff, and go right (west). Follow the road around the reservoir for about 4.25 miles. Pueblo Reservoir sees more than 1.5 million visitors a year. The reservoir covers 4,646 acres, is 11 miles long, and has 60 miles of shoreline. Five campgrounds are near the lake; in general, shade is sparse, privacy is poor, and sites are on the open prairie. Only a few are very close to the lake, but many have good views of it. Boats cannot be docked on shore overnight. **Arkansas Point,** the very popular **Prairie Ridge,** and **Yucca Flats** offer flush toilets, showers, laundry facilities, electrical hookups, and dump stations. **Juniper Breaks** and **Kettle Creek** are primitive and have vault toilets and drinking water. Most sites will accommodate RVs of up to 30 feet, but some pull-thrus will accept RVs over 40 feet. Reservations are accepted. **(719) 561-9320.**

18. Lathrop State Park (100 sites); 3 miles west of Walsenburg on Highway 160. The attractions at this park are Martin Lake (206 acres) and Horseshoe Lake (176 acres). Two campgrounds are in a setting of high grasslands away from the lakes. Piñons, junipers, and yucca provide little shade for campers. **Yucca Campground** (21 sites) is very primitive, but offers spacious sites. **Piñon** (79 sites) is very modern, with paved pull-thrus, electrical hookups, a dump station, tent pads, flush toilets, showers, laundry facilities, a playground, and an amphitheater. Maximum RV length is 45 feet. Reservations accepted. **(719) 738-2376.**

19. Trinidad State Park (62 sites); 3 miles west of Trinidad on Highway 12. Trinidad Lake (800 acres) offers fun for water enthusiasts, although swimming is prohibited. The campground sits above the lake and has two loops. Piñons and junipers provide limited shade. Hookups and a dump station are available for RVs. Modern facilities include flush toilets, laundry facilities, and showers. Maximum RV length is 40 feet. Reservations accepted. **(719) 846-6951.**

SOUTHEASTERN PLAINS AREA

20. John Martin Reservoir State Park (213 sites. Map coordinates: *Colorado Atlas & Gazetteer,* page 99, D5.5. *Colorado Recreational Road Atlas,* page 32, A1); 20 miles east of Las Animas. Take Highway 50 east 15.5 miles from Las Animas. Turn right (south) at Hasty on County Road 24, and go for 2 miles. This large Eastern Plains reservoir varies in size between 3,000 to 10,000 acres, with about 65 miles of shoreline. It is a great destination for lovers of water sports and warm-water fishing. Two developed campgrounds exist within the park. **Lake Hasty Campground** (109 sites) lies below John Martin Dam, adjacent to small Lake Hasty (75 acres). Pleasant camping abounds under a canopy of mature deciduous trees (although about 30 sites have no natural shade) in a grassy, parklike setting. Recently renovated, sites have been enlarged and will handle any RV (20 are pull-thrus), and all sites have electrical hookups (but not water). Tenters will find tent pads at most sites and must use them when available. Amenities include sheltered picnic tables at some sites, flush toilets, water faucets, pay showers, laundry facilities, a playground, and a dump station. **The Point** (104 sites) is a new, primitive campground on a ridge that overlooks John Martin Reservoir. Set in a dry, natural grassland there are no trees to provide shade. Sites are large and will accommodate any RV (59 pull-thrus), and tenters will find tent pads at all sites. There are vault toilets but no drinking water. Dispersed and free camping can be found within John Martin State Wildlife Area. Reservations accepted. **(719) 829-1801**.

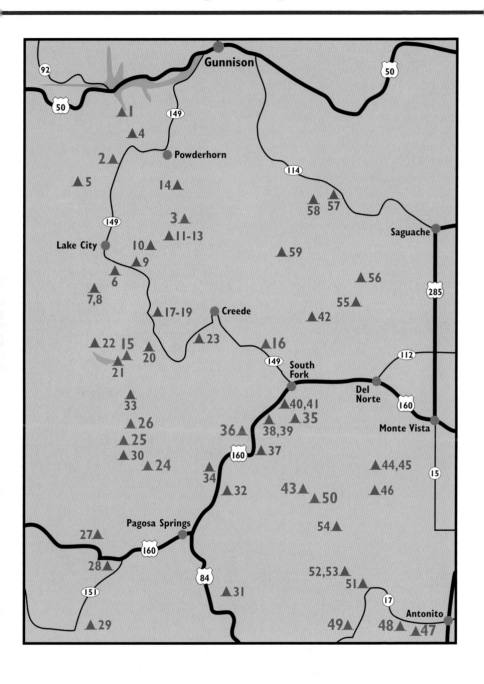

Most destinations in this area are quite remote and require an effort to discover them. Lake City is on the northeastern boundary of one of the top jeeping areas in the country. The most exciting recreational pursuits are centered around this vast network of jeep roads. Engineer Pass and Cinnamon Pass form the famous Alpine Loop—offering sweeping mountain vistas and well-preserved ghost towns. Anglers will discover Colorado's second largest natural lake, San Cristobal, only a few miles south of Lake City. The Powderhorn Primitive Area and La Garita Wilderness Area east of Lake City offer challenging trails for hikers, backpackers, and horseback riders.

In the Creede area, the Rio Grande Reservoir and Rio Grande River draw anglers, boaters, and whitewater rafting enthusiasts. Anglers and other water-lovers also frequent the Big Meadows and Beaver Creek Reservoirs southwest of South Fork.

Pagosa Springs is home to the world's largest and hottest spring. The town's name derives from the Ute word "Pagosah" or "Healing Waters." Visitors from all over the world soak in these therapeutic waters after a day of too much fun. Northwest of Pagosa Springs, several popular campgrounds are located in a stunningly beautiful area near the Williams Creek Reservoir and the magnificent hiking opportunities that await in the Weminuche Wilderness. Southwest is Navajo Reservoir, often considered a mini-Lake Powell, with miles of boating and angling possibilities.

Fishing the Conejos River and the lakes northwest of Antonito is a favorite pastime of visitors to this area. Forest Road 250 is a marvelous loop that journeys past several lovely campgrounds, Platoro Reservoir, and Stunner Pass. The scenery along this drive is a treat for the eyes. The Cumbres & Toltec Scenic Railroad offers train and scenery buffs a wonderful 64-mile narrow-gauge train ride from Antonito to Chama, New Mexico.

▲100 BEST   ▲ All The Rest

▲1 Gateview	▲4 Red Bridge	▲27 Lower Piedra	▲52 Spectacle Lake
▲2 The Gate	▲5 Big Blue	▲28 Ute	▲53 Conejos
▲3 Mason Family State Wildlife Area	▲6 Wupperman	▲29 Navajo State Park	▲54 Lake Fork
▲15 River Hill	▲7 Williams Creek	▲30 Williams Creek	▲55 Poso
▲16 Palisade	▲8 Mill Creek	▲31 Blanco River	▲56 Storm King
▲24 Bridge	▲9 Slumgullion	▲32 East Fork	▲57 Buffalo Pass
▲25 Teal	▲10 Deer Lakes	▲33 Palisades Horse	▲58 Luders Creek
▲26 Cimarrona	▲11 Hidden Valley	▲34 West Fork	▲59 Stone Cellar
▲35 Cross Creek	▲12 Spruce	▲37 Tucker Ponds	
▲36 Big Meadows	▲13 Cebolla	▲38 Park Creek	
▲43 Stunner	▲14 Cebolla Creek	▲39 Highway Springs	
▲47 Mogote	▲17 North Clear Creek	▲40 Lower Beaver Creek	
▲48 Aspen Glade	▲18 Silver Thread	▲41 Upper Beaver Creek	
▲49 Trujillo Meadows	▲19 Bristol Head	▲42 Cathedral	
▲50 Mix Lake	▲20 Road Canyon	▲44 Rock Creek	
	▲21 Thirty Mile	▲45 Comstock	
	▲22 Lost Trail	▲46 Alamosa	
	▲23 Marshall Park	▲51 Elk Creek	

LAKE CITY AREA

1. Gateview

Location: 27 miles north of Lake City
Elevation: 7,500 feet
Number of Sites: 7
Recommended RV Length: Up to 25 feet
Season: May through November
Maps: *Colorado Atlas & Gazetteer*, page 67, A7
Colorado Recreational Road Atlas, page 27, B3
Phone: 970-641-2337

Scenery: ★★★★★
RVs: ★
Tents: ★★★
Shade: ★
Privacy: ★★★★

Directions

From Lake City, go about 20 miles north on Highway 149 to County Road 25 and turn left (north). After about 2.5 miles, County Road 25 will veer off sharply to the left. Keep going straight ahead (north) for 4.5 miles on what is now County Road 64.

Distinguishing Features

The drive to Gateview Campground is one of the most spectacular canyon stretches in Colorado. No fee is required for Gateview Campground, and remember: some of the best things in life are free! Seven sites are located in a deep, narrow, rocky canyon. Gateview is for true canyon connoisseurs. Campers can close their eyes for a moment, and try to imagine the sound of a narrow-gauge train rattling and hissing as it passed through this canyon from 1889 to 1933.

I found five walk-in tent sites scattered along a rocky hillside, all spaced fairly closely together. Shade provided by spruce and fir trees ranges from poor to fair, but the views are magnificent. A sixth spot—the best in the campground—is on the river and has good shade. The mythical seventh spot eluded me.

Popularity

Gateview is so isolated that it reportedly never fills. Campers needn't call for reservations.

Facilities

Despite Gateview's isolation, you'll find picnic tables, fire grates, a water faucet, and vault toilets equipped for wheelchair access.

RV Notes

One back-in spot on the river accommodates a medium-sized RV up to 25 feet, but that's it. No dispersed camping is allowed along the last 4 miles of the road within park boundaries.

Tent Notes

The views will drive shutterbugs crazy! Though most sites are spaced closely together, this camp receives such little usage that the chance for privacy is excellent.

Recreational Opportunities

Anglers can try their luck at catching brown and rainbow trout in the Gunnison River. The last 5 miles, ending near the campground, is considered a difficult Class IV to V rafting and kayaking thriller; the river is at its best from mid-May to mid-July. A 0.75-mile walk along the river leads farther into the canyon, but Blue Mesa Reservoir isn't accessible from here.

2. The Gate

Location: 16.5 miles north of Lake City
Elevation: 8,400 feet
Number of Sites: 8
Recommended RV Length: Up to 21 feet
Season: Early May through October
Maps: *Colorado Atlas & Gazetteer*, page 67, C7
Colorado Recreational Road Atlas, page 22, B4
Phone: 970-641-0471

Scenery: ★★★★
RVs: ★★★
Tents: ★★★
Shade: ★★★
Privacy: ★★

Directions
From Lake City, go 16.5 miles north on Highway 149. Between mile markers 88 and 89, look for a dramatic narrowing of the canyon; just before the cliffs, look for a sign on the left that says "The Gate, Recreation Area." Turn left.

Distinguishing Features
"The Gate" is an opening in the cliffs caused by erosion from the Lake Fork of the Gunnison River, and what a beautiful place it is. Situated just down off the highway, six of the eight sites are on the river. The other two are only a few feet away. On either side of the river, awe-inspiring rock formations run along the tops of the hillsides. Sites are fairly spacious, and most have a nice mix of sun and shade. Trees are mainly spruce.

Popularity

From July 4 through mid-August, this campground fills around 60 percent of the time. Campers can usually find a spot. No reservations.

Facilities

Facilities include picnic tables, fire grates, and wheelchair-accessible vault toilets; there is no drinking water.

RV Notes

Good medium to long back-ins are available. Sites are fairly level. The campground is a little tight to maneuver large rigs. The nearest dump station is at Wupperman Campground, about 4 miles south of Lake City along Lake San Cristobal.

Tent Notes

All spots are great for tents.

Recreational Opportunities

Fishing in the river for rainbow and possibly brown trout is a few yards away. Anglers take note: artificial flies and lures only. Rainbows are catch-and-release only, but you can keep two browns over 16 inches. This is also a rafting and kayaking put-in for a 5-mile Class II run to Red Bridge Campground. Beyond Red Bridge is a difficult 5-mile Class III to V stretch of water to Gateview Campground.

Independence Trailhead to the south goes almost all the way to Lake City along Highway 149. The trail leads west into the Big Blue Wilderness, sometimes following Independence Creek. Lake City is the northeastern portal to the most fabulous four-wheeling and OHVing in the country.

---

3. Mason Family State Wildlife Area

Location: 24 miles northeast of Lake City
Elevation: 9,200 feet
Number of Sites: Undesignated
Recommended RV Length: Up to 35 feet
Season: Year-round
Maps: *Colorado Atlas & Gazetteer*, page 68, D1
Colorado Recreational Road Atlas, page 28, B1
Phone: 970-641-7060

Scenery: ★★★★
RVs: ★★★
Tents: ★★★
Shade: ★★★
Privacy: ★★★★★

Directions

From Lake City, take Highway 149 south 9 miles to Forest Road 788 (a.k.a. County Road 5 or Los Pinos-Cebolla Road), and turn left (north). Continue for 15 miles to the state wildlife area, just north of Cathedral.

Distinguishing Features

This place is easy to get to, yet far from civilization. The campground (used loosely) stretches for 0.6 mile off the main road along Cebolla Creek. Some areas are simply grassy meadows. Driving through here, you're surrounded by beautiful, mature trees in a very flat area, with many spots on the creek that make dynamite campsites. On the other side of the creek, fascinating rock formations and sharp, jagged pinnacles jut out of steep hills. Nobody is around and the only sounds are the creek and the chirping birds. This is one of those truly peaceful camping experiences that gives you a taste of what camping was like long ago.

Popularity

No reservations are needed. This campground is very remote, and crowding should never be a problem.

Facilities

Port-a-potties are available, but no potable water or trash service.

RV Notes

Very level, flat areas should accommodate most RVs.

Tent Notes

Campsites couldn't get much better than this! This is as close to a backcountry experience as you can have while keeping the luxury of your vehicle—along with all the stuff it can carry—only a few feet away.

Recreational Opportunities

Relax by the stream and enjoy the trout fishing. For ambitious hikers or equestrians, several trailheads are only a few miles to the southwest. The Powderhorn Park Trail leads west into the Powderhorn Primitive Area and branches off in many directions. Less than a mile south of this trailhead lies the Mineral Creek Trailhead, where you'll find bathrooms, picnic tables, and drinking water. The trail goes south into the La Garita Wilderness and for several miles follows Mineral Creek, connecting to countless other trails. Many trails also lead out from Forest Road 788.

photo by Gil Folsom

Other Nearby Campgrounds

4. Red Bridge (5 sites); 22.5 miles north of Lake City. Take Highway 149 north for 20 miles, and turn left (north) on County Road 25. Go 2.5 miles. This pretty little campground is best suited for tents and small RVs. Well-shaded sites are close to the river and tightly spaced. No drinking water is provided. No reservations. **(970) 641-0471.**

5. Big Blue (11 sites); 21 miles northwest of Lake City. Take Highway 149 north for 11 miles, and turn left (west) on Forest Road 868 (Alpine Road). The steep, rough, narrow, 10-mile dirt road leading to Big Blue—one of the most remote campgrounds in Colorado—is not recommended for RVs. Big Blue is next to the Big Blue Wilderness, offering plenty of seclusion in a nice but unremarkable setting. No water. No reservations. **(970) 641-0471.**

6. Wupperman (32 sites); 4 miles south of Lake City. Take Highway 149 south for 2.25 miles, and turn right (south) onto County Road 30. Proceed for 1 mile, and turn left (southeast) onto County Road 7. Go 0.5 mile. An interesting campground, Wupperman is made up of several loops spaced far apart from each other. Many of the sites perch high on the steep banks of stunning Lake San Cristobal (346 acres). Sites vary considerably, but most can accommodate medium-sized RVs and offer little shade or privacy. A dump station is available. No reservations. **(970) 944-2225.**

7. Williams Creek (24 sites); 9 miles southwest of Lake City. Go south on Highway 149 for 2.25 miles, and turn right (south) onto County Road 30. Go 6.5 miles. This mix of open and shaded sites near Williams Creek is a good base camp from which to explore some of the most breathtaking four-wheel-drive roads (many open to OHVs) in the country. Most sites can accommodate medium-sized RVs. No reservations. **(970) 641-0471.**

8. Mill Creek (22 sites); 13 miles southwest of Lake City. Take Highway 149 south for 2.25 miles, and turn right (south) onto County Road 30. Go 10.5 miles. Set above a river, a steep access trail leads campers down to the water. The mix of open and shaded sites works best for smaller RVs. Many sites offer views of the surrounding mountains. No reservations. **(970) 641-0471.**

9. Slumgullion (22 sites); 9.1 miles southeast of Lake City. Take Highway 149 south about 9 miles, and turn left (north) on Forest Road 788. The second highest campground in Colorado, Slumgullion is heavily forested and consists of two paved but tight loops on either side of the road. Some sites are RV-friendly and can accommodate smaller RVs, but none offer scenic views. No reservations. **(970) 641-0471.**

10. Deer Lakes (12 sites); 13 miles east of Lake City. Take Highway 149 south 9 miles to Forest Road 788. Turn left (north), and go 3.5 miles. This renovated, RV-friendly campground with four small, stocked lakes attracts many families. Most sites are well shaded, but none adjoin the lakes or offer views of them. Maximum RV length is 30 feet. No reservations. **(970) 641-0471.**

11. Hidden Valley (4 sites); 16 miles east of Lake City. Take Highway 149 south 9 miles to Forest Road 788. Turn left (north), and go 7 miles. This lovely little tent-only campground consists of three lightly shaded sites on a creek. No reservations. **(970) 641-0471.**

12. Spruce (9 sites); 17 miles east of Lake City. Take Highway 149 south 9 miles to Forest Road 788. Turn left (north), and go 8 miles. All sites are in a single row near Cebolla Creek, but thick underbrush prevents easy creek access from most. Half the sites are open and sunny, while the rest are more secluded and shady. This isn't the best place for RVs, but several spots work for short to medium-sized rigs. No reservations. **(970) 641-0471.**

13. Cebolla (4 sites); 18.25 miles east of Lake City. Take Highway 149 south 9 miles to Forest Road 788. Turn left (north), and go 9.25 miles. These five wonderful, well-shaded, tent-oriented creekside sites are set in a picturesque corner of a small canyon. Cebolla is not a good choice for RVs, as they'd be stuck side by side in a central parking area. No reservations. **(970) 641-0471.**

14. Cebolla Creek (3 sites); 35 miles northeast of Lake City. Go 26.5 miles north on Highway 149 to County Road 29. Turn right (southeast), and proceed for 1.75 miles to County Road 27 in Powderhorn. Turn right (south) on County Road 27, and go 6.5 miles. This tiny little roadside campground has three delightful, shaded, creekside spots suitable for most RVs. No reservations. **(970) 641-0471.**

CREEDE AREA

15. River Hill

Location: 31 miles southwest of Creede
Elevation: 9,200 feet
Number of Sites: 23
Recommended RV Length: Up to 32 feet
Season: Memorial Day through September
Maps: *Colorado Atlas & Gazetteer*, page 77, C7
Colorado Recreational Road Atlas, page 28, B2
Phone: 719-658-2556

Scenery: ★★★
RVs: ★★★
Tents: ★★★
Shade: ★★★
Privacy: ★★

Directions
From Creede, go southwest on Highway 149 for about 21 miles, then turn left (west) on gravel Forest Road 520 (Rio Grande Reservoir Road). Go 10.5 miles.

Distinguishing Features

River Hill's attraction is the Rio Grande River—a fast-moving, honest-to-God river. Parents, be careful not to let small children out of sight. Nestled at the bottom of a canyon between hills rising 1,500 feet, River Hill is a long campground running alongside the river. The six riverside sites are exceptional, and the campground is designed to take advantage of its riverfront property. Nobody is ever far from the water. Large, spacious sites with good spacing are the rule. Pine, fir, and spruce trees provide fair shade. River Hill is very secluded and private, and often there are beavers in the river and moose in the area.

Popularity

This is a busy campground from July 4 through mid-August, but it typically only fills during the first two weeks of July. The popular riverside spots—sites 6-12—do disappear quickly, so plan accordingly. No reservations.

Facilities

Facilities include picnic tables, fire grates, firewood for sale, hand-pumped water, vault toilets (with lights and exhaust fans), dishwater disposal, and anglers' parking.

RV Notes

Fairly level medium to long back-ins and pull-thrus make life easy. The campground has a total of three double sites. Riverside site 11 (a double) is a super-long pull-thru with a double table. The nearest dump station is just south of Creede on the first large curve on Highway 149 as you leave town.

Tent Notes

Try for one of the river sites, and a happy camper you'll be!

Recreational Opportunities

Anglers, you'll have too many cookies in the cookie jar to choose from! Fish on the river from the campground, or try 5-mile-long Rio Grande Reservoir, Road Canyon Reservoir (1.25 miles long), or Squaw Creek. Depending on your choice, you can catch brook, brown, cutthroat, or rainbow trout.

The campground serves as a put-in for rafters and kayakers for a Class III to IV 5-mile run. Hikers and equestrians can access the Weminuche and Squaw Creek Trails near Thirty Mile Campground 1.5 miles west. Mountain bikers can ride a loop trip via Forest Road 533 (Sawmill Canyon Road). Forest Road 520 (Stony Pass Road), a moderate 60-mile four-wheel-drive road, continues west of Rio Grande Reservoir, eventually ending up in Silverton. It's suitable for all off-road enthusiasts (including gonzo mountain bikers). The campground sponsors programs on Friday evenings.

16. Palisade

Location: 12 miles southeast of Creede
Elevation: 8,300 feet
Number of Sites: 12
Recommended RV Length: Up to 32 feet
Season: Year-round
Maps: *Colorado Atlas & Gazetteer,* page 78, B3.5
Colorado Recreational Road Atlas, page 28, C2
Phone: 719-658-2556

Scenery: ★★★★
RVs: ★★★
Tents: ★★★
Shade: ★★
Privacy: ★★

Directions
From Creede, go southeast on Highway 149 for 12.1 miles. Alternately, from South Fork, go 9 miles northwest on Highway 149.

Distinguishing Features
Palisade is conveniently located just off Highway 149 (Silver Thread Scenic Byway). In a lovely valley near the spectacular Wheeler Geologic Area and beside the Rio Grande River, with the jagged Palisade Rock Formation jutting out of the forested hillsides, this is one beautiful campground. Abandoned railroad tracks cut through a meadow in the center of the campground, adding to the charm. The six riverside sites are great. Most spots are medium to large sites with good separation. Some are in the open, while others are

shaded by a combination of cottonwood, aspen, spruce, and fir trees. Noise from the highway can sometimes be a bit much—just tune it out and focus on the sound of the river.

Popularity
Heavily used by overnighters and retired campers, this campground fills frequently from July 4 through August. Showing up early in the day should ensure campers of a spot. No reservations.

Facilities
Facilities include picnic tables, fire grates, firewood for sale, hand-pumped water, a lighted vault toilet, and parking for anglers and rafters.

RV Notes
Fairly level medium to long back-ins and pull-thrus (three) make this a good place for RVs. The nearest dump station is just southwest of Creede on the first large curve on Highway 149 as you leave town, or at the Rainbow Grocery in South Fork.

Tent Notes
Campers will find that any spot is great.

Recreational Opportunities
The portion of the Rio Grande River that flows through this campground is Gold Medal water, and only artificial flies and lures are permitted. Trout fishing is popular, but watch out for watercraft. This is a take-out spot for some rafters.

The Wheeler Geologic Area was once a national monument, but that status was rescinded during the Great Depression due to the area's inaccessibility to vehicles. Many visitors report that the area reminds them of the rock formations in Bryce Canyon, Utah. An easy 7-mile trail leads to these unusual formations. To get there, go about 5 miles northwest on Highway 149 toward Creede, and turn right (east) on Forest Road 600 (Pool Table Road). Continue for about 10 miles to a sign marking the old Hanson Mill site. Park here and enjoy the hike!

Other Nearby Campgrounds

17. North Clear Creek (27 sites); 26 miles west of Creede. Take Highway 149 for 23 miles to Forest Road 510. Turn right (northeast), and go about 2.5 miles. Located in a fairly open mountain meadow with some shade (mainly aspens), this campground offers good views of the surrounding mountains, but not much privacy. Sites are fairly level, and work fine for tents and medium-sized RVs. Two sites are on the creek. No reservations. **(719) 658-2556.**

18. Silver Thread (13 sites); 25 miles west of Creede on Highway 149. This never-busy campground is open and grassy, with a few trees. Campers have little privacy and are subject to heavy highway noise. Maximum RV length is 30 feet. No reservations. **(719) 658-2556.**

19. Bristol Head (16 sites); 23 miles west of Creede. Take Highway 149 about 23 miles, and turn right (northeast) on Forest Road 510. Bristol Head offers every camper a magnificent 180-degree view of Bristol Hill Mountain and the surrounding mountains. Sites are lined up single-file against the back of a large meadow. Shade ranges from poor to fair, and 13 pull-thrus accommodate medium-sized RVs. No reservations. **(719) 658-2556.**

20. Road Canyon (5 sites); 27 miles southwest of Creede. Take Highway 149 for 21 miles, and turn left (west) on Forest Road 520. Go 6 miles. Just 0.25 mile from the southern end of Road Canyon Reservoir in an open meadow without trees, this campground offers good views of the reservoir and mountains from every site. Generally large parking spaces work fine for most RVs. No drinking water is provided. No reservations. **(719) 658-2556.**

21. Thirty Mile (39 sites); 33 miles southwest of Creede. Take Highway 149 for 21 miles, and turn left (west) on Forest Road 520. Go about 12 miles. This very popular and excellent campground fills often. Campers will find spacious, shaded sites with excellent spacing and lots of privacy. Set at the confluence of the Rio Grande and Squaw Creek, four sites are on the river and seven are on the creek. Maximum RV length is 32 feet. Reservations accepted. **(719) 658-2556.**

22. Lost Trail (16 sites); 38.2 miles southwest of Creede. Take Highway 149 for 21 miles, and turn left (west) on Forest Road 520 (gravel road with some rough spots). Go about 18 miles. Set in an open meadow with sparse shade and little screening from fellow campers, Lost Trail offers wonderful mountain views. Sites work best for tents and small RVs. Lost Trail Creek runs near the campground. No reservations. **(719) 658-2556.**

23. Marshall Park (18 sites); 6.5 miles southwest of Creede on Highway 149. Just off the main highway and by the Rio Grande River, this campground is in an open meadow with no shade and little privacy. The campground road is paved, 10 sites are on the river, and this busy spot is especially popular with RVers. Maximum RV length is 32 feet. Reservations accepted. **(719) 658-2556.**

PAGOSA SPRINGS AREA

24. Bridge
Location: 21 miles northwest of Pagosa Springs
Elevation: 7,900 feet
Number of Sites: 19
Recommended RV Length: Up to 50 feet
Season: Memorial Day through October
Maps: *Colorado Atlas & Gazetteer,* page 87, A7
Colorado Recreational Road Atlas, page 28, B3
Phone: 970-264-2268

Scenery: ★★★★
RVs: ★★★★
Tents: ★★★
Shade: ★
Privacy: ★★★

Directions
From Pagosa Springs, go 2.5 miles west on Highway 160. Turn right (northwest) onto County Road 600 (Piedra Road), and go about 19 miles north (after 6 miles, the pavement ends and County Road 600 becomes gravel Forest Road 631).

Distinguishing Features

Campsites are nestled on Williams Creek, with pretty views of low bluffs across the creek. And would you believe all 19 sites are on the river? Sites are large and spacious, with excellent separation for campers who enjoy a degree of privacy. Bridge is split into two campgrounds, with a long road connecting them. To the west and away from the creek is a large, grassy meadow, with beautiful fields of iris and larkspur, and to the north are impressive views of the high peaks of the San Juans. Cottonwoods shade a few sites.

Popularity

Campers, this is your lucky day! This campground rarely fills. In fact, the Forest Service has extended the normal 14-day stay limit to 30 days to help promote it. No reservations required.

Facilities

Facilities include many picnic tables, fire grates, hand-pumped water, and vault toilets.

RV Notes

A mix of fairly level, long back-ins and pull-thrus awaits RV campers. The nearest dump station is near Williams Creek Reservoir and Teal Campground to the north.

Tent Notes

Bridge offers great tent-pitching options. Excellent spacing between sites equates to privacy, even with the lack of trees. Showers, firewood, and a convenience store are all nearby at Sportsman's Supply, a couple of miles back up the road.

Recreational Opportunities

Anglers can catch brown and rainbow trout in the creek, or drive up to Williams Creek Reservoir to snag some kokanee salmon. The most popular trail in the area is the Ice Cave Ridge Trail, which leads to a beautiful overlook of the confluence of the Weminuche and Piedra Rivers. Hikers are urged to be cautious where ice collects around the area's deep crevasses! To find the trail, go about 4 miles back up the main road toward Pagosa Springs to the Piedra River Trailhead. Instead of taking the Piedra River Trail, head west on an old road for about 1.5 miles.

Piedra Falls is roughly 12 miles away via Forest Roads 636 and 637. Take the mountain bike instead of the car, and experience a pleasant ride. Hikers can access the Middle Fork Trail about 7 miles away via Forest Road 636. Windows (6 miles) and Monument Lakes (8 miles) are up this trail.

25. Teal

Location: About 27 miles northwest of Pagosa Springs
Elevation: 8,300 feet
Number of Sites: 16
Recommended RV Length: Up to 35 feet
Season: Memorial Day through October
Maps: *Colorado Atlas & Gazetteer,* page 77, D7
Colorado Recreational Road Atlas, page 28, B3
Phone: 970-264-2268

Scenery: ★★★★★
RVs: ★★★
Tents: ★★★
Shade: ★★
Privacy: ★★

Directions

From Pagosa Springs, go 2.5 miles west on Highway 160, then turn right onto County Road 600 (Piedra Road). After about 6 miles, the pavement ends and the road becomes Forest Road 631. Continue about 16 miles farther to Forest Road 640. Turn right, and go about 1.75 miles.

Distinguishing Features

This locale—one of the most spectacular campground views in all of Colorado—will most certainly take your breath away! Don't forget the camera and film, because photo opportunities abound. The razor-edged San Juans, with their vertical faces towering beyond Williams Creek Reservoir, provide a beautiful setting. Just above the reservoir in a grassy meadow, Teal consists of two fairly open loops with most sites offering excellent lake and mountain views. Scattered ponderosa pines and a few small aspens provide fair shade for some sites. In one of the loops, about seven sites have unobstructed lake views.

Popularity

Get there early to grab a good spot at everyone's favorite campground near Pagosa Springs. Teal fills to 80 or 90 percent capacity every day of the summer. This is a destination campground, where people come but never want to leave! No reservations.

Facilities

Facilities include picnic tables, fire grates, firewood for sale, hand-pumped water, and vault toilets.

RV Notes

Several sites accommodate large RVs, and most are fairly level. The nearest dump station is on the west side of the road near the campground.

Tent Notes

Plenty of perfect tent-pitching options await tenters. Hot showers are available at Indian Head Lodge just south of the campground.

Recreational Opportunities

The only boating restrictions are that waterskiing and sailboats are prohibited on Williams Creek Reservoir (343 acres). A boat ramp is adjacent to the north end of the campground. Brook and rainbow trout (stocked), and kokanee salmon are the predominant fish in the lake. Three major trailheads within a few miles of the campground (see Cimarrona) lead into the Weminuche Wilderness.

---

26. Cimarrona

Location: 29 miles northwest of Pagosa Springs
Elevation: 8,400 feet
Number of Sites: 21
Recommended RV Length: Up to 35 feet
Season: Memorial Day to mid-September
Maps: *Colorado Atlas & Gazetteer*, page 77, D7
Colorado Recreational Road Atlas, page 28, B3
Phone: 970-264-2268

Scenery: ★★★★
RVs: ★★
Tents: ★★★
Shade: ★★
Privacy: ★★★

Directions

From Pagosa Springs, go 2.5 miles west on Highway 160. Turn right on County Road 600 (Piedra Road). Go about 6 miles north (the pavement ends and the road becomes Forest Road 631). Continue for 16 more miles, turn right (north) on Forest Road 640, and go about 4 miles.

Distinguishing Features

Cimarrona is near the end of Forest Road 640 on the edge of the Weminuche

Wilderness. The ambiance is that of a remote backcountry setting. Campers will find solitude, great hiking, and fantastic vistas of mountain backdrops. On Cimarrona Creek, the views of the meadow and the reservoir to the south are beautiful. Sites are in one loop, and are generally medium-sized with good separation allowing privacy. Some sites are open, sunny, and surrounded by aspens, while others are nestled in the shade of spruce and fir trees. Horses are not allowed in the campground.

Popularity
No reservations are taken, but this campground rarely fills.

Facilities
Facilities include picnic tables, fire grates, firewood for sale, hand-pumped water, and vault toilets.

RV Notes

Large RVs can fit in a few of the sites, and many require some leveling. The nearest dump station is at Teal Campground by Williams Creek Reservoir.

Tent Notes

Campers looking for a shower can head up to Indian Head Lodge just south of Williams Creek Reservoir.

Recreational Opportunities

Equestrians, hikers, and backpackers have three trailheads to choose from. Cimarrona Trail is just across the road and leads into the Weminuche Wilderness, connecting with other trails such as the Continental Divide Trail. A mile farther down the road is the Williams Creek trailhead, with a corral and pack animal ramp. This trail also leads into the wilderness, following the creek for 14 miles before crossing the Continental Divide. The Poison Park Trail is a few miles away and leads into the wilderness too, as well as to several alpine lakes.

Other Nearby Campgrounds

27. Lower Piedra (17 sites); 23 miles west of Pagosa Springs. Take Highway 160 for about 21 miles to Forest Road 621. Turn right (east) on Forest Road 621, and go 1.5 miles. This is an attractive campground with large, level, shady sites. It's adjacent to the river, with some riverside spots. No drinking water is available. Maximum RV length is 35 feet. No reservations. **(970) 264-2268.**

28. Ute (26 sites); about 18 miles west of Pagosa Springs on Highway 160. This rustic, lightly used campground simply offers solitude and some decent shade. Maximum RV length is 35 feet. No reservations. **(970) 264-2268.**

29. Navajo State Park (138 sites); 36 miles southwest of Pagosa Springs. Take Highway 160 southwest for 15.5 miles to Highway 151. Turn left (south) on Highway 151, and go about 20 miles to County Road 982. Turn left (east) onto County Road 982. Navajo Reservoir is 35 miles long and 80% of the lake lies in New Mexico. There are three developed campgrounds and two primitive ones. The three developed ones have flush toilets, laundromat, pay showers, and dump stations. **Tiffany** (1-35) is perched high above the lake and has mature shade trees. It is good for both tents and RVs. **Caracas** (sites 51-90) offers a combination of pull-thrus and back-ins with electrical hookups at all sites. There is little shade and no lake views. **Rosa** (sites 101-147) is open and sunny with a few shade shelters. Several sites have great views of the lake. Most sites have spacious pull-thrus and electrical hookups. Eight tent sites overlook the lake. **Arboles Point** (8 sites) and **Windsurfer Beach** (12 sites) are primitive campgrounds that have vault toilets and no drinking water. Reservations accepted. **(970) 883-2208.**

30. Williams Creek (67 sites); 25 miles northwest of Pagosa Springs. Take Highway 160 west 2.5 miles to County Road 600. Turn right (northwest) onto County Road 600 (after 6 miles it becomes Forest Road 631), and go 22 miles to Forest Road 640. Turn right (north) on Forest Road 640, and go 0.5 mile. This is the most popular campground in the Pagosa area, but it's so large it rarely fills. Sites vary tremendously, but privacy is normally good. Six sites are knockout riverside spots. Many sites are under such dense tree cover that campers receive little sun and experience a deep wilderness feeling. Large RVs can always find a good spot. No reservations. **(970) 264-2268.**

31. Blanco River (6 sites); 15.4 miles southeast of Pagosa Springs. Take Highway 160 east 1 mile to Highway 84, and turn right (south). Continue for 11 miles to Forest Road 656. Turn left (east), and go 2.25 miles. This primitive but pleasant campground has one small loop, with four sites on a river and two in a meadow. Shade is good, and four sites can handle large RVs. No reservations. **(970) 264-2268.**

32. East Fork (26 sites); 12 miles northeast of Pagosa Springs. Take Highway 160 northeast about 11 miles to Forest Road 667, and turn right (east). Just 1 mile off the main highway, this is a convenient place to camp for the night. Heavily wooded with pines and oaks, sites are best for tents and small RVs. A few sites can handle larger RVs. The highway is well within earshot. No reservations. **(970) 264-2268.**

33. Palisades Horse (12 sites); Brand-new campground only open to equestrians. Situated a few hundred yards from the creek at the end of Williams Creek Road, every site has a corral. Follow the directions for Cimarrona Campground (p. 234), but go 0.5 mile farther.

34. West Fork (28 sites); 17 miles northeast of Pagosa Springs. Take Highway 160 northeast about 14.75 miles to Forest Road 648. Turn left (north) on Forest Road 648, and go 2 miles. Not heavily used, this scenic campground offers a good mix of sun and shade. Several sites are on the river. It's RV-friendly, with seven large pull-thrus and large back-ins. Maximum RV length is 35 feet. No reservations. **(970) 264-2268.**

SOUTH FORK AREA

35. Cross Creek

Location: 8 miles south of South Fork
Elevation: 8,800 feet
Number of Sites: 12
Recommended RV Length: Up to 25 feet
Season: June through September
Maps: *Colorado Atlas & Gazetteer*, page 79, D4
Colorado Recreational Road Atlas, page 29, A2
Phone: 719-657-3321

Scenery: ★★★
RVs: ★
Tents: ★★★★
Shade: ★★
Privacy: ★

Directions
From South Fork, go about 1.5 miles southwest on Highway 160. Turn left (south) on Forest Road 360 (Beaver Creek Road), and go 6 miles (pavement ends after 4 miles).

Distinguishing Features
Cross Creek is a beautiful, tent-oriented campground in an ideal location for water lovers. Seven spots are on the creek, and a couple of these have great reservoir views. Beaver Creek Reservoir—a striking, almost 2-mile-long, narrow lake—is a few hundred yards across the road. Most sites are compact and somewhat close together, but the ambiance is such that you'll overlook this transgression. Sites receive both shade (from pine, spruce, and fir trees) and sunshine, giving campers the best of both worlds.

Popularity

No reservations are taken, and this campground often fills on weekends. Arrive on Thursday to secure a weekend spot.

Facilities

Facilities include many picnic tables, fire grates, firewood for sale, water faucets, and a well-maintained vault toilet.

RV Notes

Five short back-in sites accommodate pop-up campers and smaller RVs.

Tent Notes

This is a wonderful tenting campground, and you won't see too many RVs. Five sites are walk-in tent sites.

Recreational Opportunities

Beaver Creek Reservoir tempts anglers with kokanee salmon, rainbow trout, and brown trout. A boat ramp is near the campground, and wakeless boating is permitted. The largest Douglas fir in the Rio Grande Forest—110 feet tall and 66 feet in diameter—is at the end of a short trail that leaves the road 0.25 mile south of the campground. Hikers can also access Cross Creek Trail from the campground. The trail runs alongside Cross Creek for 3 miles, eventually connecting with several other trails.

---

36. Big Meadows

Location: 13 miles southwest of South Fork
Elevation: 9,200 feet
Number of Sites: 60
Recommended RV Length: Up to 35 feet
Season: Memorial Day to Labor Day
Maps: *Colorado Atlas & Gazetteer*, page 78, D3
Colorado Recreational Road Atlas, page 28, C3
Phone: 719-657-3321

Scenery: ★★★★
RVs: ★★★★
Tents: ★★★
Shade: ★★★★
Privacy: ★★★★

Directions

From South Fork, go southwest on Highway 160 for about 11 miles. Turn right (southwest) on Forest Road 410 (a well-graded gravel road), and proceed for 1.75 miles.

Distinguishing Features

With forested hills rising 2,000 feet in the background, this campground lies adjacent to scenic Big Meadows Reservoir (113 acres) so it's no surprise that it's busy. A large campground, its three loops are in a dense, mature spruce forest that provides excellent campsite separation and privacy. Sun-worshipers won't get much sunshine, however, and just a few sites offer lake views. Several double sites are available for those with two vehicles or extra-large RVs.

Big Meadows

Popularity

In Big Meadows, 32 of the 54 campsites are reservable. This campground is the favorite destination of campers coming to the Del Norte area. Reserving in advance, especially for July, is highly recommended. From late June through the first week of August, the nonreservable sites are normally filled by morning. The most sought-after sites are 1-16, nearest the lake. Of those, try for reservable lakeside sites 1, 5, 6, or 8.

Facilities

Facilities include picnic tables, fire grates, firewood for sale, water faucets, a picnic area, a boat ramp, and wheelchair-accessible vault toilets.

RV Notes

Most sites have extra-long back-in and pull-thru spaces. These exceptionally RV-friendly sites are fairly level and private. The nearest dump station is in the Fun Valley RV Park about 5 miles away back on Highway 160, on the way to South Fork.

Tent Notes

The trees are so dense here that it's easy to pitch your tent where you'll have a wonderful feeling of seclusion.

Recreational Opportunities

Big Meadows Reservoir, where anglers can catch brookies, rainbows, and cutthroats, is a short walk from most campsites. You can also fish in the South Fork of the Rio Grande River as it exits the reservoir, or try nearby Shaw Lake.

Cascade Falls is only a 15-minute hike from the upper loop of the campground. The Archuleta Creek Trail starts from the reservoir and heads into the Weminuche Wilderness, connecting with the Continental Divide Trail and many others. Looking for a more leisurely stroll? Just follow the trail as it circles the reservoir.

Other Nearby Campgrounds

37. Tucker Ponds (16 sites); 15.75 miles southwest of South Fork. Take Highway 160 southwest 13 miles to Forest Road 390. Turn left (south) on Forest Road 390, and go 2.75 miles. This campground near Tucker Ponds is a place to fish and relax. It's busiest in July but never really fills completely. About six sites can handle RVs, and spruce trees provide good shade to most sites. Maximum RV length is 35 feet. No reservations. **(719) 657-3321.**

38. Park Creek (20 sites); 6.6 miles southwest of South Fork. Take Highway 160 southeast 7.5 miles to Forest Road 380. Turn left (south) on Forest Road 380, and go 0.5 mile. An attractive little creekside campground, Park Creek draws a lot of overnighters. It offers a nice mix of sun and shade and is RV-friendly. Campers lucky enough to snag one of the eight sites on the creek can minimize road noise. Maximum RV length is 35 feet. No reservations. **(719) 657-3321.**

39. Highway Springs (11 sites); 4 miles southwest of South Fork on Highway 160. Living up to its name, this campground is right off the highway. It's very open and sunny, offers little shade or privacy, and has plenty of highway noise. It never fills. Maximum RV length is 35 feet. No reservations. **(719) 657-3321.**

40. Lower Beaver Creek (23 sites); 5.5 miles southwest of South Fork. Take Highway 160 southwest 1.5 miles to Forest Road 360. Go left (south) on Forest Road 360, and continue for about 4 miles. This is a pleasant, quiet, sunny campground. Eight sites sit above Beaver Creek, but a steep 50- to 100-foot embankment can make access to it a bit challenging. Of the three campgrounds along this road, this is the best choice for RVs. Maximum RV length is 35 feet. No reservations. **(719) 657-3321.**

41. Upper Beaver Creek (16 sites); about 6 miles southwest of South Fork. Take Highway 160 southwest 1.5 miles to Forest Road 360. Go left (south) on Forest Road 360, and continue for about 4 miles. All sites are on or near Beaver Creek and offer easy access to the water. This is a great tenting campground, allowing campers to pitch their tents under the trees and on the creek. Only three sites are decent for RVs. No reservations. **(719) 657-3321.**

42. Cathedral (33 sites); 21 miles northeast of South Fork. Take Highway 160 east for 7 miles to County Road 18. Turn left (north), and go about 1.5 miles to County Road 15. Turn right (east) on County Road 15, go for 0.25 mile to Forest Road 650, and turn left (north). Go about 3.5 miles to Forest Road 640, and turn left (northwest). Go about 8.5 miles. This free, very primitive campground is hardly ever used. Among the aspens with pretty views of Cathedral Rock, the sites lie along Embargo Creek. As the road is very rough, RVs are not recommended. No reservations. **(719) 657-3321.**

MONTE VISTA AREA

43. Stunner

Location: 40 miles southwest of Monte Vista
Elevation: 9,700 feet
Number of Sites: 10
Recommended RV Length: Up to 25 feet
Season: Mid-May to mid-November
Maps: *Colorado Atlas & Gazetteer*, page 89, A5
Colorado Recreational Road Atlas, page 29, A3
Phone: 719-274-8971

Scenery: ★★★★
RVs: ★★★
Tents: ★★★
Shade: ★★
Privacy: ★★★★★

Directions

From Monte Vista, go about 11.5 miles south on Highway 15 to County Road 125 (becomes Forest Road 250). Turn right (west) on County Road 125, and go about 27 miles to Forest Road 380. Turn right (southwest), and go about 1 mile.

Distinguishing Features

Here's a campground with a name that really fits. With million-dollar views and a beautiful grassy meadow bordered by aspens, Stunner is a "stunner"! Shade is a bit on the sparse side, but trees would only block the views. Most sites are large, with good separation, and on a mid-August evening my only camping companions in this free campground were a few chummy cows. This is a dynamite spot for fall aspen viewing.

Close your eyes for a moment and imagine what it was like here in 1892. More than 400 starry-eyed miners, gamblers, and other hangers-on descended upon this very spot and called it home after hearing tales of get-rich-quick gold strikes. The excitement and commotion must have been infectious. But as quickly as they came, they left.

Popularity

You needn't worry about fighting the crowds at Stunner. Chances are, it'll be like having your own private campground! No reservations.

Facilities

Facilities include picnic tables, fire grates, hand-pumped water, and a vault toilet. There's no trash service.

RV Notes

Stunner has fairly level sites, with two long pull-thrus and the rest medium to long back-ins. The nearest dump station is at Gold Pan Acres in nearby Platoro. Don't let the drive deter you: the gravel road is good, and the journey is one you'll likely never forget!

Tent Notes
Pitch the tent anywhere, enjoy the sounds of silence, and feel the solitude! If civilization beckons, it's only a few miles to Platoro.

Recreational Opportunities
It's only a few short twists and turns up Stunner Pass to the Platoro area, and every recreational possibility imaginable. It's said that gold panning in this area is a good way to pass the time—so who needs the lottery when there's gold in them there hills! Be careful about fishing or using any of the stream water on this side of Stunner Pass, as heavy metals have leached into the water, rendering it unsafe.

Other Nearby Campgrounds

44. Rock Creek (23 sites); 17 miles southwest of Monte Vista. Take Highway 15 south for 1.5 miles to County Road 2S. Turn right (west), and go 2.5 miles to County Road 28 (Rock Creek Road). Turn left (south), and go about 13 miles (the road becomes Forest Road 265). This charming campground has beautiful scenery, and almost all its sites are on the creek. Shade is fair. No drinking water. Maximum RV length is 30 feet. No reservations. **(719) 657-3321.**

45. Comstock (8 sites); 20 miles southwest of Monte Vista. Take Highway 15 south for 1.5 miles to County Road 2S. Turn right (west), and go 2.5 miles to County Road 28 (Rock Creek Road). Turn left (south), and go about 15.5 miles on County Road 28 (which becomes Forest Road 265). This free, primitive campground has a stream running through its well-shaded sites. It sees some usage on weekends, and very little during the week. Maximum RV length is 30 feet. No drinking water. No reservations. **(719) 657-3321.**

46. Alamosa (10 sites); 29.4 miles southwest of Monte Vista. Take Highway 15 south about 11.5 miles to County Road 12S. Turn right (west) on County Road 12S (which becomes Forest Road 250), and go 13.5 miles. This lovely, spacious campground along the Alamosa River offers peace and seclusion. Lightly used sites are well-shaded, RV-friendly, and have good privacy. Three are wonderful riverside spots. Alas, there is one problem: mining has polluted the river, so fish are nowhere to be found. Maximum RV length is 25 feet. No reservations. **(719) 274-8971.**

ANTONITO AREA

47. Mogote

Location: 13 miles west of Antonito
Elevation: 8,400 feet
Number of Sites: 40
Recommended RV Length: Up to 90 feet
Season: Memorial Day to Labor Day
Maps: *Colorado Atlas & Gazetteer*, page 90, D1
Colorado Recreational Road Atlas, page 29, B4
Phone: 719-274-8971

Scenery: ★★★
RVs: ★★★★
Tents: ★★★
Shade: ★★
Privacy: ★★★★

Directions

From Antonito, go west on Highway 17 for 13.5 miles.

Distinguishing Features

Similar to nearby Aspen Glade but not nearly as popular, Mogote is a good choice for spontaneous campers or those seeking more solitude. Mogote lies 50 feet below the road, so you can't see the road but you can hear some traffic noise. The updated upper loop (sites 1-21) offers super-spacious open sites,

with good separation that can accommodate any rig. Ponderosa pines provide poor to fair shade. The two lower loops (sites 22-41) offer medium to large sites with fair to good separation. Cottonwood, willow, aspen, spruce, and a few pine trees provide adequate shade. Lush vegetation and beautiful wildflowers add up to a very pleasant wilderness atmosphere. Seven sites are on the lovely Conejos River, and some of the other sites are only a one- or two-minute walk through thick underbrush to the river. Two active beaver ponds add to the charm.

Popularity

Mogote is rarely more than a third full, but the most popular spots—sites 22-41 by the river—do fill, so it's a good idea to reserve them. The best are sites 38, 26, 30, and 24. On the upper loop, reserve large, wooded pull-thru sites 13, 10, or 8. The campground gate is locked from 9:00 p.m. until 7:00 a.m.; if you're arriving late, call (719) 376-5851.

Facilities

Facilities include picnic tables, fire grates, firewood for sale, water faucets (campers come here from other campgrounds to fill up on the softest, tastiest water around!), and vault toilets, one of which is wheelchair-accessible. Group camping, a picnic area, and public fishing access are also available.

RV Notes

Bring on the monster rigs, because this campground is ready for anything! Super-long back-in and pull-thru sites (18) accommodate any RV. Thirty-one sites are over 40 feet long, and 16 are 60 feet or longer (with several 90-foot parking sites). The nearest dump station is at the Conejos River RV Park 2.5 miles away, or at the Texaco gas station in Antonito.

Tent Notes

Try to get a spot in the lower loops for the most enjoyable wilderness camping. It's worth noting, though, that the upper loop is fairly open and sunny, so temperatures can be 10 to 15 degrees warmer on a cold night.

Recreational Opportunities

Anglers should have good luck catching browns or rainbows on the Conejos River from the campground (see also Aspen Glade).

48. Aspen Glade

Location: 17 miles west of Antonito
Elevation: 8,200 feet
Number of Sites: 34
Recommended RV Length: Up to 40 feet
Season: Memorial Day through September
Maps: *Colorado Atlas & Gazetteer*, page 89, D7
Colorado Recreational Road Atlas, page 29, B4
Phone: 719-274-8971

Scenery: ★★★
RVs: ★★★★
Tents: ★★★
Shade: ★★
Privacy: ★★★

Directions
From Antonito, go about 17 miles west on Highway 17. The campground gate is locked from 9:00 p.m. until 7:00 a.m.; make arrangements in advance if you're arriving during these times by calling (719) 376-2535.

Distinguishing Features
Set just below the main road, Aspen Glade is isolated from the highway. Many campers have been returning here for 15 to 20 years, and it's a favorite of retirees. Two upper loops and a lower loop on the river offer large, RV-friendly sites with good separation. Ponderosa pines dominate the upper loops, providing some shade. The lower loop has lush vegetation and is more densely wooded, providing excellent shade but not much sunshine. Campers will find appealing views of the river from the lower loop, which is popular with tent-campers. Curiously, only a few immature aspens dot "Aspen Glade" campground. Campers will find improvements to many sites and upgraded facilities in 2003.

Popularity

From the first of July until early August, Aspen Glade fills almost every night. Reservations are highly recommended. The most sought-after sites (24-34) are in the lower loop on the river. Of those, try for reservable sites 24-26 or 31.

Facilities

Facilities include picnic tables, fire grates, firewood for sale, water faucets, and vault toilets. All toilets are lighted, and one is equipped for wheelchair access.

RV Notes

You'll find marvelous, mostly level RV spots throughout the campground. Aspen Glade offers very long back-ins and 14 pull-thrus. The nearest dump station is at the Conejos River RV Park 2.5 miles away to the east.

Tent Notes

The best tent spots are in the lower loop. Sites are nice in the upper loop, but you may be a bit overwhelmed by the RVs.

Recreational Opportunities

The Conejos River is a great place for rainbow and native brown trout. Just north of the campground for about 5 miles upstream (to Menkhaven Lodge), the Conejos is classified Gold Medal water. Only fly-fishing is permitted here, and the catch is limited to two fish with a 16-inch limit. The Duck Lake and Elk Creek Trails are quite popular; both start near the Elk Creek Campground about 8 miles away. The nearby Cumbres & Toltec Scenic Railroad is North America's longest and highest narrow-gauge railroad (65 miles).

---

49. Trujillo Meadows

Location: 39 miles west of Antonito
Elevation: 10,000 feet
Number of Sites: 50
Recommended RV Length: Up to 35 feet
Season: June 15 to September 15
Maps: *Colorado Atlas & Gazetteer*, page 89, D6
Colorado Recreational Road Atlas, page 29, A4
Phone: 719-274-8971

Scenery: ★★★
RVs: ★★★
Tents: ★★★
Shade: ★★★
Privacy: ★★★

Directions

From Antonito, take Highway 17 west and south about 35 miles to Forest Road 118. Turn right (north), and go about 2.5 miles north. If you're coming

from Chama, New Mexico, take Highway 17 northeast 21.1 miles to Forest Road 118, turn left (north), and go for 2.1 miles.

Distinguishing Features

Trujillo Meadows is a wonderful place to find a cool alpine escape from the summer heat down south! With its own private little waterfall (near site 40), wildflowers, nice views of surrounding hills, and the distant sound of the narrow-gauge train whistle, it's no surprise that campers always enjoy their visit. Adjacent to 70-acre Trujillo Meadows Reservoir, this large campground is divided into a lower and an upper campground. The upper sites (1-24) are on a dividing line between a conifer-spruce forest and open meadow, offering a mix of sun and shade and views of surrounding hills. Most of the sites are medium-sized, with fair separation. The lower sites (25-49) are smaller and close together in a densely wooded area with few views. This area is best suited for tents. The prized site 49 is one of only two sites in the campground with a view of the reservoir.

Popularity

This is the second most popular campground in the area, and it fills almost completely from July 4 through mid-August. Arrive early in the day! No reservations.

Facilities

Facilities include picnic tables, fire grates, firewood for sale, water faucets, and vault toilets (one is wheelchair-accessible).

RV Notes

Stick to the upper campground (sites 1–24) and you'll be okay. The sites are fairly level, and you'll have medium-sized back-ins, pull-outs, and pull-thrus to choose from. Avoid the lower campground! The nearest dump stations are at RV parks in Chama.

Tent Notes

Any spot works fine for tents, but 49 is my top pick.

Recreational Opportunities

Anglers can catch rainbow, brown, and cutthroat trout in Trujillo Meadows Reservoir or in the stream just below it. Only small motorized and hand-propelled boats are allowed on the reservoir. The Rio de los Piños Trail near the reservoir heads northwest into the South San Juan Wilderness. The Continental Divide Trail also passes through this area. Mountain bikers and four-wheelers will find myriad adventures. The Cumbres & Toltec Scenic Railroad is nearby, and is a must for train buffs!

---

50. Mix Lake

Location: 46 miles northwest of Antonito
Elevation: 10,000 feet
Number of Sites: 22
Recommended RV Length: Up to 25 feet
Season: Mid-June to Labor Day
Maps: *Colorado Atlas & Gazetteer*, page 89, B5
Colorado Recreational Road Atlas, page 29, A3
Phone: 719-274-8971

Scenery: ★★★★
RVs: ★★
Tents: ★★★
Shade: ★★
Privacy: ★★★

Directions

From Antonito, go west on Highway 17 for 23 miles to Forest Road 250 (a well-maintained gravel road). Take this road northwest for 22.6 miles to Forest Road 247, and go 0.5 mile further.

Distinguishing Features

This campground is in a remote alpine setting just below Mix Lake, yet only a mile from modern conveniences in Platoro. Campers can turn their heads in any direction and feast on beautiful mountain views. The campground sits in a hilly area, and sites vary in elevation and size. Some are completely sunny and open with great views, and others are well-shaded. Aspens predominate at lower levels, conifer-spruce up higher.

Popularity

Unless you show up on the July Fourth weekend, finding a site should be easy. This campground rarely exceeds 50 percent occupancy. No reservations.

Facilities

Facilities include picnic tables, fire grates, firewood for sale, water faucets, and vault toilets.

RV Notes

Most sites are medium in size and not very level. A few can handle larger rigs. Many folks wouldn't drive this far up a gravel road, but the road is good and the scenery is exceptional! The nearest dump station is at Gold Pan Acres RV Park in Platoro.

Tent Notes

A good selection of tent sites makes it easy to find a relaxing spot.

Recreational Opportunities

Anglers, where do I begin? Mix Lake (22 acres) is only 100 yards from some campsites, and Platoro Reservoir (1,021 acres), the Conejos River, Lily Pond

(24 acres), and Kerr Lake (40 acres) are also nearby. The area offers brook, brown, cutthroat, and rainbow trout. A boat ramp for Platoro Reservoir lies just south of the campground. When completely full, Platoro Reservoir is almost 4 miles long.

Hikers, we wouldn't want to forget you. The Lake Fork Trail and Sawmill Gulch Trail aren't far away; both connect with many other trails. The Three Forks Trail leads to the Continental Divide and is especially popular with equestrians. A good network of four-wheel-drive roads provides mountain bikers with many choices.

Other Nearby Campgrounds

51. Elk Creek (34 sites) and **Elk Creek Overflow** (10 sites); 24 miles northwest of Antonito. Take Highway 17 west 23.75 miles to Forest Road 128. Turn right (southwest), and go 0.5 mile. This is the most popular campground in the area, especially with hikers. A pleasant place, it has four loops, large sites (RV-friendly), good separation, and a mix of open and shady sites. About four sites are on Elk Creek. Elk Creek Overflow is a parking area with side-by-side spots. No reservations. **(719) 274-8971.**

52. Spectacle Lake (24 sites); 30 miles northwest of Antonito. Go west on Highway 17 for 23 miles to Forest Road 250. Turn right (west), and go about 6.5 miles. This sunny, spacious campground is rarely more than a third full; it's light on shade but offers great mountain views. Larger RVs fit better here than in most other campgrounds on Forest Road 250. Spectacle Lake just across the road offers good youth fishing and is fairly wheelchair-friendly. No reservations. **(719) 274-8971.**

53. Conejos (16 sites); 30 miles northwest of Antonito. Take Highway 17 west for 23 miles to Forest Road 250. Turn right (west), and go 7 miles. Conejos lies along the Conejos River, with about five sites on the river and most others not far from it. A good mix of sun and shade adds a cheerful atmosphere, and many sites have beautiful mountain views. This is a very busy campground in midsummer, so arrive early in the day. Maximum RV length is 25 feet. No reservations. **(719) 274-8971.**

54. Lake Fork (18 sites); 41 miles northwest of Antonito. Take Highway 17 west for 23 miles to Forest Road 250. Turn right (west), and go about 18 miles. Yet another charming campground in a beautiful area, this one works best for tents and small RVs. With an abundance of wildflowers and aspens, it's indeed lovely. About five sites are on the Conejos River, and several others are close to it. This is a busy place, but the hosts can usually squeeze you in. Maximum RV length is 25 feet. Reservations accepted. **(719) 274-8971.**

55. Poso (11 sites); 36 miles northwest of Monte Vista. Take Highway 285 north for about 17 miles to County Road G. Turn left (west), and go about 6.5 miles to County Road 41-G. Turn right (northwest), go about 10 miles to Forest Road 675, and turn left (west). Go 2 miles. Peace and solitude out in the boonies are what campers can expect in this primitive, rather run-down campground that has few visitors. Sites are small and not good for RVs, but have good spacing and fair shade. No water. No reservations. **(719) 655-2547.**

56. Storm King (11 sites); about 37 miles northwest of Monte Vista. Take Highway 285 north for about 17 miles to County Road G. Turn left (west), and go about 6.5 miles to County Road 41-G. Turn right (northwest), and go about 14.25 miles (the road becomes Forest Road 690). This primitive campground is almost entirely in an aspen grove, and is best for tents. Sites have fair to good separation and shade. No reservations. **(719) 655-2547.**

57. Buffalo Pass (26 sites); about 29 miles northwest of Saguache. Take Highway 114 northwest for 27.6 miles, turn right (southwest) onto the gravel road that leads to the campground, and go 1.7 miles. Nestled in evergreens, this is a great place to relax and enjoy the scenery. Maximum RV length is 30 feet. No water. No reservations. **(719) 655-2547.**

58. Luders Creek (6 sites); about 32 miles northwest of Saguache. Take Highway 114 west 22 miles to Forest Road 750. Go left (west) on Forest Road 750, and go 9.5 miles. Primitive but lightly used, it has free, well-shaded sites, and Luders Creek is nearby. Maximum RV length is 25 feet. No water. No reservations. **(719) 655-2547.**

59. Stone Cellar (4 sites); about 57 miles southwest of Saguache. Go northwest on Highway 114 about 37 miles to Forest Road 804 (County Road 17-GG). Turn left (southwest), and go about 5.5 miles to County Road NN-14. Go left (east) for 1 mile, turn right (south) on County Road 17-FF (which becomes Forest Road 787), and go about 13 miles. Another remote but free campground, sites are fairly open with little shade and Saguache Creek runs through the campground. Maximum RV length is 25 feet. No reservations. **(719) 655-2547.**

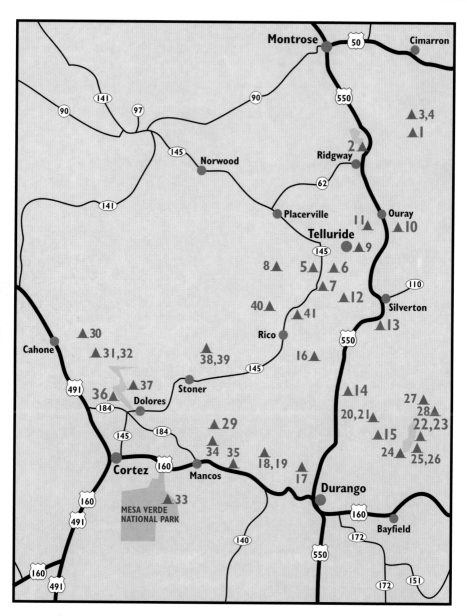

For locations of campgrounds by Ridgway Reservoir and Vallecito Reservoir, see maps on page 295.

If someone posed the question, "Where's the most dramatic mountain scenery in Colorado?" the answer would have to be southwestern Colorado and the picturesque San Juan Mountains. Shutterbugs will go nuts. Just one drive along the Million Dollar Highway (Highway 550) between Ouray and Durango will quickly convince anyone who doesn't believe. Ouray is known as the "Switzerland of America" and the "Jeep Capital of America." Visitors looking for the full menu of four-wheeling, ghost towns, and spectacular scenery won't be disappointed if they venture into the area around Ouray, Silverton, and Telluride. Guided jeep tours are an excellent alternative for those who'd rather look than drive. Fantastic hiking and mountain-biking opportunities are plentiful, although the terrain can be quite strenuous and demanding.

Area lakes include McPhee Reservoir (the second largest in the state) near Dolores; Ridgway and Silver Jack Reservoirs near Ridgway; and Vallecito and Lemon Reservoirs just north of Bayfield. Telluride arguably boasts the most stunning mountain backdrop in the state and draws thousands of visitors every summer to its festivals (campers: plan carefully!). For those seeking the ultimate train ride, the Durango & Silverton Narrow-Gauge Railroad is not to be missed. And Mesa Verde National Park near Cortez gives visitors an unforgettable look back at the most extensive and well-preserved cliff dwellings in the country.

But whatever most interests you, it's hard to go wrong when visiting this special slice of Colorado! Campgrounds along the Million Dollar Highway (Highway 550) from Montrose to Durango and those near Telluride see the heaviest usage. If you're looking for the most scenic route between Gunnison and Ridgway, try the Cimarron Road, a gravel road from Highway 50 to Owl Creek Pass. Most vehicles can make the trip.

▲ 100 BEST

- ▲ 1 Silver Jack
- ▲ 2 Ridgway State Park
- ▲ 5 Sunshine
- ▲ 6 Alta Lakes
- ▲ 7 Matterhorn
- ▲ 10 Amphitheater
- ▲ 12 South Mineral
- ▲ 13 Molas Lake Park
- ▲ 14 Haviland Lake
- ▲ 15 Miller Creek
- ▲ 22 Pine Point
- ▲ 23 Middle Mountain
- ▲ 29 Transfer
- ▲ 36 McPhee

▲ All The Rest

- ▲ 3 Big Cimarron (closed)
- ▲ 4 Beaver Lake
- ▲ 8 Woods Lake
- ▲ 9 Telluride Town Park
- ▲ 11 Canyon Creek Area
- ▲ 16 Sig Creek
- ▲ 17 Junction Creek
- ▲ 18 Snowslide
- ▲ 19 Kroeger
- ▲ 20 Florida
- ▲ 21 Transfer Park
- ▲ 24 Old Timers
- ▲ 25 Graham Creek
- ▲ 26 North Canyon

- ▲ 27 Vallecito
- ▲ 28 Pine River
- ▲ 30 Bradfield Bridge
- ▲ 31 Cabin Canyon
- ▲ 32 Ferris Canyon
- ▲ 33 Mesa Verde National Park
  Morefield Campground
- ▲ 34 Mancos State Park
- ▲ 35 Target Tree
- ▲ 37 House Creek
- ▲ 38 Mavreeso
- ▲ 39 West Dolores
- ▲ 40 Burro Bridge
- ▲ 41 Cayton

RIDGWAY AREA

1. Silver Jack

Location: 26 miles northeast of Ridgway
Elevation: 8,900 feet
Number of Sites: 60
Recommended RV Length: Up to 30 feet
Season: June through September
Maps: *Colorado Atlas & Gazetteer,* page 67, C5
Colorado Recreational Road Atlas, page 22, A4
Phone: 970-240-5300

Scenery: ★★★★
RVs: ★★★
Tents: ★★★
Shade: ★★★
Privacy: ★★★★

Directions
From Ridgway, take Highway 550 about 1.75 miles north to County Road 10. Turn right (northeast) on County Road 10, and go about 3.75 miles to County Road 8. Turn right (east) on County Road 8 (which becomes Forest Road 858), and go about 20 miles over the very scenic Owl Creek Pass. Silver Jack can also be approached from Cimarron. From Cimarron on Highway 50, go southeast for 2.25 miles, turn right (south) on Big Cimarron Road (Forest Road 858), a well-maintained gravel road, and go for about 22 miles.

Distinguishing Features
Situated in a stunning aspen grove surrounded by tall grass and magnificent wildflowers, this remote but accessible campground offers the utmost in beauty, quiet, and relaxation. The Silver Jack campground provides three paved loops and paved parking spots as well as good-sized sites with good spacing. Four sites have wheelchair access, and others offer great mountain views. An easy 0.5-mile walk or drive takes you to the Silver Jack Reservoir Overlook. This vantage point affords breathtaking views of the reservoir in its fairytale, alpine setting.

Popularity
Few people have discovered this hidden gem, thus it is rarely over half full. No reservations.

Facilities
Facilities include picnic tables, fire grates, firewood for sale, water faucets, and wheelchair-accessible vault toilets; two are lighted.

RV Notes
Paved, fairly level medium-sized back-ins and pull-thrus are available. The wide dirt road to the campground can be daunting, but it's generally in good condition. Just take your time and enjoy the scenery. The closest dump station is 21 miles away near Cimarron on Highway 50.

Tent Notes
The ground is fairly level, and some sites have pads. Showers are available 5 miles north of the campground at El Rancho, a small resort with a store and rental cabins.

Recreational Opportunities 🏃 🐾 🚣
Silver Jack Reservoir (318 acres) offers a beautiful setting for fishing and motorless boating. The fishing is excellent, and the lake is stocked with brook, rainbow, and German brown trout. A boat access area is at the southern end of the lake; anglers can access the lake from this point as well. Anglers can also fish below the dam at the north end of the reservoir.

Hiking opportunities abound. The Lou Creek Trail starts from the campground, leading to Cowboy Lake and other trails. The Alpine Trail starts across from the campground, leading into the Big Blue Wilderness.

---

2. Ridgway State Park
Location: 4 miles north of Ridgway (see map on p. 295)
Elevation: 6,880 feet
Number of Sites: 294 plus 3 yurts
Recommended RV Length: Unlimited
Season: Year-round
Maps: *Colorado Atlas & Gazetteer*, page 66, C3
Colorado Recreational Road Atlas, page 22, A4
Phone: 970-626-5822

Scenery: ★★★
RVs: ★★★★★
Tents: ★★
Shade: ★
Privacy: ★

Directions
From Ridgway, go 3.5 miles north on Highway 550. Turn left (north) into the park entrance.

Distinguishing Features
Close to Ridgway Reservoir—1,065 acres and 4.5 miles long—this park has three paved campgrounds with ultra-modern facilities. Ridgway is in a semi-arid environment, so don't expect to find many towering trees.

Elk Ridge (98 sites plus 10 walk-in tent sites) is in two loops in a piñon-juniper forest above the reservoir, with some sites providing partial views of the reservoir. Many others have views of the Cimarron and San Juan Ranges. Two-thirds of the sites have decent shade, with loop E providing the best. The lake is a 20- to 25-minute walk down a steep hill, and short trails lead to beautiful lake and mountain views.

Dakota Terraces (79 sites), an open, airy setting with three loops (A-C), is the only campground close to the reservoir. Some sites in Loop C are less than 100 yards from the water. Most have lake views, and all are within 0.5 mile of the swim beach and marina. For a five-dollar fee, campers can moor their boats. Sites 10, 12, and 50-55 provide some shade.

Pacochupuk (81 sites plus 15 walk-ins) is away from the lake, and the last of the three campgrounds to fill. Loop F offers latecomers the best chance of finding a site. This campground has two open loops and one lovely shaded tent-only area overlooking the river. A few sites in Loops F and G have some shade. Most sites are within a 10-minute walk of the Uncompahgre River and two stocked fishing ponds. Loops F and G offer full hookups.

Popularity
Ridgway consistently ranks first or second in popularity among the state parks, so reservations are practically mandatory for weekends from Memorial Day to Labor Day. Elk Ridge is the most popular campground, and sites 186, 184, and 153 (tent site) are the most requested. Walk-in sites 151-160 are also popular. In Dakota Terraces, sites 64, 66, 62, 10, 12, and 50-55 are the prime spots. In Pacochupuk, sites 257, 259, 263, 265, 267, 269, 271, 273, 274, 276, and 278 are the most popular. For tents, sites 282 and 284 are the most sought-after, but all walk-ins (281-294) go fast.

Facilities
Ridgway has it all: picnic tables, fire grates, water faucets, flush toilets, sinks, mirrors, electrical outlets, showers, laundry facilities, a playground, volley-ball, horseshoes, a group picnic area, a marina, a boat ramp, and three rental yurts. Almost all facilities are wheelchair-accessible.

RV Notes
All sites have electrical hookups, while full hookups are available at Pacochupuk. A dump station is provided, and all sites have paved pull-thru and back-in spaces.

Tent Notes

The walk-in tent sites are cheaper and go faster than any other sites in the park. They all have tent pads, and most offer decent shade. Walk-in sites 151-160 at Elk Ridge are wonderful, as are Pacochupuk's Loop H sites 281-294 up the hill. The sites in Pacochupuk are 150 to 225 yards from the parking lot; carts are available to transport your gear.

Recreational Opportunities

Boating and fishing opportunities abound at the reservoir, and campers can rent boats at the marina. The lake is stocked with rainbow trout and kokanee salmon, and brown trout are plentiful in the springtime. You might also snag a yellow perch or a sucker. Catch-and-release rules apply in the river at Pacochupuk (artificial flies and lures only!). Bait is allowed in the two small fishing ponds in this campground, which are stocked with rainbows.

The park's 15 miles of trails are well-loved by hikers and mountain bikers alike. A paved bike path runs south to the town of Ridgway. Some of the most spectacular hiking, jeeping, and sightseeing in Colorado are just 14 miles south in Ouray—the gateway to the San Juans.

Other Nearby Campgrounds

3. Big Cimarron

Since the writing of this book, this campground has been permanently closed.

4. Beaver Lake (11 sites); 28 miles northeast of Ridgway. Take Highway 550 north 1.75 miles to County Road 10, and turn right (northeast). Go about 3.75 miles to County Road 8. Turn right (east) on County Road 8 (which becomes Forest Road 858), and go about 22 miles. This campground next to pretty Beaver Lake has sites that vary from open and sunny to enclosed and shaded. Many have nice views of the lake. Privacy varies, and sites are on the shorter side for RVs. Maximum RV length is 20 feet. No reservations. **(970) 240-5300.**

TELLURIDE AREA

5. Sunshine
Location: 8 miles southwest of Telluride
Elevation: 9,500 feet
Number of Sites: 18
Season: May through September
Maps: *Colorado Atlas & Gazetteer*, page 76, A2
Colorado Recreational Road Atlas, page 27, C1.5
Phone: 970-327-4261

Scenery: ★★★★
RVs: ★★★
Tents: ★★★★
Shade: ★★★★
Privacy: ★★★

Directions
From Telluride, go west on Highway 145 for 3 miles,
then south on Highway 145 for about 5 miles.

Distinguishing Features
Located close to Telluride, Sunshine is the most pleasant campground in
this area. Sites are large and spacious, offering privacy and shade in a lush
setting. Colorful wildflowers spread across the meadow's thick grass. A few
sites provide impressive mountain views. This campground was recently
renovated to make it more RV-friendly. Two wheelchair-accessible toilets
have been added as well.

Popularity

Like all Telluride-area campgrounds, this one is busy. It fills about 22 of every 30 days, and during the early season it fills by noon. If you're staying here especially during the Bluegrass Festival, try to arrive a day or two ahead of time. Reservations accepted.

Facilities

All facilities are wheelchair-accessible, and include picnic tables, fire grates, firewood for sale, water faucets, composting toilets, lantern posts, and a group area.

RV Notes

The recent renovation now accommodates most larger RVs. The parking spaces (all back-in) have reportedly been enlarged to 45 feet in length.

Tent Notes

All sites have tent pads. Pay showers are available at Town Park Campground in Telluride and at Matterhorn Campground 4 miles south.

Recreational Opportunities

Be sure to visit Bridal Veil Falls just east of Telluride, with the longest vertical drop of any waterfall in Colorado. Mountain-biking opportunities are plentiful in the area, with rides ranging from moderate to difficult. Beginning from the Telluride airport is the scenic Last Dollar Road, which is rated difficult. The Ames to Illium Road (Forest Road 625) is an easy but very rewarding ride running parallel to the South Fork River along a beautiful valley. The ride begins a few miles south of the campground, and becomes a loop trip if you return via Highway 145. (Also see Alta Lakes and Matterhorn Campgrounds.)

---

6. Alta Lakes

Location: 13 miles southwest of Telluride
Elevation: 11,000 feet
Number of Sites: Undesignated
Recommended RV Length: Pickup campers only
Season: Late June through September
Maps: *Colorado Atlas & Gazetteer*, page 76, A3
Colorado Recreational Road Atlas, page 27, C1.5
Phone: 970-327-4261

Scenery: ★★★★★
RVs: ★
Tents: ★★★
Shade: ★★★
Privacy: ★★★★

Directions

You'll need a high-clearance vehicle to access Alta Lakes. From Telluride, go west on Highway 145 for 3 miles, then south on Highway 145 for about

5 miles. Turn left (southeast) onto Forest Road 632, and continue for about 4.5 miles up a rough high-clearance dirt road.

Distinguishing Features

Alta Lakes offers the most spectacular scenery of any campground in the area. Long a favorite of locals, it's remained a well-kept secret. The three small lakes that surround the campground add shine to this breathtaking setting. Campsites aren't designated, making this "free dispersed camping" at its finest. Evergreens provide pleasant shade and much privacy.

The town of Alta—Spanish for "high"—was a mining center from 1877 to 1948. It was also the first in the world to use alternating current (AC) electricity. Today, it's one of the most well-preserved ghost towns in Colorado.

Popularity

Since there are no designated sites, this campground never fills.
No reservations.

Facilities

The primitive facilities include two pit toilets. No water or trash service is available.

RV Notes
Suitable for high-clearance pickup campers only.

Tent Notes
Pick a spot near the lakes—any spot—and enjoy the beauty and serenity.
Just don't forget to bring water and a portable table.

Recreational Opportunities 🚶🎣
The lakes are too small for boating, but the lower lake is stocked with brook
and rainbow trout. Fishing is best just after snowmelt. The nearby ghost
town of Alta is a fascinating place to visit. (Also see Sunshine and Matterhorn
Campgrounds.)

---

7. Matterhorn
Location: 12 miles southwest of Telluride
Elevation: 9,500 feet
Number of Sites: 28
Recommended RV Length: Up to 35 feet
Season: Memorial Day through September
Maps: *Colorado Atlas & Gazetteer*, page 76, B2
Colorado Recreational Road Atlas, page 27, C2
Phone: 970-327-4261

Scenery: ★★★★★
RVs: ★★★★★
Tents: ★★★★★
Shade: ★★
Privacy: ★★

Directions
From Telluride, go west on Highway 145 for about 3 miles. Proceed south
on Highway 145 for about 9 miles.

Distinguishing Features
With almost all the creature comforts of home, Matterhorn is one of the
ritziest Forest Service campgrounds in Colorado. Spectacular backdrops and
lovely wildflowers add to its splendor. Matterhorn's campsites are all in one
paved loop with paved parking spots. Sites range from small to large, and
spacing is varied. Aspen, fir, and spruce trees provide shade, which is sparse
in many center sites but good in many on the outside of the loop. Four sites
are on a creek.

Popularity
Deluxe amenities and a prime location add up to a highly popular, desirable
campground. Resrving far in advance is advised. Sites 8, 6, 4, and 2 are all
on the creek. If Matterhorn is full, try the free, undesignated sites 1.5 miles
south at Priest Lake. Reservations accepted.

Facilities
Matterhorn offers wheelchair-accessible picnic tables, fire grates, and flush

toilets. Facilities also include water faucets and lantern posts, and bathrooms have showers, sinks, and electrical outlets. Firewood is available for sale.

RV Notes
Medium to long paved back-ins and five pull-thrus are available. Eight sites offer full hookups, but none are in the pull-thru sites.

Tent Notes
Sixteen sites have tent pads, and sites 12-14 are walk-ins. With so many amenities, there's no need for roughing it here.

Recreational Opportunities
Anglers should have good luck in stocked Priest Lake and in nearby 126-acre Trout Lake. Southeast of Trout Lake is the 3-mile Lake Hope Trail, a favorite of hikers, horseback riders, and mountain bikers. Another top pick is Lizard Head Trail, which starts a few miles south of the campground and meanders through the Lizard Head Wilderness (no bikes). Four-wheel-drive roads are everywhere, and the nearby Ophir Pass Road is a fairly easy warm-up for the more difficult ones. (Also see Sunshine and Alta Lakes Campgrounds.)

Other Nearby Campgrounds

8. Woods Lake (41 sites); 22 miles southwest of Telluride. Go about 13 miles west on Highway 145, and turn left (south) on County Road 57.P. Go 9 miles on County Road 57.P (which becomes Forest Road 618, a.k.a. Fall Creek Road). This newly renovated, fairly RV-friendly campground accommodates RVs in its three loops, one solely for campers with horses. About half the sites have views of stunning Woods Lake (17 acres). Tent sites are in an aspen forest and have pads. Facilities include a lantern post at every site. No reservations. **(970) 327-4261.**

9. Telluride Town Park (40+ sites); near the east end of Telluride. This is a crowded, cheap place to stay, close to all action. Expect very compact sites with good shade. The campground has flush toilets and pay showers, but fires are prohibited. A swimming pool, tennis courts, volleyball, horsehoe pits, and a skate ramp are nearby. Maximum RV length is 30 feet. This campground fills every weekend in summer. No reservations. **(800) 525-3455.**

OURAY AREA

10. Amphitheater
Location: 2 miles southeast of Ouray
Elevation: 8,400 feet
Number of Sites: 35
Recommended RV Length: Up to 25 feet
Season: Memorial Day through September
Maps: *Colorado Atlas & Gazetteer,* page 66, D4;
Colorado Recreational Road Atlas, page 28, A1
Phone: 970-240-5300

Scenery: ★★★★★
RVs: ★
Tents: ★★★★
Shade: ★★★
Privacy: ★★★

Directions
From Ouray, go south on Highway 550 for about a mile, then left (east) on County Road 16 (Forest Road 885), and watch for the campground sign.

Distinguishing Features
This campground's setting—beside the mountain cliffs of the Amphitheater and 600 feet above Ouray—offers amazing views of Ouray and the surrounding mountains. The road to the campground is paved, steep, hilly, and narrow. Primarily a tent-oriented campground, Amphitheater has compact sites that are well-spaced and private. Many campers use Amphitheater as a base camp for hiking and four-wheeling. A mix of spruce, scrub oak, and aspen trees shades the sites. No turnaround at end of road.

Popularity
This campground is booked months in advance, but has a

40% turnover each day. Arrive early for a better chance of finding a site. Half the sites are reservable; try reserving sites 10, 11, 14, 15, and 22–25.

Facilities

Facilities include picnic tables, lantern posts, fire grates, firewood for sale, water faucets, vault toilets, and a day-use area.

RV Notes

Several spots work for RVs under 25 feet and towables under 20 feet. Back-in site 30 and pull-thrus 15-17 are the best. No trailers or towed vehicles are allowed in the lower loop (6-14). Most parking spots are short back-ins and not very level.

Tent Notes

Amphitheater is a tent-oriented campground, and all of the sites have formal tent pads.

Recreational Opportunities

You'll find some of the most spectacular hiking in the country in this area. The Portland Trail and Upper Cascade Falls Trail start from the campground. Difficult and steep, Upper Cascade Falls is 2 miles long and gains 1,500 feet in elevation. It leads to the falls and Chief Ouray Mine and offers stunning mountain and town views as it winds its way up the side of the mountain.

Ouray takes pride in being the "Jeep Capital of the World." Engineer, Imogene, Black Bear, Ophir, and Cinnamon Passes just scratch the surface of what's available for off-road enthusiasts. A visit to Box Canyon Falls and the wildflower-rich Yankee Boy Basin are other recommended adventures. After a hard day of fun, go down to the Ouray Hot Springs Pool for a relaxing soak.

Other Nearby Campgrounds

11. Canyon Creek Area. From Ouray, go south on Highway 550 about 0.5 mile and turn right (west) onto Camp Bird Road. Three primitive camping areas are located 1.5, 2 and 4.5 miles along Camp Bird Road in the Canyon Creek Area. The road leads to the spectacular Yankee Boy Basin and Imogene Pass. A fee is required to enter. There's no picnic tables or drinking water. Some sites have fire rings and toilet facilities are available. Firewood is provided at each site. Camping is limited to these designated areas: **Angel Creek** (15 sites) has 3-4 sites good for RVs, but the road to the other sites is 4-wheel drive. Four sites are along Canyon Creek. Good privacy and shade. **Thistle Downs** (11 sites) is suitable for RVs as well as tents. Five sites are by the creek and all have good shade. **Atlas** (6 sites) is near timberline at 10,700 feet and offers great views. Access is by 4-wheel drive only. Several sites are near Sneffels Creek. No reservations. **(970) 240-5300.**

SILVERTON—DURANGO AREA

12. South Mineral
Location: 7 miles west of Silverton
Elevation: 9,800 feet
Number of Sites: 26
Recommended RV Length: Up to 45 feet
Season: Memorial Day to mid-September
Maps: *Colorado Atlas & Gazetteer,* page 76, B3
Colorado Recreational Road Atlas, page 28, A2
Phone: 970-884-2512

Scenery: ★★★★★
RVs: ★★★
Tents: ★★★★
Shade: ★★★
Privacy: ★★★

Directions
From Silverton, go about 2 miles northwest on Highway 550, then turn left (west) on Forest Road 585. Go about 5 miles on this wide, well-maintained dirt road.

Distinguishing Features
South Mineral is nestled beside a peaceful creek, with majestic peaks all around. Several sites are close to the creek, and most are large and adequately spaced apart. Fir and spruce trees provide excellent shade, and a few sunny sites are available.

Popularity
Reservations are not taken, and this campground is full most of the summer. If full, sites are usually available in the free designated camping areas between the creek and the road.

Facilities

Facilities include picnic tables, fire grates, firewood for sale, a water faucet, and vault toilets.

RV Notes

You'll find mostly long, fairly level back-ins and a few pull-thrus. Free dispersed camping is permitted at designated spots near the road leading to the campground.

Tent Notes

Marvelous campsites are available for tents.

Recreational Opportunities 🚶 🎣 🚙 🛻

Anglers will find brook and rainbow trout in the creek. Two hundred yards from the campground is the Ice Lake Trail, a difficult but rewarding hike that offers a variety of scenery. Possibilities are endless for those seeking off-road adventure, breathtaking views, and lush, wildflower-carpeted meadows. Ophir Pass Road, a few miles north on Highway 550, is an easy four-wheel-drive road, as is the road east of Silverton, which leads to the fairly well preserved ghost town of Animas Forks.

---

13. Molas Lake Park

Location: 5 miles south of Silverton
Elevation: 10,515 feet
Number of Sites: 60
Recommended RV Length: Unlimited
Season: June through September
Maps: *Colorado Atlas & Gazetteer*, page 76, C4
Colorado Recreational Road Atlas, page 28, A2
Phone: 970-387-5654 or 800-752-4494

Scenery: ★★★★★
RVs: ★★
Tents: ★★★★
Shade: ★★
Privacy: ★★

Directions

From Silverton, go 5 miles south on Highway 550.

Distinguishing Features

A few years ago, AAA called Molas Park "The Most Scenic Campground in Colorado" and it is hard to disagree. Molas Lake Park is a primitive, tent-oriented campground with awe-inspiring views in every direction. Molas has the feel of a Forest Service campground, but is owned by the town of Silverton. A rough dirt road leads up, down, and around the lake to the campsites. Average in size, sites offer poor to excellent spacing. Shade varies considerably.

Popularity

From late June through mid-August, it's best to call ahead and make a reservation, especially if you have an RV. The most popular reservable sites—9, 40, 42, and 55 around the lake edge. If the campground is full, drive 1 mile farther south on Highway 550 and check out the free dispersed sites available around Little Molas Lake. There is one vault toilet, but no other facilities. Many sites are fine for RVs, and quite a few are well-shaded.

Facilities

Facilities include picnic tables, fire pits, two water faucets, a new shower building, and vault toilets. A small camp store sells some groceries, firewood, ice, and bait.

RV Notes

About 18 sites are suitable for RVs, and about 8 of those are suitable for larger RVs. Most are not very level. The campground has a dump station ($10 fee).

Tent Notes

It gets quite chilly up here, so bundle up at night.

Recreational Opportunities 🏃 🐎 🚙 🌳

Anglers can catch cutbow and rainbow trout in the lake, and you can arrange for horseback riding next door. Small boats are permitted in the lake, but no gas motors are allowed. The Colorado Trail (a.k.a. Molas Trail) passes near the southern side of Molas Lake (25 acres). A great 3-mile hike eastbound on this trail descends 1,800 feet via 37 switchbacks to the Animas River. The last half of the hike offers postcard views of the Animas River Canyon, the Durango & Silverton Narrow-Gauge Railroad, and the rugged Grenadier Range. The Durango to Silverton train ride is the memory of a lifetime. Jeeping possibilities are unbeatable.

---

14. Haviland Lake

Location: 18 miles north of Durango
Elevation: 8,000 feet
Number of Sites: 43
Recommended RV Length: Up to 45 feet
Season: Mid-May through October
Maps: *Colorado Atlas & Gazetteer*, page 76, D3
Colorado Recreational Road Atlas, page 28, A2
Phone: 970-884-2512

Scenery: ★★★★
RVs: ★★★
Tents: ★★★
Shade: ★★★
Privacy: ★★★

Directions
From Durango, go about 17 miles north on Highway 550. Turn right (east) onto Forest Road 671, and travel about a mile.

Distinguishing Features
With the Hermosa Cliffs rising majestically in the background and 208-acre Haviland Lake in the foreground, this is another campground in a place that feels like paradise! RV-friendly and wheelchair-accessible, the campground consists of four loops, shaded by ponderosa pine, aspen, and scrub oak. Most sites are medium to large with adequate spacing, giving campers welcomed privacy. One loop is just above the lake, and nine sites sit lakeside. The other three loops are farther from the lake and higher up the hill.

Popularity
The campground is full almost every evening, so come before noon to secure a spot. This special place is very popular with the locals.

Facilities
Facilities include picnic tables, fire grates, water faucets, and firewood for sale. The campground has wheelchair-accessible picnic tables, fire grates, and vault toilets. A day-use area and boat dock are also available.

RV Notes
Medium to long back-ins and about six pull-thrus are available. Eight sites in one of the upper loops have electrical hookups.

Tent Notes
Many good spots are available, and almost all sites have tent pads.

Recreational Opportunities
Anglers will find mostly rainbow trout in the lake; boats without gas engines are allowed. For a more secluded fishing spot, take the four-wheel-drive road just southeast of the lake to Forebay Lake 1 mile away. An especially beautiful fall hike on the Goulding Creek Trail begins on the west side of Highway 550, a mile south of the Haviland turnoff. The trail climbs quickly to the top of Hermosa Cliffs. Great mountain-biking trails are in the area, and you can rent horses at the campground turnoff on Highway 550. Nine miles away, Purgatory Ski Area offers an alpine slide, scenic chairlift rides, mountain-bike trails, and more.

15. Miller Creek

Location: 18 miles northeast of Durango
Elevation: 8,000 feet
Number of Sites: 12
Recommended RV Length: Up to 35 feet
Season: May through October
Maps: *Colorado Atlas & Gazetteer,* page 86, A4
Colorado Recreational Road Atlas, page 28, A3
Phone: 970-884-2512

Scenery: ★★★
RVs: ★★
Tents: ★★★
Shade: ★★
Privacy: ★★

Directions
From Durango, go northeast on Florida Road (County Road 240) for about 14 miles. Turn left (north) on County Road 243 (Forest Road 596), and go about 3.5 miles.

Distinguishing Features
Miller Creek offers solitude. Nestled on Lemon Reservoir (622 acres), the campground is split into two areas. Sites 1-7 are pleasant spots in a small loop to the left. Sites 8-12 are on the right; in a parking-lot setting, these

sites are lakeside and close together. RVs park in the open very close to one another and with little shade. Tents can be pitched in shady spots by the lake.

Popularity
Miller Creek often fills on weekends from mid-June through mid-August; arrive by noon on Friday to get a spot. No reservations.

Facilities
Facilities include picnic tables, fire grates, firewood for sale, a water faucet, a flush toilet, and a boat ramp.

RV Notes
Sites 1-7 have small to medium back-in spaces, and sites 8-12 have short to medium pull-outs. Most are fairly level.

Tent Notes
Most sites work fine for tents, which can be pitched by the lake.

Recreational Opportunities
Lemon Reservoir is stocked with trout and kokanee salmon. There are no boating restrictions on the reservoir. Most of the hiking trails are near the Florida and Transfer Park Campgrounds a few miles to the north. Hikers can access the Burnt Timber Trail, which leads into the Weminuche Wilderness. Leading to Lost Lake and Stump Lake are two short, easy trails. Horses are available at Miller Ranch next to the reservoir.

Other Nearby Campgrounds

16. Sig Creek (9 sites); 30 miles north of Durango. Take Highway 550 north for 24 miles to Forest Road 578. Turn left (west), and go 5.5 miles. This out-of-the-way campground is best suited for tents, although it works for smaller RVs. On a south-facing hillside, it can get quite toasty during midday. A creek runs through the back of the campground. No reservations. **(970) 884-2512.**

17. Junction Creek (34 sites); about 5 miles northwest of Durango. Go northwest from Durango on County Road 204 (Junction Creek Road) for 4.5 miles. (County Road 204 becomes Forest Road 171.) This is a pleasant, spacious, RV-friendly, well-shaded campground only 10 minutes from town. This place is extremely popular—get here early! Maximum RV length is 50 feet. Reservations accepted. **(970) 884-2512.**

18. Snowslide (13 sites); 17 miles northwest of Durango. Take Highway 160 west for about 11 miles to County Road 124. Turn right (north) on County Road 124, and go about 6.5 miles. More popular than nearby Kroeger, this primitive campground is in an attractive setting on both sides of the road, and the creek runs by several sites. Decent shade is available, and parking spaces are fairly RV-friendly. Maximum RV length is 40 feet. No drinking water. No reservations. **(970) 884-2512.**

19. Kroeger (11 sites); 18 miles northwest of Durango. Take Highway 160 west for about 11 miles to County Road 124. Turn right (north) on County Road 124, and go about 7 miles. Kroeger is an off-the-beaten-path, primitive campground that rarely fills. Sites are heavily shaded and best suited for smaller RVs. No reservations. **(970) 884-2512.**

20. Florida (20 sites); 21 miles northeast of Durango. From Durango, go northeast on Florida Road (County Road 240) for about 14 miles. Turn left (north) on County Road 243, and go about 7 miles. Florida is a delightful riverside campground, with 12 sites on the river. Douglas fir and some aspen provide good shade. Back-ins and a few pull-thrus can handle large RVs. Reservations accepted. **(970) 884-2512.**

21. Transfer Park (25 sites); 22 miles northeast of Durango. From Durango, go northeast on Florida Road (County Road 240) for about 14 miles. Turn left (north) on County Road 243, and go about 7 miles. Turn left on Forest Road 597, and go 1 mile north. Of the three campgrounds in the area, this one offers the best chances for solitude. The upper loop is fairly RV-friendly. The lower loop is closer to the river and is best for tents. Most sites have adequate shade. Maximum RV length is 35 feet. Reservations are accepted. **(970) 884-2512.**

VALLECITO RESERVOIR AREA

22. Pine Point
Location: 18 miles north of Bayfield (see map on p. 295)
Elevation: 7,900 feet
Number of Sites: 30
Recommended RV Length: Up to 35 feet
Season: May to mid-September
Maps: *Colorado Atlas & Gazetteer,* page 87, A5
Colorado Recreational Road Atlas, page 28, A3
Phone: 970-884-2512

Scenery: ★★★
RVs: ★★★★
Tents: ★★★
Shade: ★★★
Privacy: ★★★

Directions
From Bayfield, go north on County Road 501 (Vallecito Road) for about 13.5 miles to Vallecito Dam. Turn right (east) on Forest Road 603, and go about 4 miles.

Distinguishing Features
This campground suffered a lot of damage from a forest fire in 2002. About a third of the campground is gone. Pine Point is one of four Forest Service campgrounds on the east shore of Vallecito Reservoir. This campground is wonderful for RVs. Sites are large and well-separated, and ponderosa pines provide plenty of shade. Ten sites are lakeside with nice views, and many non-lakeside sites offer pretty views of the lake through the trees.

Popularity
Pine Point is very popular, so arrive early in the day (especially on weekends) to secure a site. No reservations.

Facilities

Facilities include picnic tables, fire grates, firewood for sale, water faucets, and two vault toilets and one mini-flush toilet.

RV Notes

Long, fairly level back-ins and four long pull-thrus are available. A dump station requiring no fee is by the Bayfield town park on the south side of Highway 160 near Pine River.

Tent Notes

Many sites are wonderful for tents.

Recreational Opportunities

You'll find some of the best fishing in the country right here at Vallecito Reservoir. State-record catches of northern pike and brown trout are just part of the story; you may also hook a native trout, rainbow trout, or kokanee salmon. A sheltered area for mooring boats, along with a playground, is just south of the campground.

   Three hiking trails start nearby: Graham Creek, North Canyon, and East Creek. A 0.5-mile hike up Graham Creek Trail leads to an excellent view of the reservoir. North Canyon and East Creek Trails are especially popular with horseback riders. (Also see Middle Mountain Campground below.)

---

23. Middle Mountain

Location: 23 miles north of Bayfield (see map on p. 295)
Elevation: 7,900 feet
Number of Sites: 24
Recommended RV Length: Up to 40 feet
Season: May through October
Maps: *Colorado Atlas & Gazetteer*, page 87, A5
Colorado Recreational Road Atlas, page 28, A3
Phone: 970-884-2512

Scenery: ★★★
RVs: ★★
Tents: ★★★
Shade: ★★
Privacy: ★★★

Directions

From Bayfield, go north on County Road 501 (Vallecito Road) for 23 miles. Proceed around the north end of Vallecito Reservoir to the campground.

Distinguishing Features

Located on a gently sloping hill on the east side of Vallecito Reservoir, this campground offers great lake views from many sites and easy water access. Half the sites are lakeside or close to the water. Sites are medium to large, with generally good separation. A good balance between sunshine and shade exists, with ponderosa pine and aspen the dominant trees. Vallecito Reservoir (2,718 acres) is a large lake, 5 miles long with 22 miles of shoreline.

Popularity
This campground fills almost every night during the peak summer months, and reservations are not taken. Campers should arrive before 2:00 p.m. to find a spot. Arriving Sunday or Monday is best.

Facilities
Facilities include picnic tables, fire grates, firewood for sale, water faucets, and vault toilets.

RV Notes
Of the mostly medium back-ins and five pull-thrus, about half accommodate larger RVs. Many sites are not level. A free dump station is at the Bayfield town park on the south side of Highway 160 near Pine River.

Tent Notes
There's no shortage of great tenting spots.

Recreational Opportunities
Anglers have snagged state-record northern pike and German brown trout at Vallecito Reservoir, as well as the plentiful native and rainbow trout and kokanee salmon. The streams that feed Vallecito Reservoir offer great fishing as well. There are no water recreation restrictions, and boats can be rented at Five Branches Camper Park just south of the campground. Many nearby trails offer excellent hiking, and several commercial outfitters, including nearby Five Branches Camper Park, offer horseback rides. (Also see Pine Point Campground.)

Other Nearby Campgrounds

24. Old Timers (10 sites; see map on p. 295); 15.5 miles north of Bayfield. Take County Road 501 (Vallecito Road) 13.5 miles north to Forest Road 603. Turn right (east) on Forest Road 603, and go 1.75 miles. Old Timers is a charming place, offering some of the best lake access of all the campgrounds in the area. The well-shaded sites are best for tents and small RVs. There are no reservations. **(970) 884-2512.**

25. Graham Creek (25 sites; see map on p. 295); 17 miles north of Bayfield. Take County Road 501 (Vallecito Road) 13.5 miles north to Forest Road 603. Turn right (east) on Forest Road 603, and go 3.5 miles. This campground is the only one on Vallecito Reservoir with a boat launch and a beach area (when the reservoir is low). Small RVs and tents work best here. On a hillside 100 yards above the water are nine spots with unobstructed lake views. Some sites are shaded. Wildflowers are magnificent in May and June. No reservations. **(970) 884-2512.**

26. North Canyon (21 sites; see map on p. 295); Suffered some fire damage in 2002, might be closed for 2003. 17 miles north of Bayfield. Take County Road 501 (Vallecito Road) 13.5 miles north to Forest Road 603. Turn right (east) on Forest Road 603, and go 3 miles. Typically less busy than the other Vallecito Reservoir campgrounds, here you can find more solitude and a wilderness setting. Sites are nestled under tall ponderosa pines and offer good privacy. Several accommodate large RVs. No reservations. **(970) 884-2512.**

27. Vallecito (80 sites); 22 miles north of Bayfield. Go north on County Road 501 (Vallecito Road) about 18.5 miles to County Road 500. Go left (north), and go about 2.75 miles. More than 2 miles north of the reservoir, this busy campground is a favorite of hikers and equestrians venturing into the Weminuche Wilderness. Heavily wooded, it's fairly level and RV-friendly, with a dozen prime creekside sites. Maximum RV length is 40 feet. No reservations. **(970) 884-2512.**

28. Pine River (6 sites); 22 miles northeast of Bayfield. Take County Road 501 (Vallecito Road) 13.5 miles north to Forest Road 603. Turn right (east) on Forest Road 603, and go 4.5 miles to Forest Road 602. Turn right on Forest Road 602, and go about 3.5 miles. In a spectacular location with views of Runlett Peak rising 3,000 feet from the Pine River valley floor, this primitive campground is best suited for tents. Pines and a few aspens provide adequate shade. No drinking water is available. No reservations. **(970) 884-2512.**

CORTEZ—MANCOS AREA

29. Transfer
Location: 10 miles northeast of Mancos
Elevation: 8,500 feet
Number of Sites: 12
Recommended RV Length: Up to 45 feet
Season: Memorial Day through October
Maps: *Colorado Atlas & Gazetteer,* page 85, A7
Colorado Recreational Road Atlas, page 27, B3
Phone: 970-882-7296

Scenery: ★★★
RVs: ★★★★
Tents: ★★★★
Shade: ★★
Privacy: ★★★★

Directions
From Mancos, go 0.5 mile north on Highway 184. Turn right (east) on County Road 42 (Forest Road 561), a well-maintained gravel road. Proceed about 10 miles.

Distinguishing Features
This is a remote, peaceful campground in a small and lovely aspen grove. Visitors to Mesa Verde will find it a quiet spot to camp away from the crowds. The sites are large and especially RV-friendly, and the aspens offer morning and evening shade. A nearby overlook provides spectacular views of the sheer-walled West Mancos River Canyon and La Plata Mountains.

Popularity

This campground rarely fills. No reservations.

Facilities

Facilities include a group picnic area and amphitheater, picnic tables, fire grates, hand-pumped water, and wheelchair-accessible vault toilets.

RV Notes

The Forest Service has done an excellent job of accommodating RVs. Long, level back-ins that are quite wide give you plenty of room, even if you have slide-outs.

Tent Notes

Fairly level ground makes Transfer a pleasant place for tents. Two sites have tent pads.

Recreational Opportunities

In only 0.75 mile, Transfer Trail switchbacks steeply down to the West Mancos River and some good fishing. The Chicken Creek Trail leads to Jackson Gulch Reservoir, and the connecting Morrison and Transfer Trails hook up with many others. Beginning from the campground is the Transfer Park/Windy Gap intermediate mountain-bike trail—a 22-mile loop along Forest Service roads. Also starting near the campground, the 39-mile Aspen Loop multipurpose trail is suitable for ATVs, trail bikes, mountain bikes, hikers, and equestrians. A horse corral is just across the way, and equestrians may camp there.

Other Nearby Campgrounds

30. Bradfield Bridge (22 sites); 25 miles north of Cortez. Take Highway 491 northwest for 19.5 miles to County Road DD. Turn right (east), and go about 1 mile to County Road 16. Turn left (north), and go about 2 miles. Remote Bradfield Bridge is used sparingly by rafters in May and June. Most sites sit above the Dolores River, and a few are located by it. Shelters (in some sites) over the picnic tables provide a little shade. Above the bridge, fishing is catch-and-release, but below the bridge, anglers may catch and keep. No reservations. **(970) 882-7296.**

31. Cabin Canyon (11 sites); 28 miles north of Cortez. Take Highway 491 northwest for 19.5 miles to County Road DD. Turn right (east) on County Road DD, and go 1 mile to County Road 16. Go left (north) on County Road 16 for 2.75 miles to County Road S.00 (Forest Road 504). Go right (east) on County Road S.00 for about 4 miles. Rustic and isolated, this campground on the Dolores River offers a barrier-free trail for fishing access. Sites have nice shade and are secluded, and one site is on the river. Gold Medal fishing rules apply. Maximum RV length is 45 feet. No reservations. **(970) 882-7296.**

32. Ferris Canyon (7 sites); 31 miles north of Cortez. Take Highway 491 northwest for 19.5 miles to County Road DD. Turn right (east) on County Road DD, and go 1 mile to County Road 16. Turn left (north) on County Road 16, and go 2.75 miles to County Road S.00 (Forest Road 504). Turn right (east) on County Road S.00, and go about 7 miles. Situated at the bottom of the Dolores River Canyon and on the river, Ferris Canyon is a scenic locale. Sites are large, private, well-shaded, and work best for tents and smaller RVs. Gold Medal fishing rules apply. No reservations. **(970) 882-7296.**

33. Mesa Verde National Park/Morefield Campground (477 sites); 11 miles southwest of Mancos. Take Highway 160 east 9.5 miles from Cortez or west 7 miles from Mancos to Ruins Road. Go south on Ruins Road for about 4 miles. This is the largest public campground in Colorado. Nine crowded loops contain generally small sites squeezed in tightly. Sites offer little privacy and poor to adequate shade. The first loop on the left as you enter, the Navajo Loop (sites 396-477), is for tents only. Sites have pads. The best loop for RVs is the Ute Loop (sites 139-222). Full hookups are available at 15 of the sites. There are no pull-thrus in the campground.

Don't feed the deer—human food can make them sick, or even kill them. Modern facilities include flush toilets, sinks, and outlets in the bathrooms as well as laundry facilities, an amphitheater, store, cafe, gas station, and dump station. Showers are near the store and gas station. Maximum RV length is 40 feet. No reservations. **(970) 529-4461.**

34. Mancos State Park (34 sites with 2 yurts); 5 miles north of Mancos. Take Highway 184 north about 0.5 mile to County Road 42. Turn right (east) on County Road 42, and go 4 miles to County Road N. Go left (west), and proceed 0.5 mile. Two small campgrounds are near charming Jackson Lake (217 acres), and wakeless boating is allowed. Sites 1-24 are in a loop just south of the lake. These large sites have adequate shade and spacing. The rest of the sites are very close to the lake. All are shaded, and some are very private. Sites 25-29 are tent-only, and 30-33 are suitable for smaller RVs. A dump station is provided. Reservations accepted. **(970) 883-2208.**

35. Target Tree (25 sites); 7 miles east of Mancos on Highway 160. Just off and above the highway, this modern campground offers excellent RV spots. Many long pull-thrus are available. Sites contain tent pads, and shade is adequate. Indians once used the trees for target practice. Maximum RV length is 45 feet. No reservations. **(970) 882-7296.**

DOLORES AREA

36. McPhee

Location: 11 miles northwest of Dolores
Elevation: 7,400 feet
Number of Sites: 71
Recommended RV Length: Up to 50 feet
Season: Mid-May to mid-November
Map: *Colorado Atlas & Gazetteer,* page 85, A4
Colorado Recreational Road Atlas, page 27, B3
Phone: 970-882-7296

Scenery: ★★★
RVs: ★★★★
Tents: ★★★★
Shade: ★★★
Privacy: ★★★

Directions

From Dolores, go southwest on Highway 145 for 2 miles to the intersection with Highway 184 West. Turn right (north), and go 7 miles. Turn right (north) onto County Road 25. Go 0.1 mile and turn right onto Forest Road 271. Continue for about 2 miles.

Distinguishing Features

Campers looking for a remote campground with modern facilities beside a large lake need look no further. McPhee Reservoir (4,470 acres) is suitable for all types of water recreation. McPhee Campground sits on a high bluff 500 feet above the reservoir. The main campground consists of two paved, wooded loops with large sites and good privacy. Several sites have covered picnic tables. A third loop leads to several group sites set in the open with minimal shade. The only sites with any views of the reservoir are a few of the walk-in tent sites. The now-submerged town of McPhee was once Colorado's largest lumber town.

Popularity
Even on busy holiday weekends, McPhee is usually only 30 percent full. Campers can reserve the sites in the Pinyon Loop.

Facilities
Facilities include picnic tables, fire grates, firewood for sale, water faucets, pay showers, sinks, electrical outlets, and wheelchair-accessible flush toilets. There is a nearby boat ramp, but the marina was destroyed by arson in 2002.

RV Notes
Campers will find mostly long, fairly level paved back-ins and about 14 pull-thrus and pull-outs. Many back-ins have side-by-side parking spaces to accommodate boats or a second vehicle. Site 2 in both loops offers full hookups. In the Juniper Loop, sites 1, 4, 11, 14, 21, 23, 29, and 37 have electrical hookups. In the Pinyon Loop, sites 4, 7, 16, 28, and 31 have electrical hookups. A dump station is nearby.

Tent Notes
Tent campers have all the best views! Each loop has six walk-in sites, and these are the place to be. Site 3W in the Juniper Loop has the best lake view, while several other sites have partial lake views.

Recreational Opportunities
With Mesa Verde only 25 miles away, many campers use McPhee as a long-term base camp when exploring the Four Corners area. But the reservoir is the biggest attraction. McPhee Reservoir is almost nine miles long, with a few long arms and 50 miles of shoreline. With no water recreation restrictions, anything goes. McPhee has been stocked with more than 4.5 million fish, and it's said to have the highest catch ratio per hour in southwestern Colorado! It's rare to find both cold- and warm-water fishing in one place, but anglers will discover it at McPhee. The reservoir has its own strain of rainbow trout, as well as large and smallmouth bass, brown trout, crappie, panfish, and catfish. Although anglers have five access points, many spots on the reservoir are quite remote, so bringing a boat is a good idea. The lower Dolores River from the dam to 12 miles downstream is considered Gold Medal water (catch-and-release only). A short overlook trail from the Pinyon Loop leads to a 360-degree panorama of the reservoir and surrounding countryside.

Other Nearby Campgrounds

37. House Creek (72 sites); 13 miles north of Dolores. From Dolores, go northeast on County Road 31 (which becomes Forest Road 526). Go north for 7.25 miles to Forest Road 528. Turn left (southwest) on Forest Road 528, and go about 6 miles. On the eastern shore of McPhee Reservoir, Colorado's second largest lake, this is a popular place for boaters, and the campground rarely fills. With few trees, all campers have a lake view. Sites are RV-friendly, and many have electrical hookups. A dump station is available. The most popular sites are 34-39, closest to the lake. Some sites have covered picnic tables to provide a little shade. Maximum RV length is 50 feet. Reservations accepted. **(970) 882-7296.**

38. Mavreeso (14 sites); 21 miles northeast of Dolores. Take Highway 145 northeast for 12.5 miles to Forest Road 535. Turn left (north) on Forest Road 535, and go 8 miles. Mavreeso is a picturesque campground on the Dolores River. Most sites are either on the river or very close to it, and offer excellent shade and good privacy. Medium-sized sites are available for RVs, and some have pull-thru spaces. Five sites have electrical hookups. Maximum RV length is 35 feet. No reservations. **(970) 882-7296.**

39. West Dolores (18 sites); 19 miles northeast of Dolores. Take Highway 145 northeast for 12.5 miles to Forest Road 535. Turn left (north) on Forest Road 535, and go 6 miles. Another popular campground on the Dolores River, this one offers larger RV sites than does nearby Mavreeso. Half the sites are on or very close to the river. Shade is wonderful, and six sites have electrical hookups. Maximum RV length is 35 feet. No reservations. **(970) 882-7296.**

40. Burro Bridge (12 sites); 39 miles northeast of Dolores. Take Highway 145 northeast for 12.5 miles to Forest Road 535. Turn left (north) on Forest Road 535, and go 26.5 miles. Offering a horse corral, Burro Bridge is a favorite of equestrians and hikers. Sites are small and don't accommodate RVs well. Half are well-shaded, while the rest have no shade. If approaching from the north end of Forest Road 535, RV travel is discouraged. No reservations. **(970) 882-7296.**

41. Cayton (27 sites); 44.5 miles northeast of Dolores. Take Highway 145 northeast for 44 miles to Forest Road 578. Turn right (east), and go 0.5 mile. Attracting a loyal following, this is a busy campground. As it's surrounded by beautiful mountain views and sits beside the Dolores River, it's no wonder this is a popular spot. The lower loop is nearest the river and offers better shade. Site size, shade, and privacy vary widely. The campground has a dump station. Maximum RV length is 35 feet. No reservations. **(970) 882-7296.**

LAKES and RESERVOIRS

These illustrations of lakes and reservoirs are organized by region and show the location of campgrounds around them. These are major reservoirs and lakes I've described that have multiple campgrounds around them. Red indicates Top 100 Campgrounds mentioned in this book; blue indicates other nearby campgrounds (including some not listed in this book).

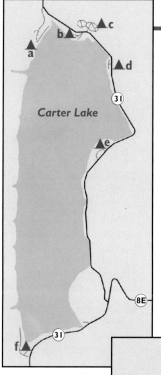

North Region (East)

Carter Lake p. 21
Campgrounds: a. North Pines
b. Lowell's Campground
c. Eagle
d. Big Thompson
e. Carter Knolls
f. South Shore

Green Mountain Reservoir pp. 55-56
Campgrounds: 64. Prairie Point
65. Willows
66. Davis Springs
67. McDonald Flats
68. Elliot Creek
69. Cataract Creek
a. Cow Creek

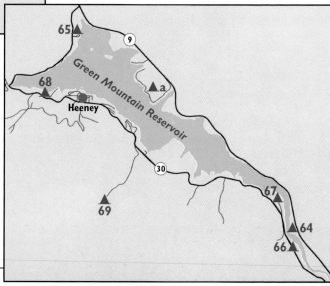

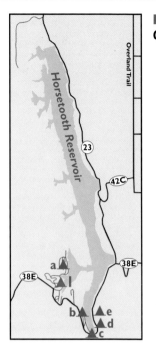

Horsetooth Reservoir p. 18

Campgrounds: 1. Shoreline
a. North Inlet Bay
b. South Bay
c. Turkey Point
d. Little Turkey
e. East Shore

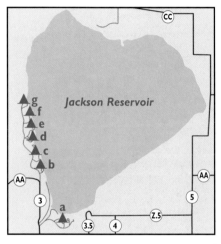

Jackson Reservoir p. 58

Campgrounds: a. Dunes
b. Lakeside
c. Cove
d. Pelican
e. Sandpiper
f. Fox Hills
g. Northview

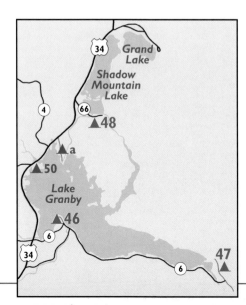

Lake Granby pp. 47-52

Campgrounds: 46. Sunset Point
47. Arapaho Bay
48. Green Ridge
50. Stillwater
a. Cutthroat Bay (group)

LAKES and RESERVOIRS

North Region (West)

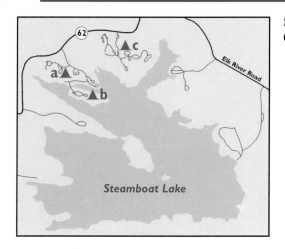

Steamboat Lake p. 67
Campgrounds: a. Dutch Hill
                b. Bridge Island
                c. Sunrise Vista

Central Region (East)

Bonny Reservoir p. 115
Campgrounds: a. Wagon Wheel
                b. East Beach
                c. North Cove
                d. Foster Grove

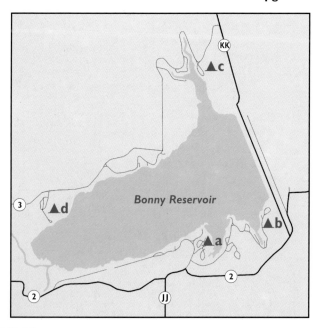

Central Region (East)

Elevenmile Reservoir

pp. 109, 112, 114

Campgrounds:
36. Spillway
38a. Riverside
38b. Springer Gulch
38c. Cove
39a. Rocky Ridge
39b. North Shore
39c. Stoll Mountain
39d. Cross Creek
39e. Lazy Boy
39f. Rocking Chair
39g. Howbert Point
39h. Witcher Cove

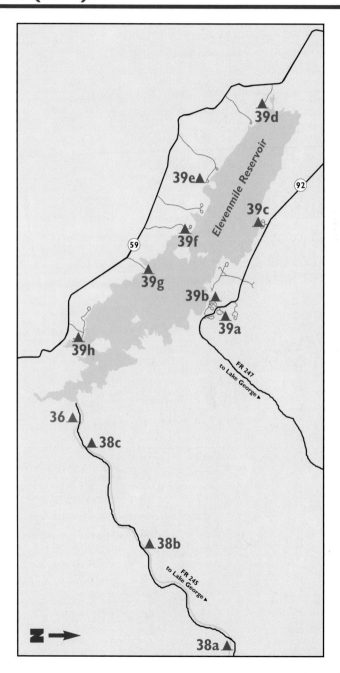

LAKES and RESERVOIRS

Central Region (A)

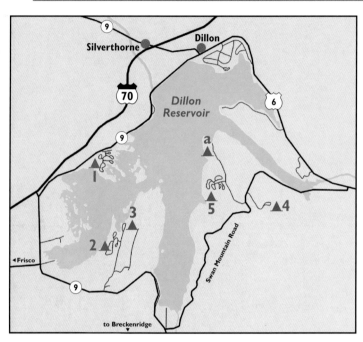

Dillon Reservoir pp. 118-122

Campgrounds:
1. Heaton Bay
2. Peak One
3. Pine Cove
4. Lowry
5. Prospector
a. Windy Point (group)

Turquoise Lake pp. 124-129

Campgrounds:
12. Baby Doe
13. Belle of Colorado
15. Molly Brown
16. Tabor
17. Silver Dollar
18. Father Dyer
19. May Queen
a. Printerboy Group

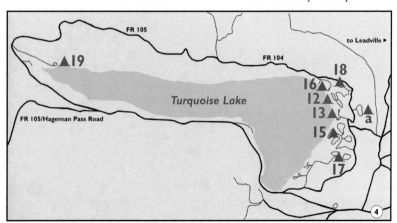

Central Region (B)

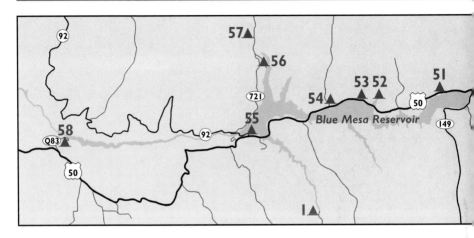

Blue Mesa Reservoir pp. 182-183, 218

Campgrounds: 1. Gateview   55. Lake Fork
51. Stevens Creek   56. Ponderosa
52. Elk Creek   57. Soap Creek
53. Dry Gulch   58. Cimarron
54. Red Creek

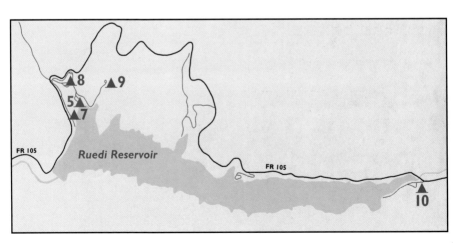

Ruedi Reservoir pp. 149-152

Campgrounds: 5. Mollie B   9. Little Mattie
7. Ruedi Marina   10. Dearhamer
8. Little Maud

South Region (East)

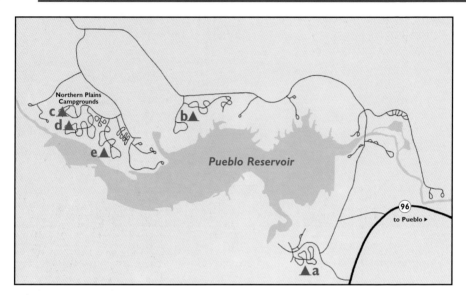

Pueblo Reservoir p. 214
Campgrounds: a. Arkansas Point
b. Juniper Breaks
c. Kettle Creek (Northern Plains Campground)
d. Yucca Flats (Northern Plains Campground)
e. Prairie Ridge (Northern Plains Campground)

South Region (West)

Ridgway Reservoir p. 258
Campgrounds: a. Elk Ridge
b. Dakota Terraces
c. Pacochupuk

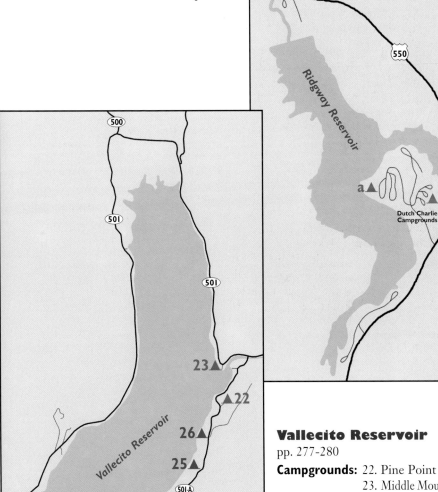

Vallecito Reservoir
pp. 277-280

Campgrounds: 22. Pine Point
23. Middle Mountain
24. Old Timers
25. Graham Creek
26. North Canyon

Index

Note: Citations followed by the letter "p" denote photos; "m" denotes maps.

About the Author

Gil Folsom has lived in Colorado since he was a teenager and became an avid camper through his experience as a Boy Scout. He attended Western State College in Gunnison before receiving a degree in marketing and business administration from the University of Northern Colorado.

He has camped all over the world, from as far north as Alaska to as far south as New Zealand. Reaching these campsites by foot, bicycle, canoe, sea kayak, car, four-wheel-drive vehicle, or RV, he has learned to appreciate camping from many different perspectives. In addition to camping, his interests include backpacking, canoeing, dirt-bike riding, jeeping, mountain biking, sea kayaking, skiing, and traveling.

About the Photographer

Bill Bonebrake has lived in Colorado most of his life and, through his work as a nature photographer, has acquired a vast knowledge of the state. While Bill has photographed in more than 50 countries around the world, he concentrates his efforts in the Rocky Mountains and in the Four Corners region.

Bill travels close to 30,000 miles each year along Colorado's highways and backroads. His photographs appear in books, and on greeting cards and postcards he and his wife, Lorraine, produce through their company, JAMIT Publishing. Bill's work also gains international exposure through stock agencies.